This Book is Due...

QUEST FOR THE AFRICAN DINOSAURS

QUEST FOR THE AFRICAN DINOSAURS

Ancient Roots of the Modern World

Louis Jacobs, Ph.D.

VILLARD BOOKS   NEW YORK   1993

All rights reserved under International and Pan-American Copyright Conventions.
Published in the United States by Villard Books, a division of Random House,
Inc., New York, and simultaneously in Canada by Random House of Canada
Limited, Toronto.

VILLARD BOOKS is a registered trademark of Random House, Inc.

Library of Congress Cataloging-in-Publication Data
Jacobs, Louis L.
    Quest for the African dinosaurs/by Louis L. Jacobs.—1st ed.
       p.   cm.
    Includes bibliographical references.
    ISBN 0-679-41270-0
    1. Dinosaurs—Africa.   2. Dinosaurs—Research—Africa.   I. Title.
QE862.D5J28   1993   567.9′1′096—dc20   92-15080

Manufactured in the United States of America
9 8 7 6 5 4 3 2
First edition

To my family, past, present, and future, great and grand, in-law and out, close and distant, father and mother, sisters (no brothers), nieces and nephews, aunts, uncles, and cousins, and with special dedication to
Bonnie, Matthew, and Melissa

This thing we call existence; is it not a something which has its roots far down below in the dark, and its branches stretching out into the immensity above, which we among the branches cannot see?

—Olive Schreiner (*nom de plume,* Ralph Iron), 1883
The Story of an African Farm

PREFACE

T HIS BOOK is about fossils and about Africa. Thanks to the generous support of the National Geographic Society, most of it is based on my experiences and fieldwork excavating fossils on the African continent. But it is about more than bones dug from the Earth. It is also about the people of Africa and how their legacies have shaped their lives. And it is about how such a thing as an expedition to find the ancient bones of the past can be put to use now to help build the future.

The fossils in this book are those of dinosaurs and the animals that lived with them—weird crocodiles, strange mammals, and more familiar beasts, such as frogs and turtles. It is the whole suite, the once living community, that is most important, but dinosaurs catch the imagination first. Dinosaurs and Africa are two subjects that have a strange, if not sinister, appeal. Dinosaurs are scary giants; Africa is the Dark Continent. Those perceptions of dinosaurs and of Africa are partly myth, partly true; nevertheless the appeal they engender seems to be enduring for each. They are both exciting, true enough. But the view of Africa as the Dark Unknown is an old idea indeed. Africa is no longer as it was in the nineteenth century. How could it be? While some things never seem to change, in reality almost everything does. In Africa as elsewhere it is important to appreciate the past, and to enjoy the present, and it is necessary to build for the future. Does digging for fossils in Africa fit that bill? You bet it does.

In Western eyes Africa is perceived as a land for adventurers and explorers. It seems that every outlander who has ever gone to Africa assumes that he or she has found something. Each has "discovered" some part of the continent. But while Africa is undeniably diverse and different, it has never been a lost continent—only unfamiliar, underappreciated, misunderstood, or forgotten. Every outlander who has ever gone to Africa has taken a part of it away and left something behind. The results have not always been good, nor have they always been bad, but they have all gone into the mix that makes up African society. I want to put in something good. I want to use my work on the bones of Africa to build the capabilities of one small place, right in the heart of Africa, so that the people can do on their own what I do with them now. I want to drive myself extinct, at least in terms of the paleontological development of the tiny country of Malaŵi. This book tells how I am doing it.

But is it a good thing for Africa to focus the talents of a limited number of educated people on the study of fossils? Is that not frivolous? Is it necessary that a poor African nation devote resources to such a thing as fossils? That is for Africans to decide. At least we know that fossils are good, in a very warm sense, no matter where they are found, even Africa. Just ask a kid. Besides, it can be no more frivolous and no more unnecessary than in developed countries, where very respectable profits are made from the sale of dinosaurian accouterments and many an eager mind has opened to the wonders of science after being tapped by the excitement of the Lost World of the past. Moreover, by way of example, paleontology has certainly been good for the African nation of Kenya, judging from the lasting value of the Leakeys' work built there using the fossils of our collective human ancestry.

The first chapter of this book defines the scientific issues involved in my African work and discusses how I got to Africa in the first place. It also provides the background of evolution and geology necessary for a fuller appreciation of why this paleontological work in Africa is worth doing. The second chapter is devoted to the major earthly feature of this part of Africa—a giant lake. The lake influences everything and everyone in the country, including its early European explorers, who marveled at it even as resident citizens and visitors do today. But the lake is also a geological feature, and understanding how it formed is essential to understanding why the fossils are there at all. This theme is continued by detailing how to find a fossil and, once found, how to get it out of the ground. The third chapter presents the country of Malaŵi in more detail and narrates the day-to-day activities of a fossil-hunting expedition in Africa. The human setting and its history are woven into the fieldwork, and that thread is carried through in later chapters. Drafts of Chapter 3 (and parts of several other chapters) were written in the field. I hope this imparts an immediacy, a spirit of real time and excitement, to my descriptions of fieldwork.

The next four chapters are devoted to specific groups of fossils and their significance. Chapter 4 examines the sauropod dinosaurs, while Chapter 5 covers the other dinosaurs and their roles in the Mesozoic world. Chapter 6 discusses the very interesting crocodiles from Malaŵi and their relationships to those discovered in South America. Chapter 7 is devoted to the search for early mammals. Chapter 8 covers some familiar but rather poorly understood animals and outlines some enigmatic patterns in living species that trace their roots to more ancient times.

The ninth chapter, which deals with rumors of living dinosaurs in Africa, is a bit of a sideline, but a necessary one. Africa and its remoteness is often misunderstood in the West. Science is also often misunderstood. These two phenomena manifest themselves in some strange ways. One particularly odd way is the search for living dinosaurs in the swamps of the Congo. There are good reasons to look at Africa as a continent ever changing through geologic time, which it is, rather than as a stagnant refugium where life, that of dinosaurs or people, never changes.

Science never ends. Each experiment attempted, each analysis performed, each fossil measured only leads to more questions, more experiments, more analyses, and more measurements. Science never stops, but my work in Africa is entering a new phase, and that provides a convenient milepost from which to reflect. The final chapter, an afterword, is designed to meld my feelings for the country with the scientific results of the expeditions, and to present some aspirations for the future. My Malaŵian colleagues are well on their way toward managing their own paleontological resources in a profes-sional, world-class way without needing the expertise of outlanders. They are becoming the experts on their own dinosaurs. That is the way it should be, and this phase of my African work must happily yield to more appropriate strategies that African paleontologists will write about in the future.

None of the work reported in this book could have been accomplished without the goodwill and companionship of colleagues in the field. I have listed the members of the various African dinosaur expeditions at the end, but I also wish to express my appreciation to all the colleagues of many nations on other expeditions in which I have been a party on three continents. Among these are the people who have had the greatest influence on my career through their actions during my training and formative years, especially Everett H. Lindsay, Robert F. Butler, George Gaylord Simpson, Edwin H. Colbert, Noye M. Johnson, David Pilbeam, and my fellow graduate students, all of whom have left on me an indelible stamp. And now I appreciate the graduate students who teach me today. It is with a great deal of fun that I acknowledge them all.

Further, I must acknowledge the friendship and cordial cooperation of Gadi Mgomezulu, now Secretary for Education and Culture, but previously the Principal Conservator of Antiquities in Malaŵi. When he moved on, he was replaced by Yusuf Juwayeyi. Without these two fine gentlemen there would have been no Malaŵi Project. I must also thank Zefe Kaufulu, now at the University of Malaŵi, in this regard. In Cameroon I had the exceptional good fortune to be associated with Joseph Victor Hell. I am also grateful, for various reasons, to W. J. Anderson, Netta Blanchard, James E. Brooks, Carolyn Brown, Michel Brunet, L. Sprague de Camp, Edwin H. Colbert, William R. Downs, Max Fine, Lawrence J. Flynn, Brian M. Foy, Elizabeth Gomani, John Goodge, Robert T. Gregory, Vicki Hansen, Harvey Herr, Paula Herr, Rodney L. Honeycutt, Nicholas Hotton III, Bonnie F. Jacobs, Richard E. Leakey, David James Maxwell (also known as Village Headman Makonganya), A. Lee McAlester, Phillip A. Murry, Morris Mwafulira, Oliver Mwenifumbo, Kent Newman, David Pilbeam, Louis H. Taylor, Mary Taylor, Alisa J. Winkler, and Dale A. Winkler. Gerhard Maier provided valuable information about Tendaguru. I am pleased to mention the National Geographic Society, National Science Foundation, Margolis Foundation, Carl B. & Florence E. King Foundation, Institute for the Study of Earth and Man, Johnson & Johnson Orthopaedics, Caltex Petroleum Corporation, and Caltex Oil Malaŵi Limited for supporting this African fieldwork. Three gentlemen at Caltex, Brian Foy, Steve Carson, and J.B.R. Allen, deserve special thanks for facilitating work in Malaŵi. The Huntingfield Corporation, through the good offices of Owen Henderson and H. Russell Morrison, provided for the training of a Malaŵian technician in my Dallas laboratories. The Dallas Aquarium allowed access to their extraordinarily interesting collection of species. My literary agent, John A. Ware, my editor, Douglas Stumpf, and the staff at Villard Books, have been exceedingly skillful and supportive in bringing this book to fruition. The illustrations were cheerfully, pleasantly, enthusiastically, and realistically rendered by Mary Ann Zapalac. My wife, Bonnie, read and commented upon several drafts, even appearing to enjoy the process. While it must have been hard on her, it was encouraging to me, and I thank her for it. My son, Matthew, and my daughter, Melissa, were great helps, especially on the computer.

Finally I wish to offer my profound thanks to Africa, and in particular to the people and the governments of Malaŵi, Cameroon, and Kenya.

ZIKOMO!

CONTENTS

LIST OF ILLUSTRATIONS

QUEST FOR THE AFRICAN DINOSAURS

1

THE FORGOTTEN DINOSAURS OF AFRICA

"I BEG TO DRAW your attention to Africa." Those are the words of the missionary David Livingstone. He was trying to focus the eyes of the nineteenth-century world on the interior of the Dark Continent. He wanted to develop the economic potential of its downtrodden slaving grounds as a means of saving it.

One of those who followed Livingstone in his mission was Henry Drummond, an influential Scottish theologian and scientist. In 1883, ten years after Livingstone died, Drummond conducted a brief natural-history survey in British Central Africa to determine what species of plants and animals inhabited the region, which might be of economic significance, and how suitable the area might be for agricultural and mineral development. According to his contemporaries, Drummond, while exceedingly pleasant to be around, was more infatuated with the idea of being a famous African naturalist than endowed with the attributes to be one. His efforts in Africa came to very little. Nevertheless it is important for this story that Drummond discovered fossils—the first from this part of what used to be Livingstone's landscape. No others were found until the next century, when a British planter stumbled across some scraps of petrified bones and reported them to colonial authorities. They turned out to be dinosaurs.

In 1930, five decades after Drummond first found fossils, the British Museum (Natural History) sent an expedition to investigate the reports of dinosaurs. It, too, found some. They were dug up and shipped back to England. Since then those old dinosaur bones from Africa have been lying comatose, virtually ignored, doing nothing but haunting the basement of the natural-history museum on Cromwell Road, London. For over fifty years no serious dinosaur hunter returned to find more bones, or to make sense of the rocks that entomb them. The dinosaurs from the Warm Heart of Africa, the country now called Malaŵi, were for all practical purposes forgotten.

If you want to know about dinosaurs, more specifically African dinosaurs, I suppose you could start in the basement of the British Museum. Or, in a very broad sort of way, you could take the advice of the kolokolo bird: "Go to the banks of the great gray-green, greasy Limpopo River, all set about with fever-trees, and find out." If you are curious about African fossils, go there. There are more bones in the ground. The African dinosaurs in the British Museum may be moldering in a state of seclusion, but in the tiny country of Malaŵi (Figure 1) more bones are starting to emerge from the badlands visited so long ago by the British expedition.

There are three reasons why the fossil bones from Malaŵi are significant: First is their age, second is their location, and third is the species they represent. At about 100 million years old, the bones from Malaŵi represent animals living at the very time the modern world, as we know it, was beginning to take on its own definition, even as the dinosaurs remained in apogee. Their place is significant because at that time the continents and oceans of the world were rearranging themselves dramatically. Africa was once a part of a gigantic southern supercontinent. The once-living species that inhabited it, and their fossil bones, are descended from animals that were at one time part of a widespread community living on the huge landmass. But Africa was breaking away. Members of the global animal community evolved their separate ways after Africa, South America, Australia, India, and Antarctica became separate. Malaŵi is particularly important because the bones that are emerging there are abundant and well preserved, and it is the only place where some unique species can be found. That brings us to the third reason why the bones in Malaŵi are significant: They represent a window into the past, a view of an ancient community, that has not been seen elsewhere.

The Republic of Malaŵi in southeastern Africa is a bit larger than Louisiana, but nearly a quarter of its area is water. A lake, Lake Malaŵi, dominates the country. It is 360 miles long. The whole country is not all that much

FIGURE 1: *Location map of Africa. Malaŵi, a part of the Interior explored by David Livingstone, is stippled. The major lakes of Africa are shown in black. The string of lakes in eastern Africa owe their existence to the Great Rift Valley.*

longer. At its widest, the shores are 50 miles apart, at its narrowest, 11. The total area of Lake Malaŵi is almost equal to that of the state of New Hampshire, but not all of it belongs to Malaŵi; part of the lake is in Mozambiquan territory. It is the world's third deepest lake, behind Lake Tanganyika, which lies just to the north, and Lake Baikal in Asia, which is the deepest. Lake Malaŵi is 2,300 feet deep, nearly half a mile, with the surface at an elevation of 1,550 feet above sea level, and its deepest point at 750 feet below sea level. The Lake is fresh and blue, filled by yearly rains. It drains to the south, via the Shiré River to the Zambezi. The Zambezi flows into the Indian Ocean south of Chinde in Mozambique. Malaŵi is a beautiful setting, and it has bones—lots of them.

AFRICA HAS BEEN forever the most introverted of inhabited continents. There is no way around the cliché. It has a mystique, a legacy of exotic tribes, wild animals, diseases, the unknown. For centuries the Arabs, British, French, Germans, and Portuguese were held at bay by the fevers of Darkest Africa. Still the slavers and explorers, traders and planters, and the men like Livingstone—whites with a mission of God—invaded the continent. They came, and they took, and some of them believed they saved. But Africa, though changed, was not assimilated.

A century has passed. Africa, its people, and its animals are exotic to this day. It remains unknown to us in the West. The mystique remains. But the mystique evolves. There are still snakes, and scorpions, and malaria. There is more wild game than anywhere else on Earth. But a new set of problems has taken over the continent. Starvation replaces slavery. The reality of AIDS surpasses the dread of other diseases. The specter of extinction supplants the excitement of discovery. On safari, strings of porters have lost their jobs to Land Cruisers. And now we shoot with cameras. But the mystique remains.

The mystique of Africa attracted me, yet how I got there was as much an accident, an unpredictable set of circumstances, as it was anything else. For the kinds of things I wanted to do, getting to Africa has never been particularly easy. As it ended up, in 1981 I went to work for Richard Leakey as head of the Division of Palaeontology at the National Museums of Kenya.

The Leakey family and Kenya, firmly set in the Cradle of Humankind, are famous for their discoveries of the remains of our early ancestors at Olduvai Gorge, Lake Turkana, and other places in East Africa. Consequently there is a superb collection of old bones from the Rift Valley and Lake Victoria stored in the National Museum in Nairobi, where Richard was director. It was my responsibility—my great fun—to oversee them.

I got the job in Nairobi because I was in the right place at the right time. The small museum in Arizona where I had been working for the three years since getting my Ph.D. was laying off researchers, and I was one marked to go. I figured I would be out of the bone business altogether and into something else, maybe selling shoes. It really did not matter what I did if I was not doing fossils. I rationalized that the fieldwork I had done previously in the western United States, Mexico, and Pakistan during the time that I was lucky enough to be a paleontologist had been its own reward. Circumstances were just moving me on.

My ongoing fieldwork at the time was in Pakistan. I had been going there for the past six years as part of a larger project trying to unravel the Asian chapter of human evolution, that of the last eighteen million years, from fossils found in the southern foothills of the Himalayas. There are similarities in the fossil record between Asia and Africa indicating that there was in the past a certain amount of migration involving a number of kinds of animals, including primates, some of which are closely associated with human ancestry. There are many kinds of fossils found in Pakistan, and my particular responsibility was to find, collect, and interpret the evolutionary patterns of all the tiny mammals, such as mice, the ones so small that they had been overlooked before. Because they can be found in much greater abundance than hominoid primates when searched for with the appropriate techniques, the small mammals provide useful models for evolution in southern Asia generally, and they reflect close ties to Africa.

I had at least one more trip to Pakistan left while I still had a job. It occurred to me that, since I was going to be out of the business anyway, I should have a final fling and do what I had long wanted to do. I should have my last plane ticket home from Karachi written through Africa because, I thought, I would never get another chance to see it.

As circumstances would have it, at this same time Leakey's head of paleontology just happened to be moving on as well. Unbeknownst to me, Leakey was in London. So was David Pilbeam, the leader of the Pakistan project. Leakey mentioned that he needed a replacement to fill the vacant position. David gave my name. Meanwhile, while they were talking in London, I was in the field in Pakistan talking about Africa with Andrew Hill, one of Leakey's employees from the museum in Nairobi. Andrew would not be in Nairobi when I went through, but he gave me the keys to his flat and a letter of introduction to take to Richard.

I met Leakey for the first time on that trip. It was in his office at the museum. I thought it was just an opportunity to meet him as a colleague. But it was a job interview. There I was, informal, untucked, rolled up, and bethonged. Because I did not know of the words between David, Andrew, and Richard, I was ignorant, unaware, and anything but nervous. That must have been what did it.

"I am looking to hire someone," said Leakey.

THE NEXT NOVEMBER Bonnie and I got married. She was still in graduate school at the University of Arizona, studying fossil pollen and what it tells about ancient plants and environments. A month after we got married, I left for Africa while Bonnie stayed behind to work on her research. In April, after her Ph.D. dissertation took shape, Bonnie joined me in Nairobi. Our African experience had begun, and it was exciting for us both. Bonnie set up a pollen laboratory and I worked with bones. And I never had to get out of the fossil business.

Many of my duties in Kenya ran automatically. The staff was well trained and quite pleasant. All the curators knew their functions long before I arrived. Alfreda, Mary, Emma, Alice, and the others needed little supervision. They looked after the collections and I helped look after foreign researchers. I conducted training classes that helped the staff in their work and helped me to learn African fossils. One of my great responsibilities—and pleasures—in Leakey's absence was to show visitors through the cathedrallike vault holding the sacred fossilized remains of human ancestors. Sometimes the visitors were dignitaries, such as the former secretary general of the United Nations from Venezuela, Javier Pérez de Cuellar, or the Crown Prince, now Emperor Akihito, of Japan.

The viewing of the primate fossils, those most majestic relics of human evolution, each one delicately cushioned in a custom-made protective box, is a solemn ceremony indeed. One by one the boxes are removed from steel cabinets and placed on padded tables. Then slowly, a top is lifted, a specimen is bathed in soft light. During that first moment everyone in the vault, everyone without exception, is struck with the same awesome emotion. It is a blow that reverberates through the reaches of human consciousness, like thunder but more pleasant, deafening yet stirring deep into the soul. To be in the presence of such tremendous fossil reminders of our common and distant past is a moving experience like no other, not religious but inspiring all the more. From that vantage point, with the vast evolutionary distances our species has traveled clearly in view, tangible and credible, it is but a short step to the future. No other set of fossils so forcefully emphasizes the notion that the world of tomorrow will be shaped by the actions of those living today because no other set of fossils demonstrates so frankly that we ourselves are the earthly product of the lives of distant and equally earthly antecedents.

ON SAFARI INTO the African bush I saw vast herds of antelope, families of elephants, and prides of lions. Crocodiles basked on the warm banks of watercourses. I traveled through deep red soil on dusty roads that hung like native necklaces around Mount Kenya, stringing together small vegetable plots and steep, hillside maize *shambas*, dangling from the byways like bangles in the cool Kikuyu highlands. The magnificent volcano Kilimanjaro, the molehill of the gods, and the splendid scar that is the Great Rift Valley testified to the geological tension concealed beneath the African landscape, creating in places the conditions just right for fossils. Even at our home, in view of the Ngong Hills, giraffe browsed below our house outside the Nairobi suburb of Karen. Duikers ate the best cabbages from our garden. Eagle owls roosted in the trees and grunted like pigs in the night. Yet while I was surrounded by this vibrant wildlife and superb scenery, in my work at the museum I was immersed in life's history—the remains, excavated from the Earth, of beasts and humans that existed in past millennia. I dug fossils myself from the musty mudstone of the Tugen Hills. Dirt from the rocky graves of ancient animals ground under my fingernails.

Africa is a very important piece of the puzzle that is the fossil record, and my time in Nairobi complemented what I had already observed in my fieldwork in both North America and Asia. I enjoyed being in the African setting, learning what Africa had to say about how life changed from the bones of the past to the flesh and blood of today.

Most of my research experience was with mammals—those animals that, while living, have fur, produce milk, and show parental care of their young. In fact, as I mentioned earlier, I was a specialist on rats due to my doctoral research on fossil rodent teeth from Pakistan. It seems odd to say it now, so much out of context, but that is what I got my Ph.D. for—fossil rats, millions of years old. It may seem odd also, but they are very, very interesting. Their fossils speak of their own special evolutionary history, but because they are often abundant as fossils, they can serve to resolve geologic time. They can even tell us about evolutionary phenomena that might also affect other kinds of animals, analogous to the way laboratory mice are used in medical experiments as models for humans.

There are plenty of fossil mammals in Africa, and studying fossil rats would have been the logical way for me to proceed. And in fact I have kept an interest in them. But I was interested in other things and other animals as well. I wanted another research project. One that was new to me and out of the ordinary. That is a big order in Africa, where all projects are, by nature of their venue, out of the ordinary. I wanted something that would make a difference in the world of fossils.

At the time, there was only one dinosaur bone known from all of Kenya, and it was from an extremely remote area west of Lake Turkana. I could see it every day because it was on display at the Museum in Nairobi. It had been found years earlier, but no paleontologist since had been back to the spot. I was not, at that time, particularly interested in dinosaurs. They were for kids, and much too popular for an egghead scientist like me. Besides, did we not already know everything worth knowing about dinosaurs? What I was interested in was what might be found with them. There could be early mammals in the same strata.

I knew that unless Africa was different from the rest of the world during the Age of Reptiles, the rocks that the Kenyan dinosaur bone had come from could be no younger than 66 million years old. That was when dinosaurs went extinct, long before any of the fossil mammals known from Kenya had lived. If dinosaur bones were preserved in those ancient sediments, other bones could be as well. If I could find mammals, any mammals, from that part of the Age of Reptiles in Africa, I would make a significant scientific contribution toward knowing how the kinds of animals we see today evolved. Such a find would be very, very important. The fossils would be tiny. They would be strange. They would be very different from anything known today, but just how they would be different I could not say because no one had ever seen them before. Most likely only their teeth, the hardest, most durable parts of the body, would be preserved. They would be minute. Each specimen would nestle snugly on the head of a pin. But I knew I could find them; I would use the same techniques I had used previously to find single, isolated rat teeth in much younger rocks.

I approached Leakey for permission to search for mammals in the dinosaur beds west of Lake Turkana. It was not forthcoming. He said no. The reasons were legitimate, but I was shattered. What was I to do? I was convinced of the scientific importance of finding early mammals in Africa, yet I could not go to the spot I had picked to search.

I examined maps of Kenya to find suitable rocks somewhere else. There were some down by the coast, a bit old, but still interesting, about forty miles inland from the old Arab port city of Mombasa. Bonnie searched with me. No luck. Disappointed but not defeated, it was not in the cards for me to find early mammals in Kenya. I retreated from the Kenya coast.

Still I could not give up. I read about other African dinosaurs, trying to locate another place to go in search of early mammals. African dinosaurs have not been found in all that many places. Fish-eating *Spinosaurus* (Figure 2) and a few others were known from Egypt. They had been collected by Germans and shipped off to Europe, but most of their bones were destroyed in World War II when Stuttgart was bombed by Allied forces. The French had a few localities in remote North Africa. The star dinosaur locality in francophone (French-speaking) West Africa is Gadoufaoua in Niger. At Gadoufaoua beautiful bones of the two-legged, sail-backed, herbivorous *Ouranosaurus* (Figure 3) were found, along with bits and pieces and skeletons of fish, turtles, crocodiles, and other dinosaurs. The French were rumored to be searching for mammals there.

Of the age I was interested in, one leg bone was known from Mozambique, a few scraps were reported from Zambia, and a few more from Zimbabwe. A small handful of localities were scattered around southern Africa, each containing only the fragmentary parts of single skeletons. Together they added up to a meager record. What I needed was a locality rich in bone so that tiny mammals might have a greater chance of being entombed in the sediments along with any dinosaur parts. Even with all these reports, and despite a long history of expeditions, there was no denying that Africa was very nearly a forgotten land for dinosaurs and the animals that lived with them. I decided that the best place for me to go for what I wanted to do was Tendaguru in southern Tanzania. The grandest collection of dinosaur bones ever to come out of Africa is from there. It is hard to imagine a site richer in dinosaurs. It ranks as one of the truly great dinosaur localities of the world.

Tendaguru! Its name conjures up the African mystique. Everything about Tendaguru and its long history made me want to go there. There was even a tradition linking it to the museum in Nairobi. Louis Leakey, Richard's father, served on the first British expedition to Tendaguru in 1924 when this part of Tanzania was called Tanganyika.

Fate took Louis Leakey to Tendaguru. While a student at Cambridge, he

FIGURE 2: SPINOSAURUS, a carnivorous dinosaur from Africa, eating a large lungfish. Bones of this beast were found in Egypt by German expeditions, who shipped them to Europe, where they were destroyed in the Allied bombing of Stuttgart during World War II. SPINOSAURUS has a long, narrow snout, which suggests it might have eaten fish, and a saillike hump on its back supported by long projections from the vertebrae. Like other carnivorous dinosaurs, the footprints of SPINOSAURUS would show three pointed toes.

FIGURE 3: OURANOSAURUS, an herbivorous dinosaur from Africa. This dinosaur was first discovered by the French in West Africa. Although it has long projections off the vertebrae supporting a saillike hump similar to that seen in meat-eating SPINOSAURUS, the two are not closely related. OURANOSAURUS is a plant-eater grouped with the duck-billed dinosaurs. Its footprints would show blunter toes, less formidably clawed than those of carnivorous dinosaurs.

was kicked in the head, twice, in a rugby match. This caused his cranium to ache whenever he concentrated. Studies were out; he was forced to take a year's leave. Being born in Kenya of missionary parents, and being fluent in Kiswahili, a language used widely across East Africa, he had the African experience the expedition needed and the time off from his studies to allow him to take part in the work of excavating dinosaurs in the continent that was his home.

Even before Louis Leakey, Tendaguru had an illustrious history in the annals of paleontology. Bones were first discovered there by a German mining engineer in 1907, in what was then called German East Africa, *Deutsch-Ostafrika*. By 1909 there was an expedition under way, well financed, for German honor, through the dogged determination of the director of Berlin's natural-history museum. Excavations continued for five years until January 1913. At the height of fieldwork nearly five hundred laborers were employed, all of whom, and many of their families, had to be provided with food and water. Imagine the logistics of supplying a small townful of excavators in tropical Africa eighty years ago.

African crews worked in the pits under the watchful eyes of their white supervisors, scratching huge bones from the Earth. Each fossil was encased in plaster or covered with red mud to protect it from damage. Then it was cushioned in dry grass and crated in cylinders of bamboo slats and round cross-sections of logs. More than 250 tons, well over five thousand man-loads of fossils, each carried on an aching shoulder or teetering atop a throbbing head, were transported over fifty miles from Tendaguru to the Indian Ocean at Lindi to be shipped to Europe. Imagine the endless lines of porters snaking their way for days toward the coast. This was the Africa of the movies. Never before has there been a dinosaur expedition of such magnitude. It is difficult to conceive of there ever being one like it again.

In 1914, at the height of the German Tendaguru expeditions, the First World War spread to Africa from Europe. For most of us this is also the Africa of the movies, because our only familiarity with it is Bogart and Hepburn in *The African Queen*. But the war was real. The commander of German forces in East Africa was Paul von Lettow-Vorbeck, whose namesake is the Tendaguru dinosaur *Dryosaurus lettowvorbecki*. Lake Malaŵi in August 1914 was the venue of the first British naval victory of the war. The British steamship *Guendolen* fired upon a German gunboat, the *Hermann von Wissman*, while it was beached for repairs. The German captain, who knew the British captain as a friend, rowed out to the *Guendolen* to find out what was happening. He was placed under arrest.

Germany lost the war and its African colonies. The Cameroons were divided between Britain and France. Namibia became a South African protectorate. *Deutsch-Ostafrika* became Tanganyika Territory in British East Africa. Thus the stage was set for the British Museum to enter Tendaguru, which it did a decade later. And, with the British entry into Tendaguru, the Leakey family, because of Louis's aching head, entered into the world of dinosaurs.

The leader of the first British Tendaguru expedition was a Canadian dinosaur hunter named W. E. Cutler. He had never been to Africa before, and that is why Louis Leakey, with his knowledge of Africa as a native-born Kenyan, was so valuable to the expedition. Leakey proceeded before Cutler from London to Lindi on the African coast, then, with fifteen porters, he set off up-country to Tendaguru. Eight weeks later, in June 1924, Leakey guided Cutler to the camp he had built. The two *wazungu,* whites, hired about a hundred laborers, some from as far away as Nyasaland, now Malaŵi. In October Leakey left for England while Cutler remained. Nine months later Cutler was dead of malaria.

Cutler was replaced by F.W.H. Migeod. He had African experience from his civil service background, but he was not a paleontologist. In 1930 Migeod and an assistant, Rex Parrington, a young Cambridge student, made an exploratory side trip from Tendaguru to Nyasaland to determine if bones reported from the northwestern shore of Lake Nyasa, Livingstone's lake, were like those of Tendaguru. They crossed the lake on the *Guendolen,* the same ship that sixteen years earlier had scored the World War I naval victory against the Germans. Migeod not only found dinosaurs, he also found other kinds of bones in rocks older and younger than the dinosaur beds. After two months he returned to Tendaguru. In January 1931 the British Museum abandoned Tendaguru and East African dinosaurs. No one has seriously worked there since.

The British effort was nowhere nearly so well financed as the German expeditions. Consequently the two were of different scales, and their results were of different magnitude. Nevertheless, held up against any digs except those of the Germans at Tendaguru, the British expeditions were exceptional. Both the Germans and the British opened quarries in the hilly countryside for a two-mile stretch from north to south, and almost the same distance from east to west. All through the area dinosaur bones lay entombed in river sediments 145 million years old. The dinosaurs of Tendaguru are not so different from those of the same age in Utah, or Wyoming, or Colorado. Like their Northern Hemisphere cousins, the bones belonged to menacing car- nivores, giant herbivores, light-boned coelurosaurs, and other extinct mem- bers of the dinosaur community (Figure 4).

North American *Stegosaurus,* with its rows of triangular plates running down its back to the spiked end of its tail, has its Tendaguru counterpart in *Kentrosaurus,* with an equally small, long head, but with spikes replacing plates higher up along the rump. These animals fed on vegetation low to the ground.

FIGURE 4: *African life 145 million years ago. This scene is a reconstruction of the famous fossil beds at Tendaguru, Tanzania. Dinosaurs lived along the shores and bays of the ancient East African coast. Here* ALLOSAURUS, *a carnivore, spies a group of the giraffe-necked sauropod* BRACHIOSAURUS. *The plated stegosaur* KENTROSAURUS

and the lightly built carnivore ELAPHROSAURUS are in the lower left. Plant-eating DRYOSAURUS is in the far left. The trees are related to living monkey puzzles. There are also cycads related to sego palms, horsetails, and low-growing conifers—relatives of pines. Notably missing are the flowering plants or angiosperms.

Also low to the ground was the small, primitive herbivore *Dryosaurus,* scampering in goatlike flocks, common to both sides of the equator. *Dicraeosaurus,* with its long, sinuous neck, mirrored *Diplodocus,* and so, too, but to a lesser degree, did *Janenschia.* Big *Barosaurus* lived on both continents. These were huge, four-footed beasts. As gigantic herbivores, they worried the trees for fodder to fill their bellies. Ferocious *Allosaurus,* with daggers for teeth that were half a foot long, preyed on whichever victim failed to parry its thrust.

At Tendaguru *Brachiosaurus* towered over them all, its spectacular forty-foot height embarrassing its neighbors. It stood on all fours with its forelimbs longer than the hind. That raised its chest, giving it what some of us might call a proud stature. At the summit of its vertical, giraffelike neck balanced its grotesquely small head, about the size of a not-so-large beach ball. The forehead was high and domed, with nostrils at the apex. The prognathous jaws extended forward into an absurd, toothy duck's bill. The crowns of the teeth were hardly the size of teaspoons. Ten large bull elephants, or a family herd of females and young, would barely equal the weight of one of these giants. This beast could weigh more than fifty tons, perhaps as much as eighty. How could this animal maintain its bulk feeding, as it had to do, through such a small head?

The bones at Tendaguru are so common, and the look of the dinosaurs so familiar, at least in a general sort of way, that it is amusing, if not informative, to speculate about their lives. Imagine *Brachiosaurus,* its huge size making it appear to move as if in slow motion, head erect on a thin obelisk of a neck, the body resting on legs like the columns of an animate temple. It stops walking and dips its head slightly to pluck sprigs and needles from the top of a conifer. The deep green foliage rides a peristaltic wave down its fire-hose esophagus. The bolus halts at the gizzard to be ground by millstones called gastroliths before sliding on to become engulfed in the roiling, hot mass of compost fermenting in the cavernous gut. Energy for the great body piggybacked on billions of commensal microbes. *Brachiosaurus* is always warm. The fermenting compost in its belly and the thickness of insulating flesh assure a high temperature. Hot blood from deep in the coelomic cavity flows through pumping arteries, thick as ropes, then passes through capillaries and veins that carry the heat to the body's dry surface. This dinosaur likes the cooling feel of rain washing the dust from its rough skin. It likes the cool taste of water. Imagine *Brachiosaurus* alive!

. . .

THEY NO LONGER breathe, but five skeletons from Tendaguru—*Kentrosaurus, Dryosaurus, Dicraeosaurus, Elaphrosaurus,* and the noble *Brachiosaurus*—can be seen today at the Museum für Naturkunde on public display in what was formerly East Berlin. They were all once alive and members of the same community. What else could have been living with them? With so many dinosaur bones, there had to be small animals as well. And in fact there were. The Germans collected a number of animals besides dinosaurs including sharks, fish, crocodiles, flying pterosaurs, and one small, broken fragment of a jaw with the bone missing on one side and all the teeth gone. But that was enough to show it was a mammal. Tendaguru had just what I was looking for in a new project. I could go into Tendaguru with my techniques, I thought, virtually assured of finding what I wanted. I did not need huge expeditions. All I needed was a few tons of good, fossiliferous dirt. I could extract tiny mammal teeth from that. The dinosaurs were all known anyway, right? What I would find would be new. It did not occur to me at the time, even though I was working in a museum, how important the dinosaurs ought to be in educating the general public about the life of the past and about this work in particular. Nor did I realize at the time the truly exciting scientific questions that dinosaurs posed. I should have, but I did not. I was too involved with the thought of tiny mammals.

Living in Kenya as I did, the logistics of working at Tendaguru would be manageable. Even though the border with Tanzania was officially closed, if I got clearance to work at Tendaguru, permission to cross the border would follow. After all, had not Bonnie and I been allowed to cross the border and visit Mary Leakey at Olduvai Gorge? I would drive down to Tendaguru from Nairobi, taking everything I needed—food, collecting equipment, a drum of diesel—because nothing was available on the open market in Tanzania at that time. I looked forward anxiously to driving the length of the country. I was ready to go.

By this time I had some familiarity with how African bureaucracies work. They are different from American bureaucracies, but not necessarily worse. Both can be equally frustrating. I set about the slow process of obtaining permission from Tanzanian authorities. My first overtures were encouragingly received.

"An excellent project," I was told. "Please contact the next administrator."

This continued for some time. I was lulled into an unwarranted sense of impending success. I should have known better. The door slammed shut when I was told that it was a great project, and someone else was doing it.

No one else has.

WHAT NEXT? Two times now, in Kenya and in Tanzania, I had been unable to get where I wanted to go. Two strikes. Should I just hang it up?

There was no way I could do that no matter how discouraged I was. And then, wouldn't you know it, just at that time, as fate would have it, a Berkeley student, an African studying in California, was visiting the Museum in Nairobi in connection with his doctoral research. I thought he was Tanzanian. I explained the situation to him, searching for some lead in his responses that might give a clue as to how I could surmount the obstacles between me and the fossils. Zefe looked at me quizzically as I spoke to him of Tanzania.

"I am from Malaŵi," he said. "Come there. We have dinosaur beds."

THE ROCKS ZEFE was talking about, the same ones Migeod and Parrington had visited along Livingstone's lake in 1930, the same ones that had yielded specimens to the British Museum, sounded almost too good. True, they did not have the reputation of Tendaguru for vast quantities of bone, but on the other hand, the area was more remote. It had been visited but never seriously worked by a paleontologist. Younger than the Dinosaur Beds were rocks of the right age to contain *Australopithecus,* humankind's ancestor. Zefe was doing his Ph.D. dissertation on them, and he had found many bones weathering out already. Still younger, there was interesting archaeology, cultural remains from the African Stone Age. Still older than the Dinosaur Beds were rocks with fossils of animals that were traditionally considered sort of evolutionarily "half way" between reptiles and mammals because, although they are on the mammalian limb of the evolutionary tree, they have a primitive, reptilian look to them.

All of these different aged rocks with their wealth of fossils were found in the same area of northern Malaŵi. Surely an expedition to such a place would pay off. If I did not get exactly what I wanted in the Dinosaur Beds, I would just move into younger rocks. If that did not work, I would go older. The state of knowledge of African paleontology being what it was, I was sure to find something significant. It was a no-lose situation.

Yes, Malaŵi was the place to go. Zefe had a job waiting for him at the Department of Antiquities in the capital, Lilongwe, when he finished his Ph.D. We got along well. He was probably as happy to have a colleague interested in coming to work in Malaŵi as I was in going there. I would study the bones, Zefe would study the rocks they came from. Together we would unravel the geological history of Malaŵi, and put its fossils into the who's who of ancient life. All that remained was to do it.

Zefe and I decided that we would wait for his imminent graduation from Berkeley. Then, with Ph.D. in hand, he would return to Malaŵi. I would submit a proposal to the National Geographic Society for funds to support our work. If we got funded, we would be off.

It was two years before the plan was put into action.

MY COMMITMENT TO investigating the fossils of Malaŵi stems from a deep and considered calculation that they would provide an important chapter in the history of life. Serious study of the history of life goes back a long, long way, but a good place to start looking at it is with Charles Darwin (Figure 5). David Livingstone was a contemporary of Darwin's whose masterful work provided a foundation for understanding evolution and for making sense out of fossils. Livingstone first visited the shores of Lake Malaŵi in 1859, the same year Darwin published *The Origin of Species*. It was an exciting time in the development of great ideas.

FIGURE 5: *David Livingstone, whose explorations and opposition to slavery opened the Interior of Africa to the Western world, and Charles Darwin, who elucidated natural selection as the mechanism for evolution.*

Livingstone was trained in theology and medicine, but he had a broad interest in natural history fostered by his studies with the great British anatomist Sir Richard Owen. It was Sir Richard Owen who coined the term *dinosaur,* an event that occurred just after Livingstone first departed for Africa. Livingstone admired Owen, and the admiration was reciprocated by the teacher. Years after being a pupil, Livingstone brought to Owen, all the way from Africa, an interesting but heavy specimen. It was an elephant tusk with a strange spiral curve.

Sir Richard was very influential in building the British Museum. He was an accomplished and recognized scientist. Darwin repeatedly cites his works and opinions in the *Origin of Species.* Moreover Darwin refers to Owen's former student by name in Chapter 1 of the *Origin,* stating in his discussion of biological variation under domestication, in a passage on the widespread use of selective breeding of livestock, "Livingstone shows how much good domestic breeds [of animals] are valued by the negroes of the interior of Africa who have not associated with Europeans."

Still, long before Darwin published the *Origin of Species,* Livingstone, in his own way, concluded that science and religion were not opposed. Both, thought Livingstone, were mutually necessary and helpful revelations of the Divine. He remained, however, like Owen, unsympathetic to Darwin's views on evolution. His conclusion was reached not so much by the study of Darwin's work—there is no evidence he ever studied it—but rather because nothing in his travels suggested to him that humans descended from apelike ancestors. That view is held by some even now, but with much less justification than in Livingstone's day.

Evolution provides a framework within which we can view the interrelatedness of life, of all the myriad different species that have ever existed. The Earth through time provides the setting in which evolution takes place. The world as we know it today results from a vast amalgam of intertwined physical and biological processes acting forever under the ambient circumstances of the times. The future, in its turn, will be molded by these same immanent processes. There is an unbroken continuity in Earth history. However, in the final measure, the Earth and life are continually changing. No time is exactly the same as any other, and no place is ever exactly the same twice.

Life changes through the millennia. No species has remained unchanged since the beginning of life on Earth. Most species, the overwhelming majority, are different and distinct in successive epochs of Earth history. That is an empirical fact. Even so, although apparently great differences exist between, say, jellyfish and whippoorwills, or between kelp and rhododendrons, each distinct species is related to all others. Of this Darwin said, "It is a truly wonderful fact—the wonder of which we are apt to overlook from familiarity—that all animals and plants throughout all time and space should be related to each other."

There is continuity in the spectrum of life. All species, whether extinct or still living, are related, in greater or lesser degree, in much the same way as we as individuals are related through family genealogy to great-grandparents or second cousins twice removed. The change of life through time, this historical parade of related species, is evolution.

The big difference between an evolutionary tree and a genealogical tree is that the branches of an evolutionary tree, unlike family histories, cannot join and merge the way families can, with the marriage of a Smith to a Jones, for instance. Contemporary species cannot interbreed. Neither can time sequential species, but the transformation of an ancestral species to a descendant species is a process that takes place through time. Ancestral species evolve into descendant species, or they go extinct.

The continuity of life is obvious and logical when read in the fossil record, or even when viewed in the immense array of living species. Moreover, it has adequate testimony in the fundamental molecules of life, perhaps most prominently in DNA, the substance that carries the genetic code from generation to generation. The complex molecules of life are surprisingly uniform in their basic structural plans throughout the panoply of species alive today, even though in less fundamental details the molecules of different species differ slightly. Molecules such as DNA and proteins are the basic functional and structural components of cells. No life exists without them. In practical terms it is this similarity, this basic uniformity in both composition and function at the molecular level, independent of the diversity of species, that allows, for example, the use of laboratory rats as substitutes for humans in experimental medicine. It is the basis for the biotechnology revolution, allowing for the genetic engineering of improved agricultural stocks, or the mass production of medicines as by-products of modified bacteria. These advances derive from the recognition of the basic continuity, the relatedness, of life, the fact that species have changed over time notwithstanding.

As species of organisms have changed through the millennia, so has the level of biotic sophistication, for want of better words, changed. The simpler basic divisions of life, such as single-celled protozoans for instance, have been around longer than more complex, multicellular organisms with differentiated tissues and organ systems. This is not an inexorable transcendental progression from single-celled bacterium in primordial ooze to lofty, godlike humans in the Garden of Eden. It is a generality. Besides, there are still lots and lots of different kinds of bacteria around. And yeasts. And algae. And sponges. And all kinds of simple organisms. A few kinds of simple organisms, such as some parasites, are simple because they are degenerate. All these species have a role in the community of living creatures. Nevertheless, in general, the more simple a creature is, if it has parts that will fossilize, the farther back in time fossils representative of its level of sophistication can be found. Those simple organisms that are still around—the bacteria, yeast, and other primitive creatures—belong to species that evolved along lineages that have not branched as significantly, or so greatly, from the ancestral stock.

Thus, single-celled bacteria, as a group, not any particular living species, have been on Earth much longer than multicellular sponges. These have been around longer than fishes, and they longer than reptiles and mammals, and among mammals, humans are late on the scene. In this sense there is a progression, but only very generally. This is not to say that fish and reptiles and invertebrates are not sophisticated. They obviously are, having evolved along their own evolutionary pathways. They live as members of complicated ecological communities that have changed with time. Compare, for instance, the dinosaur-dominated landscapes of the Mesozoic with the mammal-dominated communities of today. To fully understand the origin of the modern world, the evolution of the species involved, and the evolution of the communities to which they belong must be brought to light. And ordering species in the dimension of time is necessary for both.

Comparison of the DNA or certain proteins among living species can lead to conclusions regarding the antiquity of species just as the study of fossils can lead to such conclusions. All species have DNA with essentially the same architecture, but more closely related species have more similar DNA; less closely related species have increasingly more, albeit minor, differences. The basic structure of the molecules is constant, but relatively small submolecular differences occur. Among species, these add up more and more with the increasing distance of relationship and remoteness of common ancestry. The total difference in the DNA of two species is generally related to the length of time that their evolutionary lineages have been separate and distinct. That means that fossils or molecules can sometimes be used to test and verify conclusions based on one or the other. And that is part of the reason why recent discoveries of plant and insect DNA fragments preserved in fossils are so exciting. They have the potential to meld molecular evolution and paleontology in a way never before possible. It is science with the excitement, and therefore the appeal, of fiction, seemingly a move toward real-life *Jurassic Park.*

Evolution is the basic fact of life for all species. Living things change through the millennia, but because of the continuity necessary for life to beget life, living things in their most basic mechanisms remain similar. The more things change, the more things stay the same.

AT THE TIME David Livingstone first reached the shores of Lake Malaŵi in 1859, Charles Darwin was presenting the world with a mechanism for evolution. That was well over one hundred years ago. We have learned much since then that Darwin did not know—for instance that the genetic code of a cell, passed on each time the cell divides, is carried by DNA. Nevertheless Darwin made lasting and surprisingly resilient contributions to the study of evolution. His genius was recognized by his countrymen; ten years after Livingstone died, Darwin, too, was buried in Westminster Abbey.

Darwin's mechanism for evolution is natural selection, a wonderfully elegant concept. More reproductive cells, sperm and egg, are produced in any species than will ever successfully produce progeny. Add to that the fact that each individual of a species is different. Darwin knew that, and he knew from domesticated animals that certain traits breed true. Not knowing about DNA, or the genetic code, Darwin's theory had a weakness that is overcome to some degree by modern genetics. We know much more now about the nature of genetic variation, how it is maintained, and how it is passed from generation to generation. If it is important to know about evolution, it is necessary to know about genetics.

The next premise of natural selection is that resources for each species are limited. Food, or suitable habitat, or mates—there will never be enough of something to go around. So some individuals and some sex cells are better able to cope with the environment by virtue of the nature of their variation. Those that can reproduce more than others will be naturally selected for by the environment. In that sense reproductive success, leaving more of your own genes, is a measure of evolutionary success.

The logic of natural selection is simple and easy to understand. It does have a significant role in evolution. But clearly there has to be much more that we do not yet understand about the feedback from the environment to the genetic code and about the control of embryological development, for instance. And above all, about the genetic code itself. That is where the study of life's molecules and their role in evolution is leading today. The process of evolution, when it is more fully understood, will encompass generalities of far-ranging significance to how life works because it will be a synthesis of results from genetics, molecular biology, embryology, ecology, and all other branches of the life sciences. That is truly elegant.

For any living species, as we have seen, we can already learn much of its evolutionary history written at the molecular level in its DNA and proteins. But that is only part of the picture of life's development on Earth. These things can never tell us the whole story about the wonderful variety of life, completely vanished, lost to our eyes through extinction. Only fossils can tell us about the tremendous numbers of once-living biological success stories, now gone. Only fossils can tell us the pathways that evolution did take, in addition to where they ended up. And it is only through the fossil record that we can observe, empirically, the results of the admixture of Earth and life processes. If we are wise enough to read the record, it can help us, as a species, predict the global outcome of our environmental actions, for better or worse, through an understanding of how fossil organisms responded to environmental changes imposed upon them by the Earth in times long past.

UNDERSTANDING EVOLUTIONARY history requires understanding geologic time because evolution is, by definition, change through time. So we have to have a way to measure geologic time. How do we do it? How do we know how old a fossil is? How can we tell?

Old bones, or shells, or petrified wood—any fossils—are usually found in sedimentary rocks formed from deposits of mud, sand, or lime at the bottom of lakes and rivers, beaches and seas. Animal or plant remains get caught up in the depositional process, more or less as geological particles themselves. Some rocks, such as chalk, or coal, are made up almost completely of fossils. As a part of a sedimentary system, the fossils we find tell us about the geological conditions of the past. But they are also components of a once-living community and as such they tell us of the environment and ecology in which they were a part before they entered the geological realm. These extremes—conditions of life, conditions of fossilization—grade one into the other, and each tells us something about the other. The age of a bed of rock, formed from the hardening of the sediments, represents the time the fossils were entombed and, in a geological sense, is taken in most instances as the time when the fossilized organism lived.

Any bed of sediment must be younger than the surface on which it is deposited. Therefore, it is obvious that in a sequence of sedimentary rocks, the oldest bed is on the bottom, the youngest at the top, and the age decreases progressively from the former to the latter. This concept of superposition (Figure 6) is the simple basis for being able to determine the relative age of fossils. Those at the bottom are older than those at the top. That is also the fundamental principle underlying the empirical statement that life changes through time. Different fossils occur in lower and higher beds; in other words, older and younger rocks. That is the concept of faunal—or floral—succession. Different species of organisms succeed each other in stacked layers of rock, and through time.

But it is not enough to know the relative age of a fossil. We really want to know how old, in numbers of years, a particular fossil is. The key to telling that kind of geologic time is through the natural radioactivity in rocks. After rocks such as basalt crystallize from molten lava, radioactive potassium or other elements will decay, through radioactivity, into another kind of matter. By knowing how rapidly a particular kind of radioactive element decays, the age of the cooled rock can be calculated. The idea is simple. But it only works on the right kinds of rocks, and then only if they do not get adversely affected by other Earth processes. Unfortunately the appropriate rocks for dating are not generally the ones that contain fossils. The technique of radiocarbon dating can actually date fossils, but not very old ones, and it is useless for things as old as dinosaurs.

It is easy to imagine a volcano such as Mount Saint Helens spewing ash, or lava oozing down a hillside to the sea, as happens in Hawaii. Particles of ash or flows of lava become incorporated in the sequence of sedimentary rock being formed. Radioactive elements in the volcanic rocks can be assayed, providing a minimum age for all the rock layers, and their contained fossils, below the dated rock and a maximum age for all the rocks and fossils above the dated rock. In a sequence with a lot of fossils throughout, and many lavas or volcanic ashes interspersed with the sedimentary layers, the dating can become very accurate, geologically speaking.

There is another way to figure out the ages of rocks. It is based on the behavior of the Earth's magnetic field. Paleomagnetism depends first on knowing relative ages determined from a sequence of fossils and their superposition, and on radiometric age calculations. It is nevertheless very useful because it allows extreme, long-distance precision in identifying rocks that are of identical age but that cannot themselves be radiometrically dated.

Here is how it works. The Earth has a magnetic field, as we all know because a compass needle aligns itself with magnetic north. Because compass needles always point north, we are able to tell directions, even in the dark, and therefore we do not get lost. That is well and good for the present, but it just so happens that at various times in the past the compass needle did not point to the north. It pointed south, 180 degrees opposite from what it should. What is more, these periods of reversal appear to have taken place at random intervals, at unpredictable times in the past. Sometimes the compass pointed south for a few hundred thousand years, sometimes for millions. The lengths of time varied. We know this because many rocks contain minerals that acted as tiny compass needles while the rocks were forming. The Earth's magnetic field is recorded in the sequence of rocks at the Earth's surface.

Thus, if you were to look at the history of the Earth's magnetic field and the direction in which the north end of the compass needle would point, as if recorded on a continuous tape, you would see a series of normal and reversed polarity intervals, none of them being exactly the same length, because none of them lasted the same length of time (see Figure 6). Because of the variation in lengths of intervals of normals, then reversals, then normals, the tape would present a kind of code, rather like a digital recording. Just as the pattern of simple on-off digits can record a symphony on a laser disk, if a stratigraphic section is long enough to encompass a number of polarity reversals, and if the rocks preserve the normal-reversed "digital" signal of the Earth's magnetic field layer by layer, the magnetic pattern preserved in the rocks will be unique to the time interval in which the rocks were formed, the way a fingerprint pattern is unique to a person. The pattern can be as characteristic of that time interval as a symphony is of a composer. And just as a recorded symphony can be listened to and appreciated most anywhere, anywhere rocks exhibit a characteristic pattern of polarity changes, you can be sure they are of the age defined by that magnetic pattern. Of course, there are any number of things that make the real world more complicated than theory, but in general, that is how paleomagnetism works for telling geological time. If a specific polarity pattern can be matched up from place to place, the rocks recording the patterns are of the same age. So are the fossils they might contain.

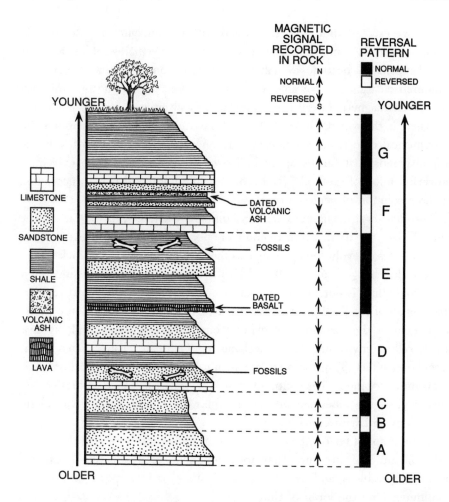

FIGURE 6: *How to date fossils. On the left is a sequence of layered rocks as shown by the patterns of lava, ash, shale, sandstone, and limestone. The rock layers are oldest at the bottom and progressively younger toward the top. Fossils that occur lower in a sequence of layered rock are older than those that occur higher in the sequence. Volcanic rocks like basalt and ash can be dated using radioactive decay of their constituent minerals. They set older and younger limits on the absolute age, in numbers of years, of a fossil that occurs above, below, or between dated rocks. The Earth's magnetic signal preserved in a sequence of rock is used to compile a reversal pattern that can be matched with other rocks of the same age anywhere in the world that the pattern might be recognized.*

So, we can tell time with fossils and with paleomagnetism. But neither technique provides an age in numbers of years. Nevertheless, if any absolute date happens to become available to a succession of strata through the radiometric dating of a volcanic rock, that date becomes applicable wherever the precise magnetic interval, or correlated fossil interval, can be identified, anywhere in the world. On the bottom of the ocean, or the top of a mountain. A numerical date is determined in only one place, but through fossils and paleomagnetism, it can be applied all over the place. This is an extremely powerful union of methods, far beyond simple floral and faunal succession, in the resolution of geologic time.

Through these techniques we can compare what is occurring at a given time all over the Earth, from region to region. We can look in excruciating detail at rates of evolutionary change as they are preserved in the rock record because the changes can be calibrated with absolute dates. This refined view of geologic time is not simply relevant to evolution. It is relevant to understanding all of the Earth's processes that benefit from the dimension of time. That includes the formation of many economic ore deposits, and, because fossils reflect environment, to mechanisms of climate change, such as the greenhouse effect. Thus the work of paleontology has broad implications. Just as evolutionary theory has continuity with the practical aspects of biology and medicine, so, too, does paleontology merge with economic and environmental geology and with climatology.

In the simplest terms, the biosphere of life and lithosphere of rocks are not independent. They are one. They are components of a perpetual tapestry of incomprehensible grandeur, the weft of stone and warp of life, woven continuously on the loom of time.

ONE DOES NOT need to go to Africa to study evolution or geologic time. That can be done anywhere. But to apply the concepts of evolution and geologic time on a global scale, Africa does have to be brought into the picture. In addition, there is another aspect of change through the millennia that must be considered: continental drift, the dance of the great Earth.

It is well accepted among geologists nowadays that the Earth's surface, the entire outer shell of the globe, is divided into rigid plates that move relative to each other. That is the concept of plate tectonics (Figure 7). The continents float on the plates, because they are made of lighter rocks, and are carried along passively as the plates move, drifting as it were across the planet.

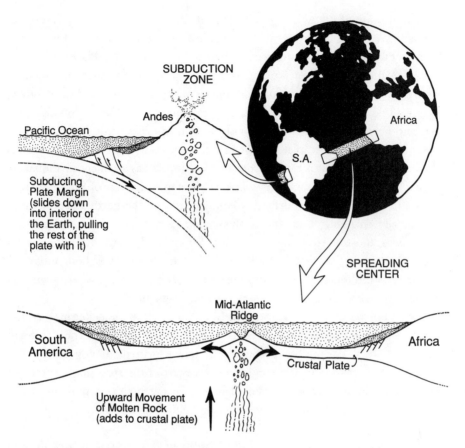

FIGURE 7: Plate tectonics and continental drift. Nowhere can this be better visualized than with South America, Africa, and the ocean in between. Continents under tension may form rift valleys and eventually tear apart. If that happens, an ocean will be born where the landmasses separate. That is what happened 100 million years ago as Africa and South America split. Oceans grow larger as molten rock rises from inside the Earth to form new ocean floor at spreading centers such as the Mid-Atlantic Ridge (bottom). Thus, what begins as a rift valley may end up an ocean basin, with the continents drifting away from each other as the ocean grows wider. That is why the outlines of the continents on either side of the ocean often fit together like pieces of a puzzle. On the western margin of South America (left) one plate dips deeply under another and is consumed in a subduction zone. Volcanic mountains such as the Andes are formed along the edge of the continent as a result of the subduction process and the heat it generates.

The motion of plates can go in different directions. Plates may diverge at spreading centers, such as the Mid-Atlantic Ridge deep under the ocean. Continents move away from each other as plates diverge. Plates may converge, or move toward each other, one dipping beneath another in a subduction zone. This causes the floating continents to move toward each other, even collide, forming mountains such as the Himalayas. Plates also slide past one another, as is happening now with the San Andreas Fault, a very obvious boundary between two plates right in our own backyard—or front yard, as the case may be. That is one reason why California has so many earthquakes. Someday, millions of years hence, Los Angeles may lie west of San Francisco.

If, through continental drift, the configuration of the Earth's continents is continually changing, then the configuration of oceans, which separate the continents, must be changing too. In fact, for an Earth that is 4.5 billion years old, it is absolutely startling that the oldest rocks in the ocean floor today are a mere 208 million years old. And only a few are that old. Most are younger. Some are much younger. Some are forming right now.

Why are oceans so young when the Earth is so old? Because at the mid-ocean ridges molten lava rises from deep in the earth and cools to form hard rock. New ocean floor is continually being formed. As new sea floor is formed, it pushes the continents farther away from the spreading center. At convergent boundaries subducting slabs of the Earth's crust pull the plates with their floating landmasses down along behind them. It is as if the continents are on conveyor belts.

It so happens that the movement of continents can be traced back in time using the magnetic signal preserved in the rocks of the ocean floor. As new rock is added to the Earth's crust at mid-ocean ridges, magnetic minerals align themselves with the direction of the Earth's magnetic field. As we have already seen, changes in the Earth's magnetic field can be used for deciphering geologic time. In the sea floor magnetic history is reflecting the magnetic field as new rock is formed and extruded out to become part of the sea floor itself (Figure 8). The farther from the ridge in either direction, the older the rock.

If new rock is continually added to the sea floor at mid-ocean ridges, the sea surrounding the Mid-Atlantic Ridge must have been smaller at any given time in the past. Africa and South America must have been closer together. It follows that the past position of the continents at a given point in geologic time can be easily reconstructed, theoretically anyway, by identifying specific portions in the fingerprint pattern of the paleomagnetic record of the ocean floor. It is like running a tape in reverse.

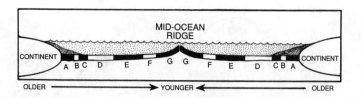

Figure 8: Magnetic stripes aligned symmetrically along spreading centers such as the Mid-Atlantic Ridge demonstrate that new ocean floor is formed at spreading centers. Compare the magnetic reversal pattern seen here aligned horizontally with the vertical pattern in Figure 6. The patterns are the same because the rocks, formed at the same time, acquired the signature of the Earth's magnetic field at the time of their formation. If rocks are of the same age, and if they clearly preserve the record of the Earth's magnetic field at the time of their formation, they will exhibit virtually identical magnetic patterns wherever they are formed, whether it be in the sea floor or on the continents.

Because the magnetic field affects the whole world, the same signal at any given point in time, past or present, will be recorded in sedimentary rocks piling up on continents, or in sea-floor rocks cooling along a mid-ocean ridge. So if the same magnetic fingerprint can be identified simultaneously on land and sea, we should be able to determine where a continent was at the precise time that a particular suite of fossils was living on land. That is truly amazing.

If all the oceans are young, geologically speaking, and if we can trace the movement of continents backward in time, we will discover that at one time all the landmasses were assembled, puzzlelike, into a super-supercontinent, Pangaea. It had itself been assembled from component continental parts in much earlier times. In its ultimate breakup to form the continents as we know them now (Figure 9), Pangaea first began to split into a major but complicated supercontinent in the north, Laurasia, and into a second supercontinent, called Gondwana, in the south. These great landmasses were separated in the east by an ocean, a remnant of which is familiar to us as the Mediterranean Sea. As time progressed, the Atlantic began to form, at first dividing eastern North America from northwestern Africa. At this stage there was no southern Atlantic because Africa and South America were still joined in Gondwana.

Africa became progressively isolated from the rest of Gondwana, first on its eastern margin, then down to the south, then up the west side. It was as if a gigantic zipper around Africa became unfastened. The South Atlantic Ocean formed as South America separated from Africa's west coast.

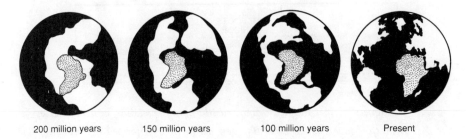

FIGURE 9: *Approximate geographic arrangements of the continents from 200 million years ago to the present (Africa is stippled). All of the continents were joined into the super-supercontinent of Pangaea 200 million years ago. Pangaea split into Gondwana, comprising the modern southern continents plus India, and another large landmass called Laurasia. By 100 million years ago Africa was beginning to split from South America, and since then the continents and oceans have achieved their modern distributions. The geographic arrangement of continents and oceans through time is a fundamental element of the evolution of the Earth and the life on it. It explains why we should expect similarities between African and South American dinosaurs (and other animals) prior to 100 million years ago.*

The last detachment of Africa from remnants of Gondwana occurred 100 million years ago. At that time what is now Brazil in South America slid away from West Africa. Imagine, if you can, standing on the beach in the Gulf of Guinea on the African coast, watching South America sailing across the ocean, the captain of its own tectonic plate, speeding away from you at the same rate at which your fingernails grow! At that time, one hundred million years ago, in what may seem a slow, inexorable process, the Atlantic Ocean was completed from south to north. Africa and its animals became isolated from all other continents.

What happens when continents become isolated from each other? All continents have their own characteristic plants and animals. When we think of Australia, we think of kangaroos, and we think of the duck-billed platypus, its scientific name, *Ornithorhynchus anatinus,* made into a children's song by Mr. Rogers. For South America, we might think of opossums, and sloths, and armadillos. Africa has vast herds of antelope and zebra on the plains, and lions, and aardvarks. Why should there be characteristic animals on different continents?

When a continent becomes isolated geographically, its inhabitants lose the opportunity to interact in any way with the members of their own species on other continents from which they have been separated, unless mixing occurs later for some reason or another. From that point onward in time evolution performs in a separate theater, distinct from what may happen on other continents, yet dependent for its raw talent on the legacy of previous distributions of species across the globe. The current geographical distribution of antelopes has little to do with continental positions in the Age of Reptiles because antelopes, as clearly recognizable antelopes, are evolutionarily much younger than the plate-tectonic events of the Mesozoic. Where antelopes live today is a reflection of more recent influences. The platypus, however, is a different story. Its roots, and its geography, may very well extend into the Age of Reptiles. Its forebears were around in Australia when the common ancestor of antelopes and humans was little more than a furry grubber of worms and bugs.

By 100 million years ago, when Africa became isolated, flowering plants were beginning to develop into the myriad species that now abound. Because of that it was a time of transition, from the earth tones of previous epochs to a fragrant world splashed with color—color provided by flowers.

Flowers have a purpose. They attract insects that inadvertently pollinate the flowers and thereby facilitate sexual reproduction. How clever! And the insects get a meal. The beauty of flowers is part of a major shift in strategy for plant evolution, but it could not have worked unless insects could see colors. They could, and they speciated, increasing their diversity and their numbers, along with the flowers.

The new diversity and abundance of flowering plants and insects provided an expanded larder for plant-eating herbivores, insect eaters, and predators that ate them both. Among these were animals that would ultimately become familiar to us in the modern world. There were frogs and lizards and mammals. Each of these major groups of vertebrates had been around much longer, but now they were making evolutionary leaps that would suit them in the modern world. They still remained somewhat minor characters in the community of species, viewing the flowers from the shadows of the dinosaurs. But important changes were under way. There was a blossoming of life beginning one hundred million years ago, taking place on fragmenting continents and leading to the richness of the natural world that we see today. Africa, like all the other continents, had its own special role in this great play of life.

2

TAHITI
WITHOUT
SALT

AFRICA HAS BEEN shaped and molded for eons by the global processes of plate tectonics and continental drift. One result is that it has a string of great lakes running across the eastern side of the continent. Lake Malaŵi is the southernmost of the string (Figure 10). It is the third largest and second deepest. In Africa, only Victoria and Tanganyika surpass Lake Malaŵi in area. Only Tanganyika is deeper. Ranked among the other lakes of the world, it is the thirteenth largest, but it is the third deepest. Lake Malaŵi, more than any other single feature, is the essence of the country. It is pervasive. It is overpowering. Through it, the processes of the Earth and the lives of the people become intertwined in a single focus, a common perception.

Lake Malaŵi is blue, lined with boulders and sand beaches. Vertical mountains with near-perpendicular rock walls plummet into the lake, alternating with stretches of low, sometimes marshy shore. Toward the north end, the highlands form the eastern bank. There they are the splendid Livingstone Mountains of Tanzania, dropping precipitously from their height of nearly 10,000 feet headlong into the depths. Then the heights are lost to the eastern shore, and highlands are on the west.

The feet of the mountains are submerged in the depths. It is there, where ramparts begin to rise from the deep, that the lake hides its deepest holes.

FIGURE 10: *Location map of Malaŵi. Our camp is at Ngara in the north, on the shore of the lake. The Dinosaur Beds are near Mwakasyunguti.*

Seemingly sheer cliffs may climb more than a mile from the lake bed, with nearly half of their height hidden below the surface. Gradually, away from the steep banks, the lake becomes more shallow, progressing from the depths toward the opposite, low-lying shore.

Palm trees dot the lake margin. The vision is that of a Pacific island—blue water, green mountains, sand, palms. But it is, of course, very different. For one thing, Lake Malaŵi is fresh. For another, this lake is an island of water in a sea of land. The oceans have never in the history of the African continent transgressed far enough inland to inundate Malaŵi. That can be said of few countries.

No body of water the size of Lake Malaŵi is monolithic. It changes; it is dynamic. Seasonal changes come with the rains, not with the extremes of temperature that characterize the seasons of North America and Europe. When skies are cloudy, the lake is gray and somber. When the sun shines, the water is light, happy. With the clouds and the changing light, the depths take on varying hues of blue, purple, and green, with glints and sparkles, as if the lake were a giant gemstone. Waves roll on the shore. Sometimes they are slow, periodic, mesmerizing. Sometimes they are thunder. The water is pleasant for bathing. The wind feels crisp off the lake. Droplets of clean, fresh water evaporating in the breeze induce prickles of ephemeral excitement.

There is no greater vision than the lake seen from the height of the mountains. From this vantage the distant shores of Tanzania or Mozambique frame the vibrant-blue water in the pastel-purple tints of the far away. Below, the hills stretch green and verdant toward the depths. In the right phase of the moon, clouds, like smoke, rise from the surface of the lake (Figure 11). Livingstone called this *kungu.* However, these clouds are not the vapors of water; rather, they are the hatching of millions of lakeflies, all taking to wing in unison. They are a part of the scene. It adds to the vision.

A ship is occasionally seen plying the lake northward from Monkey Bay on its way to Chilumba and back through other ports. The legacy of ships on Lake Malaŵi is a pleasant distraction. Ships have a history in Malaŵi that goes back to Livingstone's day. Livingstone's first European boat was a steam launch, the *Ma-Robert,* the mother of Robert, named in African fashion for Mrs. Livingstone. He used it on the Zambezi and Shiré rivers.

The first steamship on the lake was the *Ilala,* named for the place where Livingstone died. It was brought to Africa by the Livingstonia Mission. Built in London and dismantled, the pieces were numbered and shipped to the Dark

FIGURE 11: Kungu mist, a horde of lakeflies rising from the lake after hatching. For scale notice the size of the canoes. Moistened winnowing baskets are used to collect the tiny flies for the kitchen if the swarm drifts over a lakeside village.

Continent, where it was reassembled and launched on the lake in 1875. In 1882 the African Lakes Company took it over. Subsequently it was sold and transferred out of the lake. In 1922 the original *Ilala,* after nearly fifty years' service, was working at the mouth of the Zambezi. It sank soon afterward. The *Ilala II* plows the lake today. It is diesel-powered.

There were many other ships on the lake between the two *Ilalas.* I have already spoken of the illustrious service to the British war effort, and later to paleontology, of the gunship *Guendolen.* The *Dove* was a side-paddle steamer that patrolled the upper Shiré River in 1893, later making runs on the lake. Its nickname was *Chikapa,* a Yao word referring to the circular motion of dancing buttocks. How appropriate.

There was also the *Chauncy Maples,* brought by the Universities Mission to Central Africa and launched on the lake in 1901. It was named for a martyr to the lake, Bishop Chauncy Maples. Maples went to London in 1895 to be consecrated bishop of Likoma, an island in the lake near the coast of Mozambique. The new bishop was anxious to return to his bishopric. After his consecration he rushed back to his see, boarding the *Sherriff* near sunset for the final sail across the lake to Likoma, in spite of the lateness of the hour and the crew's warnings of an impending gale. The boat capsized in the ensuing storm. The bishop clung for a while to a floating box, like a cat on flotsam. He was told that land was nearby; he could swim to safety. But he refused to remove his heavy black cassock.

"Save yourselves," he is said to have cried. "You must not die for me. I am a miserable sinner. My hour to die is come."

It certainly had. The lake kept his body for two weeks until it was washed up onto the shore, recognizable only by the black cassock.

THE FISH OF Lake Malaŵi are remarkable for their color and abundance. They abound in tremendous variety. Many, perhaps most, have not even been named. One estimate suggests that there are between five hundred and one thousand distinct species in the lake. Almost all of these are endemic, known from nowhere else, not even from the streams flowing into the lake. Most, but not all, of this spectacular variety of finny diversity is accounted for by cichlids, tropical fish most characteristic of Africa but also common in South America. The African great lakes are each home to separate evolutionary radiations of cichlids with different species evolving to fill similar ecological niches, sharing similar ways of life, but in different bodies of water. This separate evolution in areas isolated from each other is on a smaller scale but conceptually identical to the evolutionary isolation on different continents caused by continental drift.

Some of the little fish of Lake Malaŵi are the tiny swimming jewels called *mbuna* that are prized by freshwater-tropical-fish enthusiasts. In days not long past, many *mbuna* of many different species were exported to the aquaria of America each year. Now they are raised on special cichlid farms in Florida. *Mbuna* are extremely varied, some quite colorful, gold or blue, some striped. Others are drab, and not of much interest to hobbyists. People have been known to poison the waters around a rocky island lacking the colorful *mbuna* locally in order to create a vacancy for more desirable species that could then be transplanted to the waters in place of less-colorful natural residents.

There is only one place in Malaŵi where tourists are abundant. That is at Cape Maclear, at the southern end of the lake, where the original Livingstonia Mission was established, and where Lake Malaŵi National Park is now located. It is beautiful. Its major attractions are the grandeur of the countryside, the crystal-clear water, and the snorkeling around the rocks and boulders. It is like viewing the fish of a coral reef in fresh water. Although tourists frequent the national park, *mbuna* inhabit most of the lake, especially in rocky areas. There are many places other than the park that are equally suited for snorkeling.

Not surprisingly, fish comprise a significant component of the Malaŵian diet. Much of the protein consumed in Malaŵi is in the form of fish. Over forty thousand tons of it comes from the lake every year. Apparently the most desired fish for the table is *chambo,* a cichlid panfish, similar to a bream. But there are many other kinds (Figure 12). There are lake trout that are not trout at all but, like trout, are swift-swimming predators. There is a species that, like a salmon, swims up streams to lay eggs. And there are *kampango,* the giants of the lake, weighing up to around one hundred pounds. These are catfish, but of a different family from those we have in North America.

Much of the fish that is caught in Malaŵi is dried in the sun on row after row of hand-fashioned straw or reed mats supported off the ground by spindly sticks. Other fish are preserved by smoking. That is the best way to enjoy *kampango.* Fishing is done through a variety of techniques, but the use of small hand nets accounts for most noncommercial, subsistence fishing. Some of my most pleasant images of Malaŵi are of fishermen in their canoes. Fishermen on a calm lake is a good image.

The simple canoes of Lake Malaŵi impress me as they have many before my time. They are dugouts, twenty feet long or so, but not of the usual dugout design. Who knows how long they have been in use, but E. D. Young provided the following description of them in 1877:

I have never seen elsewhere, nor do I know that any previous travellers have noticed the singular build of these craft. They are of course, as in all these cases, made by felling trees and hollowing them out by axe and fire. But the Nyassa canoes have this peculiarity about them, that the gunwales are inverted, so that the paddlers have only a narrow slit down the centre

FIGURE 12: *Cichlids and a catfish (bottom) in Lake Malaŵi. Fish—fresh, smoked, or dried—are a major source of protein in Malaŵi. Colorful Lake Malaŵi cichlids are a favorite with many tropical-fish hobbyists.*

of the canoe in which to sit. If a piece of bark is stripped off a tree from its whole circumference, and dried as in the sun, it will probably assume the shape of which I speak; the two edges will curl in along the centre. Built in this way they are exceedingly buoyant and tolerably seaworthy, a very marked exception to the ordinary run of river canoes, which are brought to a standstill if there is only a good ripple on the surface; for they have no more life in them in a sea-way than a garden roller, and go down like stones as soon as they ship any water. The paddler uses a paddle about six feet long, and either stands or sits.

Down the way from my camp at Ngara, fishermen returning in the evening from the day's work wrestle their dugouts onto the beach. The hulls are laden with the catch, bushels of tiny, slender, silvery fish, not more than an inch long, strained from the waters of the lake through fine mesh nets. Women of the village, and children sent by their mothers, crowd around the boats, each clutching a pot to be filled with the fish. These bullets of protein will be boiled into the evening's meal or dried, then sold in upland markets.

One evening we were on our way back from Karonga to Lilongwe. We stopped at Nkhata Bay to camp, pulling into the campsite well after dark. The deepest point in Lake Malaŵi lies a couple of hundred feet offshore from the beach where we unrolled our sleeping bags. The mountains rose a couple of thousand feet above us. There was absolutely no moon. The water and the season were juxtaposed by inexorable probability, like the alignment of the sun, the earth, and the moon in an eclipse, into the perfect night for fishing.

We could hear the exclamations of the fishermen through the darkness. They were a small commercial concern with a long net and a lot of people to pull it in. Hissing pressure lamps were positioned to attract fish by false moonlight. The net was loaded into canoes and ferried out to the deepest part of the lake, where it was dropped. Then the men on shore pulled ropes attached to either end of the net, hauling it through the water and capturing the wealth of fish that had emerged from the depths to feed.

There was only one problem: The ropes broke. They were rotten and could not bear the strain. The net began to sink—in this case, to the deepest part of the third deepest lake in the world. Someone had to go after it. A small fleet of canoes shipped the men into the night. Over the side they went, swimming blindly through the chilly black water, down as far as they could go, for as long as they could contain their bursting lungs, searching for the slowly drifting net, hoping to swim into it. They found it. But it took time. The catch was lost.

Never mind. Things happen. The fishermen were fatalistic. The inexorable flow of time and probability would bring other nights for fishing.

WITH ALL ITS diversity of fish species, there is one kind of fish, lungfish (Figure 13), that is conspicuous by its absence from this African lake. That in itself is a significant statement about Lake Malaŵi. Lungfish inhabit most of sub-Saharan Africa, from Senegal in the west to Mombasa in the east, then south over the Congo Basin, beyond the Zambezi, to the great gray-green, greasy Limpopo River. They are Paleozoic relicts, tracing their genealogy as lungfish back in time for hundreds of millions of years (which is why *Spinosaurus* can be eating a iungfish in Figure 2). All of them are now gone from the northern continents, but they persist in South America, Australia, and of course Africa, all three of which were at one time part of Gondwana, the southern supercontinent.

Lungfish inhabit a variety of watery environments, but they seem most to favor swamps or temporary marshes flooded by seasonal rains. These plump, eellike denizens are obliged to surface periodically, thrusting their fishy snouts out of the water to gulp oxygen-rich air. Although they are most certainly fish, if they are held under water, they will drown. Their gills cannot extract enough oxygen from the water they live in. If their habitat dries up, they simply burrow into the mud, secrete a copious supply of mucus, and form a cocoon in which to sleep away the dry season.

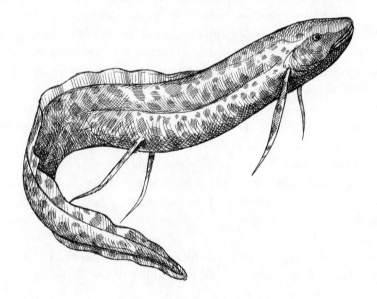

FIGURE 13: *A contemporary African lungfish. These animals have changed little in hundreds of millions of years.* SPINOSAURUS *is eating one in Figure 2. Lake Malaŵi is the only major East African Rift Valley lake where they no longer exist, even though they are found as fossils in sediments deposited in the lake as recently as a few million years ago.*

They also inhabit lakes, all the great lakes of Africa except one—Lake Malaŵi. There are no published reports of lungfish being caught in the lake. Nor do they surface among the piles of fresh, smoked, or dried fish in any of the markets I have visited in Malaŵi. In other places lungfish are eaten. Even the native markets of Nairobi, nowhere near a great lake, are stocked with lungfish from Lake Victoria.

But it has not always been the case that lungfish were absent from Lake Malaŵi. In rocks formed from the mud deposited only a few million years ago by waters of the lake soon after it was formed, my team found fossil lungfish. Clearly, as shown by the demise of the lungfish, the lake has changed. It is a monolith neither on the scale of geological time nor on the scale of a human lifetime. Lungfish in other lakes are known to venture away from shore, but generally they seem to prefer papyrus swamps along lake margins to the offshore depths. Was Lake Malaŵi bounded by more swamps in the past? Is the bottom now too firm, too free of organic debris? Are the present waters too clean and deep for lungfish? Maybe they are. One thing is sure. The lake has not remained static since it was formed. It has probably gotten deeper, and that is due to an evolving geological setting. Not only that, but as we are about to see, the geological setting has facilitated the formation of fossils.

Many of Africa's most famous lakes—Turkana, Naivasha, Victoria, Tanganyika, Malaŵi—owe their existence to the geologic structure of East Africa. Like a scar stretching from the Red Sea in the north to Mozambique in the south is the Great Rift Valley. This gash across Africa is tangible evidence of plate tectonics and continental drift: it is the rupture of the Earth as the continent is ripped apart (Figure 14). To the north it has opened to the sea. Indeed, it is the very reason why the Red Sea exists. The wound, with time, may well flood progressively to the south. One day sea water might fill a gulf that is now the Rift Valley.

In East Africa, along the Rift, the processes that tear the continents apart and send them on their way across the globe are evident. The highlands that flank the Rift, the great Ruwenzori Mountains—the Mountains of the Moon of the early explorers—Kilimanjaro, Mount Kenya, and the Aberdares are volcanic masses reflecting the upwelling of heat and lava. The Rift Valley formed along with big volcanoes as the Earth's surface was stretched, creating spectacular relief.

The climate at the bottom of the Rift Valley is hot and dry. The flanks are cooler and more pleasant. The heights surrounding the Rift Valley are much

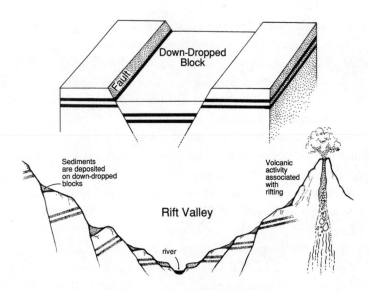

Figure 14: Formation of the Great Rift Valley. Tensional forces pull on the continent causing blocks to drop down along faults (top). The Great Rift Valley has many such faults (bottom). Volcanoes are often formed in areas of active rifting. Hillsides and mountains formed from rifting and volcanic activity are weathered and eroded. The sediments derived from them are carried downslope and downstream where they are deposited. Animals and plants entombed in the sediments become fossils.

cooler still. Mount Kenya, more properly known as Kirinyaga, reaching to an altitude of 17,058 feet, is capped with snow, yet it is on the equator. Each environment—mountain, valley, plain, desert, and everything in between—is characterized by its own climatic regime, its own geological features, and its own suite of plants and animals. Sand and soil particles and rock fragments and dust are carried downhill from the flanks and highlands by gravity, winds, and water. Finally they come to rest, deposited in the beds of the streams, rivers, and lakes of the Rift Valley.

Diatoms, single-celled plants with bodies of ornate silica, flourish in uncounted numbers in Rift Valley lakes, where they share their watery environment with species upon species of fish. As the diatoms die, their beautiful silica bodices become sediment, forming almost pure rock—diatomite, used for making toothpaste—in the clean waters near the center of a lake. Closer to the shore, along streams and deltas, diatoms mix with detritus carried down from the highlands. Pollen from flowering plants and spores from fungi sprinkle the surface of the water and join in the bottom sediments as they build up layer by layer.

Sediments such as these—river silt and lake mud—blanket bones and bodies of dead fish, hippos, crocodiles, perhaps turtles, whatever animals die in the water. Water lilies and shore grasses are buried. So are snails and clams, arthropods and crustaceans. Animals that do not live in water, but die near a lake or stream, may be washed in by rains. Occasional floods cause water levels to rise, blanketing sediments over the soil of the floodplain, covering whatever carcasses and scraps may remain on the surface after the vultures and hyaenas have had at them. The ash of a distant volcano may rain down to cover and preserve a picture of the land's surface.

After an animal dies, if it is to become a fossil, it must be buried before the elements destroy the carcass completely. Flesh may rot and putrefy. Sinews may dry and shrink, twisting the neck over the back in a death pose. It may be scavenged and eaten, or the flesh may be buried along with the bones to decompose later. Burial is done by sediments; therefore, fossils are formed in areas where rivers or lakes or oceans drop their sediment loads, just as was discussed above. After burial, minerals carried by percolating groundwater are deposited in vugs within the bone structure, or they may actually replace bone salts, literally turning the bone to stone. Millennia later, with movements of the Earth and changes in climate that transform depositional settings to those of erosion, the fossil is exhumed—resurrected. Everything about the fossil, its preservation, anatomy, the entombing sediments, what is buried with it—everything reveals something about the ancient world.

These processes are some of the ways fossils form. Each context leaves its indelible mark. Past environments and ecology are reflected in sediments turned to stone with time, in fossil organisms that show through their anatomy their habits in life, and from the behavioral relics, like the marks of scavenging carnivores, that remain on fossil bone. The constituent chemicals of bones and shells and soil may reflect the ancient climate of a region, or the diet of an animal, or the photosynthetic pathway of a plant. We can read the past from the record of the rocks. The signals change from rock layer to rock layer through time, revealing with sensitivity the history of life and the history of life's environment. That is paleoecology.

The fossilization process is occurring today in the Rift Valley. It occurred in the past. We can see the results of processes operating in the past in the famous fossil fields of Koobi Fora, east of Lake Turkana, Kenya, rich in the fossil remains of the human ancestors *Australopithecus* and *Homo,* and many, many other kinds of fossils. We can see a similar situation along the north-western shores of Lake Malaŵi, where an australopithecine has recently been found. There are also fossil snails, pigs, elephants, monkeys, crocodiles, turtles, hippos, rhinos, and fish—lots of fish—in rocks ranging back to about five million years ago. All these fossils were formed in the early stages of Lake Malaŵi. All are much, much younger than dinosaurs. So Lake Malaŵi is much younger than dinosaurs too.

The Dinosaur Beds lie cheek-by-jowl with the ancient deposits of Lake Malaŵi, but that is not because ancestral Lake Malaŵi existed with the dinosaurs. The Dinosaur Beds are much older, by about 100 million years. They were deposited by clean, swift-flowing streams and rivers that bounced sand and fresh rock eroded from adjacent hills along their channels. There were small ponds occasionally, but no evidence of a great lake. Soils on the river floodplains were thin, or stripped away by rampaging torrents. Globs of caliche, limestone left from water evaporating out of the ground, are found in the remnants of ancient soils, showing that the climate was hot. During the days of the dinosaurs the weather was seasonal, but more arid than now. The rocks of the Dinosaur Beds represent a very lost world compared with the modern world currently existing alongside the lake.

In Malaŵi the structure and geometry of the Rift is controlled by older features of the geology on which the newer Rift is superimposed. Some of the older features go back a billion years to when Africa was first assembled and ultimately conjoined with the rest of the world's landmasses into the super-supercontinent of Pangaea. As the continents as we know them now began to take shape, the seams of the original constructions became zones of weakness. These were exploited by the restless Earth as Africa unzipped from the rest of the continents beginning over 100 million years ago.

That isolation of Africa from other landmasses also began as a rift valley, just as we see happening today. The initial separation on the east side of Africa started about 150 million years ago. A bit later, but prior to 100 million years ago, Madagascar was rifting away from the east coast. The rifting process that separated Madagascar led to the formation of fault-bounded basins along the older continental seams, just in the area where the modern Rift Valley is now.

It is these old basins, associated with the split of Madagascar from East Africa, that were filled with the river sediments entombing the dinosaurs that lived in northern Malaŵi so long ago. That is why the Dinosaur Beds with their suite of fossils are found in the current Rift Valley. It is also why they are found next to the much younger deposits of Lake Malaŵi, which preserve the nearly modern fossilized remains of lungfish, hippos, elephants, and pigs.

On the other side of Africa during this same ancient time, the South Atlantic opened. Faulted basins formed in what is now Cameroon, Niger, and Nigeria. The same happened in Brazil, and at the same time, because the two areas were one. Rivers and lakes filled the basins with sediments, and in so doing preserved fossils. The whole broad region was arid, but with a complex of lakes fed by rivers draining internally to the big basins. Finally, at 100 million years ago, Brazil cruised away, by continental drift, into the sunset. The Atlantic Ocean became complete from south to north. Any river drainages that may have linked the two areas prior to the separation were forever severed. The Dinosaur Beds in Malaŵi are a reflection of life and ecology in the very heart of Africa at one hundred million years ago, the very time Africa was becoming isolated from the rest of the world.

How certain am I about the age of the fossils in the Dinosaur Beds of northern Malaŵi? Not certain at all. Clearly they belong to the Mesozoic, the Age of Reptiles. The dinosaurs tell us that. But the confidence I have in estimating their precise age is not great. All I can say to support my contentions from within Malaŵi is based on fossils. There are not yet any relevant dates or paleomagnetic determinations from within the country. The characteristic fossils from the classic dinosaur excavations at Tendaguru are lacking, suggesting a different, probably younger age for Malaŵi. Some of the fossils known from Malaŵi, but not known from Tendaguru, resemble those from Cameroon and Niger in West Africa, and from Brazil in South America. It is reasonable to speculate that these fossils are of similar, if not exactly the same, age.

Moreover, the fossil record of ocean life, which is much better than that of land-dwelling animals, plus the paleomagnetic record from the Atlantic Ocean floor, demonstrate that the northern and southern arms of the Atlantic Ocean did not conjoin until about 100 million years ago. If the bones of Brazil, Niger, Cameroon, and Malaŵi were buried while the two continents were still connected, however feebly, the completion of the Atlantic would seem to put a limit on how young the bones can be—100 million years. For the sake of discussion, that is the number I will use. The Dinosaur Beds of Malaŵi are not likely to be younger—unless there are more surprises in store. One hundred million years ago is smack in the middle of the last period of the Age of Reptiles. Technically it is late in the Early Cretaceous.

EVEN TODAY THE geology of the Rift Valley and the climate of East Africa are not uniform from north to south, and that in itself affects the fossilization process and the discovery of fossils. The big differences between searching for fossils in Malaŵi and at Leakey's Koobi Fora farther north are two. First, Malaŵi receives more rainfall than northern Kenya, so more plants grow, so it is harder to see the ground. Consequently it is harder to see fossils that might survive the rigors of soil formation in such an environment. Second, and probably more importantly in this particular comparison, the geometry of the Rift Valley is different in the two areas. At Koobi Fora, to the north, it is broad and open; in Malaŵi, to the south, it is narrow, with steep walls alternating from east to west on either side of the lake. There may be lakes in both areas, but the geology is not exactly the same, and that makes a difference. The geological setting of a region is important for finding, as well as forming and preserving fossils.

Thus, to find fossils, the rocks in which they are preserved must be visible. Many areas of the Earth are, happily, covered with deep soil and plants that, unfortunately, obscure the underlying parent rock and destroy fossils. It is often difficult to tell from a map just what the exposures of rock will be like half a world away. My heart nose-dived the first time I drove to the Dinosaur Beds in Malaŵi. I passed through a banana grove so extensive and so dense, I almost gave up hope that there would be any rocks at all open to search. Thank goodness that beyond the river bend the bananas ended and the rocks began.

Scientific expeditions to find fossils, or anything else, are not simply collecting trips. They must be pursued in the context of the questions addressed, the problems to be solved, the hypotheses tested, and the models formulated. Paleontological research is no different from research in any other scientific discipline in this regard. That, in fact, is what makes paleontology a science. The Malaŵi Project is framed in terms of the emergence of the modern world—geographically by the rearrangement of continents and bio-logically by the evolution of new groups of vertebrates that were later to emerge from the shadows of the dinosaurs to dominate the landscape.

Fossil collecting and fieldwork, especially foreign fieldwork, is fun if all goes well. But it is complicated. Logistics must be considered. How do you get to where you want to go? How do you supply a camp once you are there? The feasibility of the plan must be determined. In Malawî I was fortunate. My counterparts at the Department of Antiquities are very familiar with the logistics of fieldwork in their country. They had already set a precedent for it through their own field studies. Of course, in fieldwork as in any other aspect of science, everything hinges on getting adequate funding. That step is never easy, but once accomplished, the work can get under way.

There are two essential ingredients to a successful paleontological expedition: fossils and people. The fossils are controlled by the rocks. The people have to find the fossils. To do their best, they must want to be in the field. Even under tough conditions, a good field crew finds something pleasant to make the hardships bearable. Still, not everyone who wants to be is adequately suited for fieldwork. It takes a certain kind of temperament. The work is dirty. It is hot. There are bugs.

Obviously a prime concern is that reasonable precautions be taken for health and safety. Food must not be skimped on, diversity should be provided, and individual preferences should be accommodated so far as possible. Cook the food well and keep the dishes clean. An adequate supply of beer is welcome. People do not travel halfway around the world just to suffer; they work better when they do not.

Attacks from wild animals are not a great source of worry in Africa these days, although the threat is not completely gone: Crocodiles claim a few lives every year. However, there are other, more likely natural hazards that must be respected in fieldwork—such as snakes. When considering those sorts of dangers, it is best to follow the advice of John Moir, one of the founders of the African Lakes Company: "Fear dysentry [sic] and dissensions even more." Moir was speaking of the threat of slave raiders, but his are sage words for keeping the hazards of fieldwork in perspective as well. The crew must get along and they must stay healthy. Malaria is a real problem. Tick-borne diseases are worrisome.

Unfortunately, staying healthy is not completely within our control. One morning in camp Lou Taylor, a friend since graduate school and a great person to be in the field with, came to my tent. It was 6:00 A.M. He spoke in a calm voice. "Boss, I think I've got appendicitis." That is not how I like to wake up.

Lou had been sitting by the lake since 4:30, chewing ten aspirin to kill the pain. There was nothing that could be done until the day started, so he did not wake anyone.

Off we went down the M-1 highway on the twenty-mile trip to the regional hospital at Karonga. Lou was hurting and we were all concerned at the prospect of his having to undergo surgery. The drive heightened our anxiety. On the way the road was obstructed by an overloaded pickup that lay upside down, like a flipped turtle, on its load. We skirted around it. There was nothing we could do there.

When we arrived at the hospital Lou was given a Panadol and taken to a room where he lay on the examination table. A spider that seemed to have a spread of about eight inches emerged from a crevice near his head and climbed up the wall. Mosquitoes buzzed in the corners of the room. A used scalpel blade crusted with blood lay abandoned on the desk. At this stage no one was encouraged. The hospital at Karonga is not bad by ambient standards, but at the time of this event the prevalence of AIDS in Africa and the uncertainties inherent in the blood supply were added risks that would be avoided if Lou could just hang on until he got back to the States.

Two technicians came in. They took Lou's history and made a preliminary examination. Both were very professional. They knew what they were doing. It was now 7:00. Down the hall they went to call the doctor, who was still at his home. I overheard them saying that they were ruling out appendicitis, which gave me immediate relief, but then I wondered what the problem really was.

The doctor arrived at 7:30. He was Dutch. He took a close look at the patient, ordered a few tests, and diagnosed kidney stones. It was not appendicitis or anything life threatening that would require an immediate operation. The color diffused back into Lou's face. The doctor recommended that he return to the U.S. as soon as possible, a suggestion that made all kinds of sense. One does not do one's best digging fossils while suffering excruciating pain and pissing blood. He caught a plane the next day, his field season cut short, but only by a couple of days. He was okay, which was the only thing that really mattered, and he had done a fine job for the project.

It is not always easy to judge beforehand who is suited for foreign field-work and who is not. Supertough hombres are not necessarily right for the field. Maybe it has something to do with the inflexibility of being macho. It depends on the individual, not on gender, who will be competent, tolerant, and less prone to culture shock, which are the required attributes.

Of course, one does not have to do fieldwork to be a good paleontologist, and some very good bone people get off to a slow start in the field. Migeod wrote of the young Cambridge student, Rex Parrington, who accompanied him from Tendaguru to Nyasaland in 1930: "I am afraid that Mr. Parrington is not gifted with all the qualifications necessary for an African expedition requiring constant personal exertion. There has been from the beginning of the season a fine field for research which many men would have welcomed." Apparently Migeod thought someone else might have been better suited for the job.

I confess I have felt the same as Migeod on an occasion or two. I once took someone to Africa who, unbeknownst to me, had eccentric dietary preferences. There was little available in remote Africa that he was inclined to eat. I learned from him, a fully adult individual, but too late, that his staple food was Pop-Tarts, an item universally absent from Malaŵi menus. He had no allergies, but he had never in his life eaten a hard-boiled egg. That is all right; I presumed he just did not like the smell of them or something. When it came down to little else to eat, he decided to try one, but he had to be taught how the peeling and eating are done. All right, there is nothing really shameful in that. And once he had tried one, they became his favorite food. He ordered them at a fine restaurant in Paris on the way home. Of course, that is all right too.

The knowledge of how to eat a hard-boiled egg is not a requirement for success in paleontology, but it is telling with respect to suitability for the field, especially if the field is in a remote foreign country. Trouble does happen. These trips are not quite vacations. It could be personally dangerous to go into the bush if one is not mentally equipped for it. That can make it dangerous, or at least uncomfortable, for your companions. Each person must have confidence in the abilities of other members of the team. It can be very difficult to judge beforehand how someone will work out.

So far as Rex Parrington, Migeod's problem in the field, is concerned, in later years he led successful expeditions to Africa. He became a distinguished paleontologist, one of the top scholars in his field, and a Fellow of the Royal Society. You just never know.

PROSPECTING, the search for fossils, must take place in areas of active erosion, such as gullies and badlands, or even man-made exposures of rock, such as road cuts or mines. Once exposed on the surface by erosion, a fossil is often quickly destroyed. This seems strange. After lying protectively mantled within the earth for millions of years, a fossil exposed on the surface can be pitifully fragile and easily lost. Fossils come and go on the surface of the ground through the processes of erosion and weathering. In tropical Africa it does not take long for fossils to be destroyed. To me, worrying about fossils lost to nature is sort of like the sound of a tree falling in the wilderness: If there are no eyes present to find a bone, it might as well not exist.

The resiliency of a fossil depends to some extent on what it is, as well as on the erosional conditions that exposed it. Usually, but with many exceptions, only the hard parts of animals fossilize—shells, for example, or in vertebrates, bones and teeth. Tooth enamel is the hardest part of a skeleton, so teeth are more readily preserved and less prone to destruction even than bone. Both bones and teeth are preserved in Malaŵi.

There is no substitute for shoe leather in searching the great outdoors for fossils. Walking and looking. And patience. That is how it is done. It is quite pleasant most of the time, except that fossils seemingly have the nasty habit of coming into view only when the weather is miserable. Fossil bone retains a texture and a luster distinctly unrocklike, but definitely bonelike. Those, and shape, are what catch the prospector's eye. A fragment of fossil bone, but not modern bone, will stick to the tongue. It is a test often applied when the first scrap is found. Sometimes, if you are lucky, the fossil will be well enough preserved that it can simply be picked up after carefully noting the details of its occurrence. Other times it is much more work.

No digging is ever done without a reason. Bone must be seen on the surface of the ground to justify a greater effort. Bits and pieces of fossils, like stones and balls, roll downhill. As they weather out of the rock, gravity moves them downslope. When a piece of bone is found, the next step is to trace its path up the slope. Is there more in the ground? Hopefully, as in Malaŵi, the answer is yes. Then the excavation starts.

Taking fossil bones out of the ground is really rather simple in principle (Figure 15). First, using awls and fine needles, the bone is uncovered bit by bit until its outline is determined. This is often enough of a clue to determine its identity. Glue is applied all over to harden the specimen. I use polyvinyl acetate (supplied by my brother-in-law) dissolved in acetone or nail polish remover and thin enough to penetrate the bone. After it dries, a trench is cut around the fossil, slightly undercutting the bone, so that it stands on a pedestal. Once a bone is on its pedestal, it is covered with paleontological tissue. This invaluable supply is readily accessible in lavatories, in two-ply

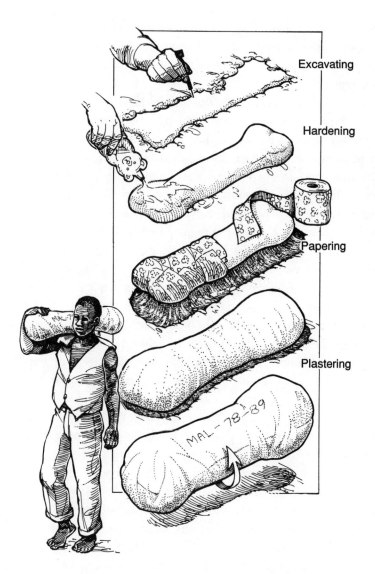

Excavating

Hardening

Papering

Plastering

FIGURE 15: How to collect a fossil. A fossil bone is painstakingly cleared of its enclosing earth (top), then impregnated with hardener. After the hardener dries, the bone, resting on a pillar of rock, is covered in paper—"paleontological tissue" if you prefer—which cushions the fossil and prevents plaster from sticking to it. The bone is then covered with plaster-soaked bandages. After the plaster sets, the fossil is flipped over, capped with plaster bandages, labeled, and then removed from the field.

rolls of four-inch squares that tear easily along perforations. It is also called toilet paper. Color or floral pattern does not matter, nor does it matter if the brand is scented or unscented. Once the paper is applied, the fossil is ready for jacketing.

Because fossils are usually cracked and broken, you treat them like what they are—broken bones. Jacketing is the process by which a fossil is encased in plaster bandages to protect it, just as if your arm were broken and the doctor put it in a cast. In fact, for hand-sized fossils I use medical bandages of gauze and quick-setting plaster of Paris, generously supplied to the Malaŵi Project by Johnson & Johnson Orthopaedics. If a specimen is too large for medical bandages, strips of burlap cut from gunnysacks or loosely woven cloth are used. These strips are first impregnated with plaster, then applied to the fossil. The jacket prevents the broken edges of bones from rubbing against each other so that they can be glued tightly together along clean breaks. The tissue cushions the fossil and prevents the plaster from sticking to it.

Plaster-impregnated bandages are applied over the tissue in multiple layers to give the jacket strength. The undercutting of the pedestal provides purchase for the jacket so that it does not pull off. After the plaster has set, the block is fully undercut and flipped over onto its top, exposing the underside. The papering and plastering is then repeated on the bottom. Braces of wood or tree branches are incorporated into the jacketing if the specimen is large or awkward. The final product is a fully protected fossil, swaddled in gleaming-white plaster. This bone and bandage ''biscuit'' is ready for transport to the lab.

Substitutes for plaster can be found in dire necessity. At Tendaguru the Germans often had to use mud and straw. In 1987 the Malaŵi Project resorted to using cloth soaked in thick, white wood glue to jacket dinosaur bones and a very large, but geologically much younger, rhinoceros skull.

If only a single bone is found, the jacketing process is straightforward enough. If there are a number of bones, you have a quarry on your hands. Then the fun really starts. A quarry is a big hole in the ground, big enough to allow for the removal of all the bones you find. The more bones there are, the larger it is, and very often the harder it is to work. The stratum containing the bones is discovered on the surface, but the bones found subsequently are entombed in sediments protected by overlying rock. The sterile rock above the quarry is the overburden. It has to be removed with picks, shovels, power tools, or sometimes even backhoes, in order to come down on top of the fossils and to excavate them properly. The effort to remove overburden can be considerable, especially if the payload dives into the side of a hill. That is what happened in Malaŵi. If the hill is steep, the difficulties can be prohibitive. That has not happened in Malaŵi yet. Knock on wood . . .

After the overburden is removed, excavation begins on each individual bone just as if it were an isolated find. If the bones are small enough, several might be taken out in a single manageable jacket. Excavation is a complicated task if the bones are abundant and jack-strawed one on top of the other. That is often how it is in Malaŵi. Bones are mapped as they become exposed to provide information as to the spatial relationships of each to the others and to sedimentary features. This is very important because bones are more often jumbled together than laid out as whole skeletons articulated as in life. That does happen, but the usual situation is that mixed-up bones must be sorted out. Maps help do that because they highlight associations of particular bones that are not obvious in the field. The jumbling that mixes bones occurs for a reason. Mapping also helps the investigator to puzzle out what the cause might be.

Quarry work is fun, but it can get old, digging day after day in the same hole, sometimes on the same bone, with awls and needles and whiskbrooms and brushes. Sitting for hours on the damp, musty earth causes an irritating itchy butt. The work is tedious. Tedium leads to boredom. Distraction creeps in. Flies are stalked with needle points. Unwarranted attention is paid to individual sand grains, not enough to other important details. By then it is time for a day off. Better that than damage fossils or let tempers flare.

Most trying in the quarry are aggressive, biting insects adapted to drinking from the corners of a paleontologist's eyes and from sweat-lined creases of skin, such as behind the knees or in the armpits. They like to crawl into ears and buzz. Every time the black flies get bad in Malaŵi, I think back to 1979, hurriedly and not very enthusiastically, to when I led my first National Geographic dig in the Painted Desert of Arizona. We were digging in rocks formed at the time when all the continents were coalesced into Pangaea and when some of the earliest-known dinosaurs roamed the Earth. The fossils were good, but getting them out had its aggravations. Gnatlike biting flies were persistent and painful. Insect repellent was their ambrosia. The whole crew had welts and allergic reactions. Rubber bands were used to close sleeves and pantlegs. Collar buttons were fastened despite the sweltering heat. Still the flies zeroed in on the tight lines where clothes met skin. We were driven to the edge. Extreme actions were in order. Finally we resorted to fashioning makeshift smudge pots. The idea to use them was my wife Bonnie's, brought from her work in Mexico. Our smudge pots were piles of dry, smoldering cow dung, collected early in the morning before the flies came out and placed in each corner of every three-meter-square of the excavation. The smoke provided some relief from the insects—but it subjected us to dung-lung!

A kind of good-natured, friendly, degenerate camaraderie develops in a quarry, catalyzed by familiarity and close quarters. There is an otherwise unusual candidness characterized by bad songs, bad jokes, bad farts, and a general discussion of bodily functions and dysfunctions, especially as concerns the digestive system. I do not know why that is, but it always seems to happen. After a field season in the quarry, friends invariably go away with a pleasant feeling of closeness, a sort of secret society of common experience. It always happens that way.

At the end of a dig the jackets are transported back to the lab. This is no easy job if the field season has been successful. We have to hire a special lorry in Malaŵi to take the bones from the field to the facilities we established at the Department of Antiquities at the other end of the country. Once in the laboratory, the plaster is removed and the fossil painstakingly resurrected. Each bone is hardened. Clinging matrix is removed. Broken edges are separated, cleaned, and fixed tightly together. Nicks and cracks are filled with plaster. Missing parts may be fabricated. Supports may be applied, and the fossil, if necessary, is cradled in a form-fitted bed to prevent it from collapsing under its own weight. Only then is the specimen ready for study, having undergone a process that may have taken years since its first discovery. If the specimen is for display, even more work is necessary. It will be some time before the bulk of the Malaŵi specimens are ready for study, and even longer before they are available for public viewing. And the whole process, from beginning to end, costs money.

Searching for tiny fossils—such as isolated rat teeth or early mammals—is a little different. The prospecting is about the same. Walk, walk, walk, scanning the ground for bone weathering out. When a likely spot is found, it is scrutinized for tiny flecks of bone, sometimes fragments of once-larger bones, but all the better if they be parts of very small bones of very small animals. It is not necessary to see much small bone, just enough to know it is there. Then gunnysack after gunnysack is filled with the fossiliferous matrix.

This bulk sample is thoroughly dried, soaked in kerosene, and finally sieved in water through boxes with sides and bottoms of fine-mesh screen. When the kerosene-soaked sediment in the boxes is first placed in water, the kerosene rushes out of it, oil being lighter than water, and water rushes in. This causes the sediment to disaggregate. The residue of this screen-washing process leaves particles in the size range of sand and gravel, just the size of small mammal teeth, captured by the screens. The silt and clay of the original sedimentary rock are washed away. The residue off the sieves is taken to the lab and the bone further concentrated by passing it through high-density liquids. These float off light sand grains while the heavier bones and teeth sink. The resulting ultraconcentrate is washed and dried, then sorted under a microscope. Good specimens of teeth and bones are glued to the heads of pins stuck in corks so that they can be handled easily. The corks slip into small glass vials for storage.

The technique of screen-washing, believe it or not, is remarkably effective. In the not-so-olden days many fossil collections were biased toward larger animals. Of course virtually every natural community of vertebrates has small species, as well as medium-sized and large ones. Where were the small ones in the fossil collections that had only larger species represented? In many cases, until the advent of screen-washing, they were simply overlooked.

Whether a fossil is from screening or from a quarry or just an isolated find, it is imperative that the locality where it was found and its position in the rock sequence be accurately determined and precisely recorded. These two pieces of data are basic to every fossil, more important even than its identification. The identity of a fossil can be repeatedly determined by whomever wishes to do so, but once a fossil is out of the ground, it is virtually impossible, except in rare circumstances, for anyone to pinpoint the exact place where it was found. The only usual exception is the original collector, and then only so well as notoriously unreliable memory serves.

Without knowing a fossil's locality accurately, its place in the rock sequence cannot be precisely determined and neither can its age by any method independent of guessing from the fossil itself. The time element—the strength of paleontology—is diminished. A fossil without time is like yesterday's doughnuts—you might survive on them for a while, but who wants to? Field records are important.

.   .   .

AND WHAT OF proper field attire? In the words of Sir Harry Johnston speaking in 1897, "Generally, I may say this about clothing, that a man should always strive to dress neatly and becomingly in Central Africa, or he will quickly lapse into a slovenly state of existence."

I find stout shoes are important.

3

JOURNALS
FROM THE
GROUND

---

7 July 1990, Saturday. The beginning of the field season.

I am on my way from the United States to Africa.

It is 5:48 in the afternoon. I am aboard Delta Flight 26 en route to Frankfurt. From there it is south, a brief transit stop in Johannesburg, then ultimately on to Malaŵi. I have two back-to-back overnight flights, one seven hours, the other fourteen. On this one the seats are filled on either side of me.

There is not much to do on an airplane, especially on an intercontinental flight, especially overnight, especially one that is crowded. You can try to sleep or try to think, but you can do neither very well. In a few minutes a travel coma will take over. For at least a full twenty-four hours I will be not quite awake, but unable to sleep. So I will write, at least for a while.

As of this writing I have made four trips to Malaŵi—three of them actually out in the field collecting fossils; one, the first one, to set it all up. The project has been good. There have been enough discoveries each time to justify another field season. We have found dinosaur bones from five different species, three kinds of crocodiles, including half a dozen skeletons of the strangest kind of croc I have ever seen. We have even found frogs. I am satisfied with what we have found so far. Now I am on the fifth trip. Will

Downs, who will be coming next week, has been with me on each field expedition to the Dinosaur Beds. For Dale Winkler and Kent Newman, traveling with me, this is the third time. The last member of the American contingent is Alisa Winkler, who will be coming over to join us in a few weeks. This is her second trip to Malaŵi. All are professionals, all are seasoned in the field, all have African experience.

That is the way I wanted it this year. The strategy is to take trustworthy professionals to Malaŵi from here, work with Department of Antiquities people there, and recruit a good Malaŵian student for fieldwork and graduate training. Then, the next time, and the next, maybe the project will be in a position to include other students and new faces. Now we must obtain enough high-quality results to make sure that there is a next time.

We know exactly where we are going. We know there are fossils. We have the localities pinpointed. We know what we are going after. We are going to quarry bones, and that means mainly dinosaurs. We know the rocks they are packed in, and we know how high the hills are. We know what it takes to move the supplies in and the finished jackets out. We have the vehicles arranged. We know where to camp and how to provision the larder. It should be just a matter of doing the work. Now, since we are no longer rookies in Malaŵi, I want to determine, through this season's fieldwork, in which direction I can lead this project.

The goals are simple. We will increase the sample of dinosaur bones. We will get more of them. That is what we are after. Dinosaur bones to study and display. Of course we will not ignore nondinosaurs. Maybe a mammal will turn up. We will quarry carefully, and we might sieve if the sediment looks good enough. But we have done that before. This year we must prove the extent of the bone layers in the ground and the completeness of the dinosaur skeletons. If they are profuse and well preserved, their value as a window into the cryptic African past will be greater. We want lots of bones, maps of their positions, samples of the enclosing sediments, and measurements of their host rocks. That should take up the time.

The field techniques will be as in previous expeditions. All the close excavation will be done with small hand tools, awls, and brushes. In the earlier field seasons picks and shovels were used to remove the overburden of sterile soil and rock. We have dug through the easy part. This year we will move the Earth. In the cargo hold of the plane, checked with our duffel bags, are two rotary and demolition hammers—we call them roto-hammers—to blast away the rock. They will be powered by a portable generator waiting for us at the Department of Antiquities in Lilongwe.

I will only have a month in the field this year. That does not seem like much, but it is all I can muster. The late twentieth century goes at a fast pace, with time being a commodity at a premium. Too bad.

Much can be accomplished in a month. The crew, including those waiting for us in Malaŵi, is large, experienced, and efficient. We can do in a month what would have taken many times longer in the earlier days of paleontological exploration. And we can collect more in a month than can be prepared in a year—several years. It is not like Tendaguru. Besides, Tendaguru is not being dug anymore. Malaŵi is. It shows us things about the past that Tendaguru cannot because the two are different windows with different views. New fossils are coming out of Malaŵi. It is the only dinosaur excavation of its kind currently under way in Africa. Everything has been done, everything we could think of, to make things go smoothly while we work it.

Toward the end of the season, after I leave, Will, Dale, and Alisa will reconnoiter the south end of the country. Maps and old reports reveal a possibility of finding dinosaurs and other fossils down there in the tsetse-fly-infested woodlands of Lengwe and Mwabvi. Even if they do not find dinosaurs, there is an even better possibility that there are lavas that can be dated to give a maximum-age estimate for the Dinosaur Beds. That is very important. My efforts to date the rocks with paleomagnetism have been unsuccessful. The fossils give an imprecise age, and anyway I need a date independent of the bones whose antiquity I want to know. I want Will, and Dale, and Alisa to find the lavas and bring back a sample. Then, with a good date, a firm handle on their age, we can really fit Malaŵi's Dinosaur Beds into the global picture of the Age of Reptiles. The bones will make better sense if their age is more precisely known.

I have butterflies in my gut. Will the generator work with the roto-hammers? Will the vehicles hold up? Will we have plaster to jacket the specimens? If we have it, will it actually set to protect the bones?

And worst of all, will the fossils play out? Will there be enough to justify the effort? Will they inspire enough to catalyze further research? Will they be good enough for display?

We will not know until we do the fieldwork.

My eyes want to close, but my mind is active. My thoughts keep returning to the evolution this project has undergone. It has been a long time developing—six years already. Has it really been that long?

My first trip to Malaŵi was in January 1984. I no longer lived in Nairobi, having taken a job in Texas. I was in Kenya doing fieldwork on the project in the Tugen Hills, but I could see signs that the plans for Malaŵi I had made with Zefe two years previously were steadily drifting off course. It was taking too long to get them implemented. I quickly flew down to Malaŵi to meet with him. He had finally finished his degree and just returned from California. I also met his bosses at the Department of Antiquities, both of whom also held Ph.D.'s from Berkeley. They were strongly behind the project. It was decided that I should submit a proposal for funding of a fossil-hunting expedition to the National Geographic Society immediately. National Geographic came through, and I returned with two other bone seekers for my first expedition in June of the same year. The project was finally getting off the ground.

I was a bit concerned my first trip down. There seemed to be a few holdover regulations on the books designed to prevent an invasion of late-surviving hippies. No long hair. No bell-bottomed trousers for the men. No pants or shorts for the women. While none of these rules posed any particular problem, I was a little apprehensive. Perhaps there were other rules that I might not be aware of. As it turned out, no one was into bell bottoms; culottes solved another problem; and whether close or not, we have never had a confrontation over hairdos. Or anything else. Knock on wood.

On that first trip to the Dinosaur Beds I became so enthusiastic about the potential for fossils that I wrote to Alan Charig, chief paleontologist in charge of the African dinosaurs in the British Museum (Natural History). I asked him if, on my way back to the States, I might arrange a visit to London to look at Migeod's collection of Malaŵian bones. Charig replied that he would be expecting me on July ninth.

In closing he offhandedly wrote, "Should you accidentally bump into the President of Malaŵi, Dr. Hastings K. Banda, kindly give him my regards. (He used to be our family doctor in the Gold Coast, thirty years ago, and a very good doctor he was too.)"

Unfortunately I have never had the opportunity.

WHAT AN INTERESTING place the world is for travelers. Everything is so new on the first visit. There are so many things to discover, to learn, and to explore. It must be that way for all travelers. In a Nairobi bookstore in 1983 I discovered a book called *Sir Apolo Kagwa Discovers Britain.* What is interesting about this book is its unique and personal perspective on African exploration. It is an edited version of *Uganda's Katikiro in England,* first published in 1904. It is a true story, written by Ham Mukasa, secretary to the prime minister of Buganda, Apolo Kagwa. In 1902 Sir Apolo was an invited witness to the coronation of King Edward VII in London. He and his secretary, through acceptance of this invitation, became explorers in Britain, strangely mimicking the history of their own continent. They were caricatures of Victorian explorers; the Europeans had gotten to Africa first. Ham Mukasa provided an account of the adventure, just as Livingstone, and Stanley, and Burton, and Young, and countless others, now including me, have done for their own travels in Africa. But Mukasa's discoveries were of turn-of-the-century Great Britain.

Mukasa's account of Great Britain is particularly auspicious in the present context because the initial European colonization of Malaŵi was by Scots. One of the chapters in his book is entitled, "Glasgow City Councillors are Drunkards." This may or may not appear ludicrous to the current inhabitants of that land; however, in the context of a discoverer of Africa, I am certain that many of my observations must appear ludicrous to Africans.

It is like a latter-day Ham Mukasa that I discovered Africa. It is a beautiful, diverse continent. The climate over much of it is tropical; the people are warm. My impressions of Africa derive from Kenya in the east, Cameroon in the French-speaking west, and Malaŵi in the southeast. All three are different, and each is internally varied. Kenya was my introduction to Africa. Malaŵi is now the focus of my African work. Cameroon has its own place in this story, as will be seen later.

Kenya, much of it, abounds with wildlife. In the south the vast herds of the Serengeti make their periodic appearance with the yearly migrations across the grasslands. Cosmopolitan Nairobi, the centrally located capital, is set high near the cool foot of the Ngong Hills. The northern half of Kenya is desert. It is sparsely inhabited by nomadic or seminomadic tribes. The tribes are varied: Cushitic Rendille and Boran, Nilotic Turkana, west of the lake to which they give their name, and Samburu. To the south of these tribes, the Rift Valley is inhabited by Pokot, fish-eating Njemps at Lake Baringo, and Masai. A large proportion of tribal people live traditionally, herding goats, cows, camels, and drinking their animals' blood mixed with milk. Many dress in skins, plait their hair with fat and ochre, fashion mud packs on the backs of their skulls, and arm themselves with spears and knobkerries. Western ways are slow to make incursions into the more remote, inhospitable areas.

Malaŵi has a different feeling from Kenya. Not better or worse, just different. It is the Interior, as Livingstone called it. It bills itself as the Warm Heart of Africa, and that is exactly the feeling it imparts.

Malaŵi has game, but lacks the vast herds of wildebeest and zebra and the great prides of lion so common in southern Kenya. Malaŵi may never have seen such huge herds as those that characterize the Serengeti. There are no giraffe. It is a different kind of land. In Malaŵi, game, except for small antelope and duiker, is mostly confined to wildlife parks and reserves. Lion, elephant, hippo, buffalo, roan, and most of the other large animals can still be seen. But animals in the bush in Malaŵi are simply better hidden and harder to see than those on the plains of Kenya.

Although a small country, Malaŵi is amazingly diverse. It has damp forested hills and verdant mountains. Dry, flat woodlands rest on the shallow soil of crystalline rocks, leveled through millennia of ceaseless erosion. Bald, straight-walled, granite inselbergs and bare-rock kopjes project skyward. Precipitous cliffs with waterfalls and convolvulus vines tumble steeply down, all headed toward the lake. The cool moorland and heather of the Nyika Plateau in the north, with more than 120 species of orchids, contrasts with the hot, dusty lakeshore plain, dotted with naked, elephantine baobabs, the cream-of-tartar tree, the trees built upside down, their leafless jagged boughs rooted in the sky (Figure 16). Rivers that run from the plateaus to the lake flow swiftly. A swaying rope and bamboo bridge provided the crossing of the North Rukuru at Nchenachena until last year. Now a concrete bridge is being built.

The people of Malaŵi are warm and friendly, curious and talkative, and above all polite. The population is a bit more than eight million, which is not a large number except when considered in relation to the size of the country. It has the atmosphere of a small town. Everyone knows everyone else. The people *really are* friendly. There appears to be little corruption by African standards. The police are strict, matter-of-fact, but they do not openly extort as a habit. There are few checkpoints on the roads, and I have never seen the guards that man them drunk. There is a placid, if superficial, aura of safety and security.

There is a mixture of cultures in Malaŵi. Many Indians, mostly descend-

FIGURE 16: *A baobab tree. According to an East African legend, the baobab was a vain and prideful tree whose vanity so disturbed the god N'gai that he uprooted the baobab and made it stand on its head for all eternity. Note the person for scale.*

ants of laborers brought to Africa by the British in colonial times, are shopkeepers and merchants in major towns. There are Muslims. They have been there ever since Arab traders from the coast sent caravans to the Interior. The original tribal religions were animalistic and naturalistic, with a strong reverence for ancestors. Most nontraditional religion nowadays follows the British missionary path. Jehovah's Witnesses have been banned since 1972 for their continued separation from the nation's only political party.

There is tribal diversity in Malaŵi, as in other African countries. But one never sees Malaŵians in traditional tribal dress. About the closest approach to it is in the brotherhood of the *Gule Wamkulu* (Figure 17). These are fearsome masked and costumed men portraying grotesque humanoids and terrifying beasts. They dance at Independence Day celebrations and the like, but they are members of a secret society, the Nyau, whose function is to maintain social order by warning and punishing miscreants. Their influence has been reduced in recent years allegedly. They are widely feared, and they maintain their secret ways. It is not uncommon to see a *Gule Wamkulu* along the road in central Malaŵi where the Nyau is prevalent, but they are to be avoided.

The name of Malaŵi prior to gaining independence was Nyasaland. In 1891, through the leadership of Sir Harry Johnston, it was proclaimed a British Protectorate; in 1953 it was in the Federation of Rhodesia and Nyasaland. The sixties was the decade of independence for Africa. Nyasaland became Malaŵi in 1964. The name Malaŵi is derived from the Chicheŵa tongue, the national language; it means "flames." It refers to images shimmering in heat. The circumflex over the *w* is the preferred transliteration to English, according to the National Chicheŵa Board. Its presence indicates that the sound of the *w* is aspirant, but it is subtle to the Western ear—mine anyway. To tell you the truth, I cannot really hear much difference between the sound of a regular *w* and an aspirant one. But the aspirant *w* and a circumflex in the spelling are correct.

Africa's independence decade, the 1960s, was awash with metaphors. One of the common themes was a new day, a fresh beginning. In Chicheŵa the word meaning "dawn" is *kwacha*. That is also the name of the fundamental unit of currency. The exchange rate is a bit less than three *kwacha* to the dollar. One hundred *tambala,* which means "rooster," make one *kwacha*. One hundred roosters to the dawn, a constant allusion to the promise of the future.

Figure 17: A Gule Wamkulu of the Nyau society. Gule Wamkulu are often seen in central Malaŵi, where their secret society is most prevalent.

The political leader of the country is His Excellency the Life President Ngwazi Dr. Hastings Kamuzu Banda. Malaŵi has a one-party, parliamentary system of government, and Banda is the only leader the country has had since independence. He was educated in the United States and Scotland. He became a medical doctor, practicing for some time in London and, for a while in the 1950s, in West Africa, before returning home to bring his country to independence. At the time of this writing, Banda is nearing ninety and still going strong.

Malaŵi has a large population for its size. It lacks significant mineral wealth, except for a bit of coal. In the recent past many young men joined migrations from their homes by choice in order to work the mines of Zambia, Zimbabwe, and especially South Africa. In centuries past many were forced to leave their homeland by Arab slavers. Banda recognized his people as a resource. Early on he emphasized agricultural development. Malaŵi grows rice, tobacco, cotton, corn (called maize in Africa), and sugar. Foodstuffs are exported to neighboring countries.

Malaŵi has maintained a policy of friendly relations with South Africa. It has open trade, which accounts for the abundance of consumer goods available on store shelves, including some rather good South African wine and other frivolous products that the population at large cannot afford. Malaŵi is one of the few places in Africa where South African tourists can go on holiday or businessmen can go on commerce. As a practical matter, the quality of life for Malaŵians probably is better with the open-trade policy than it would be otherwise. That is not to say Malaŵians approve of South African policy. In the words of Oliver Mwenifumbo, a Malaŵian businessman, "You can trade with the devil, but you don't have to like his politics." If other black African countries trade with South Africa, they do so surreptitiously.

But there is another component to Banda's policy toward South Africa that was especially important in the earlier years of the country. With open borders Malaŵians know that white South Africans, and everyone else, coming to Malaŵi can judge for themselves the effectiveness of black rule, and they can see the effect of the majority voice on the white minority. Moreover, in the struggle against apartheid, Malaŵi's black diplomats in Pretoria had to be extended the same courtesies as whites for diplomatic reasons, thus creating at least a slight chink in racist armor.

THAT FIRST MALAŴI expedition of mine in 1984 visited the same area where the British had gone before. In 1930, when Migeod made his side trip to the British Museum to the northwest side of Lake Nyasa, he stayed with a planter named Maxwell at the village of Nyungwe. In 1930 Nyungwe was in the middle of nowhere. Now the main road is paved, but Nyungwe is still in the middle of nowhere. It is located at the turnoff from the main road onto the dirt track leading to the Dinosaur Beds. Its biggest attraction is a dip tank to give cattle some measure of protection from hordes of infesting ticks. I doubt whether another white has lived in Nyungwe since Maxwell left. But he left a legacy.

In 1989, on my third Malaŵi expedition, I decided to camp at nearby Ngara, where Migeod had landed when he crossed the lake on the *Guendolen* over half a century earlier. It is a beautiful spot, right on the shore of the lake, six miles north of Nyungwe. It is a tiny but interesting fishing village. Some of the inhabitants are lighter skinned, with un-African gray eyes tinged with green. I sought the permission of the village headman to set up camp. He was quite agreeable, vacating his favorite shade tree in a magnanimous gesture of goodwill. As with many other well-to-do African men of the area, he had several wives, each with a small house scattered along the shore, about fifty yards back from the edge of the lake.

The village headman's name? Maxwell. Could it be that there is an all but forgotten branch of the Maxwell clan? The answer is yes. I learned the story from the village headman and his nephew.

William Alexander Maxwell, a young Scot, left home to escape his over-bearing father. He obtained a position with the British Cotton Growers Association and fled to Malaŵi in 1902. He acquired land at Nyungwe, where he made his home, on the Nyika Plateau, where he planted pines, and at Ngara, where he built a cotton ginnery. He returned to Scotland only once, in 1923, briefly.

William Maxwell took six native wives. He got one of them on a trip to the Nyika. A young girl of about eleven caught his eye. He asked her father how many cows he wanted for her. The answer was six. Maxwell took the horrified child right then on credit, marched back to Nyungwe, and sent the cows back to her father. The girl and her husband never talked in all the years of their long marriage. She covered her eyes when he had sex with her. His pink body looked to her like a huge mass of raw meat.

Each of Maxwell's wives bore him one child. Three were sons. Maxwell would gather them at his feet in the evenings and tell them stories. He showed them fossils he had found. One of his sons is now the village headman at Nyungwe. Another—the youngest—is David James Maxwell, also known as Village Headman Makonganya, the big man of Ngara. The patriarch of the Maxwell clan died in Malaŵi in 1963.

·   ·   ·

THE DINOSAUR DIGS are about eight miles inland from the lake near a village called Mwakasyunguti. We made friends with the locals right away on our first trip. One especially bright resident of the Mwakasyunguti area began to question Will Downs, a veteran who has hopped the globe collecting fossils, about what exactly we were doing there. Will explained our lofty goals of understanding life on Earth. The conversation turned to human origins. Will patiently explained human evolution based on the sequence of fossil remains found in Kenya. He gave the age of *Kenyapithecus,* one of Louis Leakey's early finds, as fifteen million years.

"Fourteen million," he was corrected. The Mwakasyunguti native knew the story!

The man to whom Will was speaking was Lightwell Mkwala, at the time a student and now a secondary-school teacher. I hired Lightwell to dig bones, and he has excavated alongside us for two seasons. Long hours in a quarry scratching bones gives plenty of time to get to know someone. Lightwell gave some interesting insight into contemporary life in rural Malaŵi. He also taught us history.

"What do Malaŵians think about David Livingstone, Lightwell?" I asked this question of Lightwell because I knew the standard version of the dedicated missionary who wanted to open up Central Africa to trade in order to stop the flow of slaves eastward for the insatiable appetites of the Arabs. I wanted to know if the Malaŵian perspective was different.

"Dr. David Livingstone. They like him. He stopped slavery in this part of Africa, and he brought education."

The standard version; no revisionist historical scandal for Livingstone from Lightwell.

"Do they think of him as an explorer?"

"Of course not. Africans knew they were here."

Sir Apolo Livingstone discovers Africa.

Then Lightwell went on to explain the life of Livingstone and the history of Malaŵi in very great detail. Livingstone was a man of action. Despite being an evangelist, he was self-conscious and uncomfortable at public speaking, especially in England. His voice was indistinct, perhaps unpleasant, because he had an overly long uvula. At one point he had surgery to correct the problem, but the attempt was apparently not totally successful.

At the time Livingstone first saw Lake Malaŵi, the moral issues involved with slavery were under intense and continued scrutiny. Prior to Livingstone, all trade north of Portuguese territory, what is now Mozambique, and south of British East Africa was controlled by Arabs. The major commodities were ivory, both white and black—the teeth of elephants and the lives of people. The motivation for Livingstone's exploration of the Interior was to bring trade and commerce and to open the area for whites. This was his strategy for ending the East African slave trade. In the Arab markets of Zanzibar—the cesspool of wickedness, as it was called—where cloves were cultivated with the blood of slaves, or in the markets of Oman, Muscat, Iraq, or any number of places along the Red Sea and Persian Gulf, there was no abolitionist movement. The demand for slaves remained. In the West, slavery was no longer acceptable. To stop it in the East, the supply of slaves had to be cut. That is what Livingstone set out to do. Clearly, for him, it was a mission sanctioned by God.

The tradition of slavery in East Africa goes back to the ninth century, much longer than the West African slave trade that fed the cannibalistic plantations of the New World. The East African slave trade, for much of its existence, was a minor component of coastal Swahili commerce with Arabia and points east. Along with slaves, the city-states of the East African coast exported ivory from the Interior, gold from the Zimbabwe culture, and iron. The number of slaves exported was not large, but, of course, they were still slaves. In the latter half of the ninth century those who had been shipped to the sodden land of southern Iraq revolted. So, too, in later years, did those in the small black enclaves of western India.

This early phase of the East African slave trade did not decimate the tribes. However, some centuries later the demand for slaves escalated along with the rise of labor-intensive spice and sugar plantations. Increased demand for slaves coincided with vicious if unrelated tribal hostilities, and the result was truly devastating.

So it was when Livingstone first went to Africa in 1840. In the early years his wife, Mary, and his children were with him. They shared his African hardships. It became too much. The children returned permanently to England, but Livingstone remained, set in his resolve. And resolved he was. His daughter saw him only once in her life, on one of his two visits back to England, and that when she was five years old.

By 1861 Livingstone had viewed the rotting corpses and human bones littering the charnel house that was the lakeshore. Nineteenth-century Africa was a hecatomb of slaughter. It needed help. Mrs. Livingstone, wishing to be with her husband in Africa, to share in his mission, returned once more to the Interior to join the good doctor. She was claimed by fever along the Zambezi before she could catch up with him. That was in 1862.

Also in 1862, halfway around the world, the Welshman Henry Morton Stanley, long before he found Livingstone in Africa, found himself by a circuitous route in the American Civil War. He was captured at the Battle of Shiloh while fighting for the Confederacy with Company E, Dixie Grays, Sixth Arkansas Regiment. To escape prison, he joined the Union Army. He was lucky in that war: He survived. David Livingstone's eldest son, Robert, who was also in the American Civil War, was not so lucky. He died a Union soldier in a Confederate prisoner-of-war camp not long after his mother died in Africa.

Nearly a decade later came the words, "Doctor Livingstone, I presume." Stanley, the newspaper reporter, discovered a destitute Dr. Livingstone at Ujiji on the shores of Lake Tanganyika. Stanley's search for Livingstone was one of the great media stunts of all time. He had been sent by the *New York Herald* for the story. It took him well over a year to get it, and then it was greeted with skepticism in England.

Livingstone was particularly famous in Europe, and there was considerable interest in his well-being. Consequently initial reports of his death generated quite a stir. As it turned out, they were greatly exaggerated. His porters, it seems, had had enough of Livingstone's severe life, so they deserted, presumably to return to their homes in the Comoro Islands between Madagascar and the African coast. When they reached Zanzibar after trekking out from the Interior, they were forced to explain their return without Livingstone. They did not want to get into trouble. What could they say?

They said Livingstone was dead, killed in an attack on the caravan. But they were widely disbelieved. Stanley's was the fourth of eight relief parties sent after the great man, but being only after a story, it was the one having the least connection with Livingstone's work.

David Livingstone refused to return to civilization with Stanley. He died in May 1873, south of Lake Bangweulu in what is now Zambia, west of Malaŵi. His heart was buried in Africa. His body was returned to London, where it was entombed in Westminster Abbey, the central edifice of the Church of England.

The thought of Livingstone's heart being buried in his beloved Africa is touching. However, it does not appear that it was done so much at his request as through necessity. Chuma and Susi, his most faithful native assistants, had to prepare the corpse for transport back to Zanzibar to prove his death at the British Consulate. They removed all the internal organs, including the heart, and buried them. Then they dried the eviscerated carcass for two weeks in the tropical sun so that it could be tolerated while being carried to the coast. At Zanzibar the body was positively identified as Livingstone's. It had a poorly mended broken arm. Years earlier Livingstone had been attacked and mauled by a lion. His arm was shattered by the beast and did not set properly. This bad arm provided a signature for his worldly remains.

After Livingstone's explorations of the Interior more Europeans came, disciples of Livingstone, also Scots for the most part, and mostly planters and traders. They were supplied by and sold their goods to the African Lakes Company, a Scottish firm established to carry on commerce in the area opened by Livingstone. Its African headquarters were near Blantyre, the first major town of the region, founded by the Established Church of Scotland in the Shiré highlands of the south. It is still the major city of Malaŵi. Blantyre was named by the first generation of David Livingstone's followers for the small village east of Glasgow, along the River Clyde, where Livingstone was born. The mission of the settlers remained the same as Livingstone's at first, but the decadence of some of the Europeans in subsequent decades, the abuse of the people, the cheating, the bedding of native women, were unlikely to attract the Lord's sanction, and certainly not Livingstone's.

OTHER SUBJECTS I had learned about from Lightwell pop into my mind as the airplane's turbines drone in my ears.

"Lightwell, was slavery bad here in northern Malaŵi?" I asked once.

"Oooh, yes."

"How so?"

"Well, there was an Arab in this place. His name was Mlozi. His stockade was near Karonga." Karonga is a major city in far northern Malaŵi. We go there for supplies.

For the next half hour I reflected on what Lightwell had told of the atrocities of slavery and the horrors inflicted by the barbarous half-caste Mlozi during the last two decades of the nineteenth century. Some slaves were obtained through purchase from treacherous tribal leaders. Most were captured in early-morning raids by Mlozi's *ruga-ruga,* mercenaries. Many of the men of a hapless village would be killed as they emerged, sleep still in their eyes, from their huts. Those poor few who were not killed and could not escape to the bush—women, children, boys, the remaining men—were herded together and their numbers further diminished until only those who might survive the march to the coast were left. They were stripped. The *goree,* or slave stick, a forked branch, was yoked around the neck of each. The long, polelike ends of two slave sticks were tied together so that each slave was affixed to another. At night the long end of the slave stick was tied vertically to a tree, the forked end pinning the miserable captive to the ground by the neck.

Villagers raided from the north end of the lake were kept in Mlozi's stockade until their numbers were high enough to assemble a caravan of death destined for the coast five hundred miles away (Figure 18). Each slave, near starved, was forced to carry a load, perhaps of ivory, and to step to the whip. Anyone in the coffle who became sick or infirm on the trip simply died. It is said that the condemned were often decapitated, as that was an efficient method for releasing the *goree.* Starvation continued throughout the long march, which could last three to four months.

The *ruga-ruga* were paid their daily rations, the opportunity to loot, a minor share of the slave caravan profits, and the sexual use of prisoners. In 1905 a former *ruga-ruga* from East Africa described the rewards: "Plenty food, plenty women; very lovely." They had no compassion or concern for the commodity they were transporting for profit. There was, they thought, an endless supply.

Once at the coast many of the slaves were sold to work the local planta-tions or the large sugar estates on the French islands now called Mauritius and Réunion. Females were evaluated for their potential in Turkish harems. Most of the remaining males were castrated because eunuchs were of higher market value in the courts of the Orient. Many did not survive the operation.

When the southwest monsoons began in April, Arab dhows came to ferry the slaves from the stockades of the African coast to Zanzibar. The passage was an incredible horror. Each dhow was engorged with an anguish of slaves. They were led aboard and made to lie on the deck. No room—at all—was allowed the dehumanized victims. On top of this layer was built a temporary deck. On this another stratum of slaves was deposited. This continued until the dhow was fully laden. There was absolutely no room for movement, and none was allowed until the cargo was off-loaded at Zanzibar.

At best the voyage would take a full day and night. It could go three days

FIGURE 18: A coffle of slaves. Nothing more graphically portrays the anguish of nineteenth-century Africa than yoked and shackled people driven from the Interior to the voracious slave dhows at the coast.

or more. If the winds calmed, the cargo starved. If approached by a British enforcement vessel, the cargo might be thrown overboard. The sick were dispatched, rather than pay custom on them at Zanzibar. The stench was unbearable, the misery was horrific, the inhumanity was unfathomable.

In Zanzibar the survivors were fattened in pens like cattle, then put on the market. The lucky stayed in Zanzibar to work the clove plantations of the sultan. Others had to make even longer and more horrid voyages than the one they had completed, to Turkey or China or some even to Brazil.

How many people died from all this? Who can say? How many people out of all those affected, beginning with the *ruga-ruga* raids, lived? Who can say? Only a small and sad percentage, that is certain.

. . .

"LIGHTWELL, WHAT happened to Mlozi, the big slaver in northern Malaŵi? How was he stopped?"

"Well, he battled for some time, for a long time, with the people of the African Lakes Company, for example L. Monteith Fotheringham. They had a trading station in Karonga. Then he was hanged."

"When was that?"

"Eighteen, let's see, eighteen ninety-five, I think."

ENOUGH THOUGHT OF the slave trade for a while. But Lightwell's conversation did not leave my mind.

"Excuse me," said Lightwell, "do you know about Shaka the Zulu?"

"No," I said, "tell me about him."

"Well, he was a Zulu. In fact, he was the Zulu leader. He was very fierce."

"Very fierce?"

"Oooh, yes. Very fierce."

Shaka was fierce. He brought war to southern Africa as it had never been. Some say he was responsible for two million deaths, a staggering number under any circumstances, all the more appalling considering the low population density of the time. Shaka commanded a well-disciplined and merciless army. One of his strategies was terror, wanton brutality, which he inflicted on his own people and which his army inflicted upon those he conquered.

In 1819 the Ngoni faction of the Zulus was vanquished by Shaka and driven out of their homeland of Natal in what is now South Africa. They retained their Zulu ways, murdering, pillaging, and plundering as they worked their way northward, then south again to the region of Malaŵi. Like the victims of Shaka, a pitifully small percentage survived the slaughter of the Ngoni. Tribes whose homelands lay before the invaders were splintered. Those who could, fled in advance of the onslaught. Young men of conquered tribes were conscripted into the Ngoni warrior army. Desirable young women were taken as wives. Men not conscripted were brained, bludgeoned, or speared. Undesirable women had their breasts lopped off, then were left to die.

Sixteen years after Shaka drove them from Natal, five years before Livingstone came to Africa, the Ngoni reached the Zambezi on their way north. It was the day of a solar eclipse, 2:00 P.M., 19 November 1835. Two events of interest followed. Legend has it that the chief of the Ngoni, Zwangendaba, struck the waters of the Zambezi with his spear, and like Moses at the Red Sea, the waters parted. The Ngoni were able to cross.

The second event was the premature birth of a son to one of Zwangendaba's wives, overcome with the excitement of the day. The son's name was M'Mbelwa. He was destined to become the leader of the Ngoni.

The Ngoni, who were basically pastoralists, eventually settled in the less-fertile highlands of what was to become Malaŵi. They began to face food shortages and indeed even famine. Constantly they raided the Tumbuka and especially the Tonga, who lived on the fertile grounds near the lake, taking food and slaves. It was not until years later that the Ngoni, under M'Mbelwa, relinquished their belligerent ways. In the meantime their ways, plus the actions of the slavers, created the circumstances found by Livingstone.

"So what tribe lives here at Mwakasyunguti now?" I asked.

"We are Tumbuka," Lightwell replied.

"And how did the Tumbuka come to be here?"

"We came from the north. We fled before the Ngoni invasion." Lightwell looked around at the picturesque Luwonya Hills. "The Tumbuka, Henga, Nkamanga, and other tribes escaped to the desolate regions."

I asked how the Tumbuka differed from the Ngoni.

"We are so different. We have our language."

"Well, don't the Ngoni have a language?"

"Oh, no. They adopted the languages of the tribes they conquered. The Tumbuka kept their tongue; we speak Tumbuka."

"Is that the only difference?"

"No, there are so many. But we used to be more different."

"How so?"

"Well, Ngoni are patrilineal, by which I mean if a man gets married, his wife will come to live in his house."

"Isn't that the way you do it?"

"Now it is, but in the past we were matrilineal. In the past the son-in-law was taken into the home of the daughter. Our culture has changed. It has changed in so many ways with the modern times."

A little later we began a new subject.

"Lightwell, why do you say Livingstone brought education?"

"He founded the missions, and the missions always teach."

Lightwell was certainly right about that. Educating the natives was always a major part of Livingstone's plan, and it was put into practice by his followers as well. Today Malaŵi has a decent education program, reaching everyone in the country. This legacy produces people like Lightwell, who are affected by the broad tradition of education started so long ago in this far-off part of the world. Public education in Malaŵi requires a nominal fee even though the people are very poor. Parents, by remitting fees, are thought to take a greater interest in their children's progress; they want to be sure they are getting their money's worth.

The established educational system in Malaŵi traces its roots through a remarkable pedigree, even after Livingstone. In 1875, two years after David Livingstone died, Livingstonia Mission, founded by Robert Laws of the Free Church of Scotland, was begun at the south end of the lake (Figure 19). It was a beautiful spot, but unhealthy. After the death of five missionaries within three years, Laws moved the mission to a healthier spot, Bandawe, on the west side of the lake.

Bandawe was near Ngoniland, and it was the Ngoni under M'Mbelwa (Figure 20) who first came into contact with Laws of Livingstonia Mission. Laws followed the long-standing missionary policy of not taking part in tribal matters, even to the extent of remaining neutral with respect to Ngoni raiding activities. The missionaries were not raided, probably because they were

FIGURE 19: The original Livingstonia Mission and the ILALA (based on a sketch by Captain Elton in 1877). Many of those who followed David Livingstone into the Interior shared his antislavery passion.

armed. Eventually Laws won the respect of all the local tribes and the confidence of M'Mbelwa. A long friendly relationship was begun. Laws is quoted as saying of the chief, "God seems to have called him and used him for the special purpose of admitting the Gospel to his people."

The relationship was not always smooth, however. There is the tale of M'Mbelwa's young son visiting Laws at his camp. Matronly Mrs. Laws patted him on the head and spoke kindly to him. The gesture was interpreted by some of the tribe as a hex, "so high and no higher," because soon afterward M'Mbelwa's son died. Passions ran high among the people, but M'Mbelwa refused to turn on Laws. He calmed the bloodthirsty warriors. Under M'Mbelwa's leadership, sixteen years after his first acquaintance with Laws, the Ngoni had given up the perpetration of genocide on their tribal neighbors. They were a changed people.

Laws spent five decades in Malaŵi running the Livingstonia Mission. In 1894 he moved it from Bandawe to its current home in the northwest highlands overlooking the lake. There it has faced danger as well. During the freedom movement in 1959, a political State of Emergency was declared because of widespread unrest when Banda, later to become president, was

Figure 20: The Ngoni leader M'Mbelwa. Through his vision and leadership peace finally reigned over the lake and its surroundings.

arrested and led away to gaol. The same British authorities who arrested Banda were concerned over the safety of whites at Livingstonia. The head of the mission was asked by air-dropped message if he wished to be evacuated. The reply was spelled out in whitewashed stones in a field next to Laws's old stone house: "Ephesians 2:14." Nothing more, simply reference to that passage from Paul's Letter. It reads, "For he is our peace, who has made us both one, and has broken down the dividing wall of hostility." The missionaries wanted no relief; they came to no harm.

Livingstonia Mission, through its secondary school, still turns out artisans, and teachers, and businessmen, and preachers, and leaders. In fact President Hastings Kamuzu Banda is named for one of its former missionaries. The motto of the school is, I will try.

The story of Livingstonia student Legson Kayira is particularly inspiring. He was a Tumbuka from near Karonga. The name Legson was made up because it was thought to sound British. Having completed Livingstonia in 1958, Legson decided to go to college—in the United States. Fired by the Livingstonia school motto, Legson walked 2,500 miles across Africa, with no money, few belongings, and no shoes. In Uganda he wrote to Skagit Valley College in Washington. He came across the name at the U.S. Information Service library. They responded with a promise of help. Legson walked on. At Khartoum an American consular officer befriended him and wrote to the school on his behalf. The school raised money for his studies, provided for his airfare, and found a family for him to live with—a white family that already had seven children, but welcomed this African young man. Embassy personnel gave him a suit and some shoes. In December 1960 Legson arrived in America. He got his education, first at Skagit, then at the University of Washington. He wrote a book about his travels entitled *I Will Try*. His story of perseverance is repeated in a high school history text, *World History, Patterns and Civilization,* currently in use in Texas.

To reach Livingstonia Mission, one must make an effort, even today, but it is certainly worth a visit. There is a magnificent stained-glass window, anomalous in the heart of Africa. It is a romantic portrayal of Livingstone. Behind him stand Susi and Chuma, his assistants, best known for transporting his body to Zanzibar. His hand is outstretched to a group of natives, two men and a woman. The woman has a baby on her back, snugly nestled in a cloth tied over her shoulder in typical African fashion. Lake Malaŵi is in the distance.

· · ·

"LET'S SEE IF I have this straight, Lightwell. The Ngoni invaded and were raiding other tribes at the same time Mlozi was taking slaves a bit farther to the north around Karonga?"

"It was very bad."

"Then Laws and the Livingstonia Mission worked with the Ngoni leader M'Mbelwa to pacify and educate the tribes?"

"That is right."

"And the African Lakes Company people started fighting with Mlozi and finally hanged him at about the same time?"

"Yes. And that is also about the time when Nyasaland was proclaimed a protectorate by the British."

"And Livingstonia Mission is still up there on the hill to the south of us?"

"Yes."

"Thanks, Lightwell. You have taught me a lot about your country."

"You are welcome."

THAT IS THE last I remember thinking about on the airplane before I fell into an apprehensive sleep.

9 July, Monday.

Over the Limpopo, over the Zambezi, to Kamuzu International Airport on the rolling Lilongwe Plain, etched in red dust. We have arrived in Malaŵi. It is hazy with the dry season. All our baggage arrived, checked straight through from Dallas with three transfers. No problem with customs. Yusuf, that is, Dr. Yusuf Juwayeyi, Principal Conservator of Antiquities, and Fidelis Morocco, Department of Antiquities technician, met us at the airport. On the twenty-minute drive to town I was brought up-to-date. Everything for the field season was organized. "Like cheese on bread," Kent would say. Yusuf had secured one thousand pounds of dental plaster for us from Government Medical Stores. Of course our research clearance had not come through yet, but it was at the appropriate governmental office, in good order, awaiting a signature. The formalities are proceeding smoothly and efficiently. There will be no unnecessary delay. We will soon head out to the field. But first there are a few things to do in town. We can look around the city while giving our biological clocks a chance to reset and recover from jet lag.

Lilongwe, with its specially built capital area, is a city with the vacuous ambience of a new house not quite ready for occupancy. The newer sectors, with diplomatic missions, government buildings, and the central shopping mall, have wide streets lined with vivid red poinsettias grown to bush size in the tropical climate. There are rows of yellow-green cassia trees. Lawns are manicured. Traffic is light, like a Sunday no matter what day it is. Streets bear such names as African Unity Avenue, Kamuzu Procession Drive, and Presidential Way. The flow of vehicles is controlled at intersections by traffic circles, except at one T-junction, where the Japanese recently erected a traffic signal following the death of one of their nationals in a car accident at that spot.

Everywhere red, green, and black banners proclaim the twenty-sixth anniversary of independence. LONG LIVE KAMUZU, they shout. Portals with the national colors and emblems, overseen by stylized renderings of painted buffalo, antelope, and lion, grace the roads. The *tambala* and *kwacha,* the rooster at dawn, decorate the sides of buildings.

The old town is bustling, full of shops, and noise and the central market. The air is suffused with diesel fumes and black smoke belched from lurching buses and stalled lorries. In the market, divided into sections depending on the merchandise, the din of the sheet metal workers banging and tapping out bucket after bucket, watering can after watering can, reverberates mercilessly. Piles and piles of brown smoked fish lie next to rows and rows of silvery dried fish. There are heaps of glistening moist fresh fish too. This part of the market has a distinctive odor, but it is not bad. Colorful cloth, and basketry, hardware, used nuts and bolts, axes, salvaged gears and bearings, fruits and vegetables—oranges, cabbages, onions, bananas, a few pawpaws and carrots—and the offal pile in the corner, all have territories staked out in the bazaar. Snack peddlers hawk boiled eggs, peanuts, chicken feet, and other such tidbits.

Yusuf dropped me at Country Car Hire (START WITH US AND SEE THE COUNTRY). I always rent vehicles there. The proprietor is an Asian. His family came to Malaŵi from India in the 1890s and has prospered ever since. He appears to be exceedingly shifty, but he has a strange likability if you can stand to be around him long enough to let it show through. He never has a positive word to say about anything. The world is persistently on the verge of collapse. That is, except for one thing. Ask him how business is and he will invariably reply that it is good. Having paid his prices to rent his vehicles, I am sure it is. He supplied me a Land Rover, assuring me it was in good working order.

We shall see. Last year we tried three before we switched to an Isuzu that could get us out of town.

At the Department of Antiquities Dale and Kent inventoried the project field supplies left over from last year. Everything was there. No pilferage. Tents and mattresses were being supplied to the project by the department. Most were there, but for others we had to send to Blantyre. Fidelis, along with James, the driver, is to go north to set up camp tomorrow. The departmental Land Rover has an angle-iron luggage rack that extends from the back of the cab, forward over the hood, to the front bumpers, from which it is supported by two long arms. It provides for the overloading of the vehicle so that it is excessively top-heavy. We will meet Fidelis and James at camp, after they have set it up. Our third member from the department, Elizabeth Gomani, will go north on the bus.

Today at noon we met with a representative of Caltex Oil who presented the project with a check for ten thousand *kwacha* (about three grand) to offset our vehicle expenses. He alerted the press. They reported it in the newspaper and on Radio Malaŵi, thus informing the villagers of remote Mwakasyunguti of our arrival in the country long before we will get to the field. They will be expecting us.

We seem to be happily remembered by the staff at the Lilongwe Hotel. Smily, the grinning little porter, is still there and still smiling. Last year Kent wrote a letter for him, granting permission to rummage through our tattered discards. The poor guy had been reprimanded by his boss for removing some tossed-out goods from the trash. He thought Smily had pilfered them, but he had not.

It is nice to be back in the Warm Heart of Africa. Tomorrow it will be nice to head to the field.

13 July, Friday.

Ngara camp. Lucky Friday the thirteenth.

The drive up from Lilongwe was pleasant. The weather was perfect, the skies were blue. We broke the trip into two legs. We drove to Kasungu National Park on the first day and spent the night at the lodge, taking advantage of its location for rest. It gave us a chance to watch elephant, antelope, and hippo, and to see some countryside. The rest of our stay in Malaŵi will be filled with digging bones, not sightseeing. We went for an afternoon game drive and got mired in sticky mud just as the sun was going down. It took two hours in the greasy black ooze to extricate ourselves. Luckily we had flashlights and some tools with us. We also had an armed game ranger. He, at least, felt secure from buffalo and other wild beasts with his ancient rifle. I am not sure that the rest of us were so comforted.

The road from Kasungu to Mzuzu, which we take to get up to the northern end of the country, passes through the plains and on to the spectacular forests of the Viphya Plateau. Peasant farmers sold sweet potatoes along the road. Boys and girls held out sticks of Malaŵi sausages, dried mice, for sale as lunch to travelers. The mice are caught in the fields by the children. Then they are boiled without much further ado. No skinning, no removing the heads. After boiling, their nice but nubbly little bodies are dried and salted. Half a dozen or so of the stiff sun-dried carcasses are placed in a piece of split bamboo for easy handling. Then they are ready for sale (Figure 21). And for eating—hair, bones, teeth, toenails, and tails—everything.

FIGURE 21: Malaŵi sausages—boiled, salted, and dried mice—for sale. Even if this is not your idea of lunch, the child's smile is a disarming introduction to the culture.

I have had some dealings with these sausages. I am always on the lookout for comparative skeletal material of modern species of animals to use in my studies of fossils. What a golden opportunity these Malaŵi sausages presented for making a collection of African mouse skeletons that could be used in connection with my fossil-rat interests. Last year I bought every stick of Malaŵi sausages that I could get my hands on. The children must have thought I was ravenous. I took all my specimens, for they had now become scientific, back to the Department of Antiquities in Lilongwe. I left them in the office to be shipped to me in Dallas along with some of the season's important fossils. They had not been in Lilongwe twenty-four hours before the staff, thinking I had brought them a treat, ate my entire sample of African rodents!

There are several dishes besides Malaŵi sausages that do not seem to be particularly well suited for the Western palate. For instance, *The Malaŵi Cookbook* has an entire chapter on insects. From it you learn that bee larvae should be fried with a little salt and served as a relish or appetizer. Large green crickets that swarm at streetlights should have their wings and the horned parts of their legs removed. Then they should be boiled for five minutes, dried, and panfried, just like grasshoppers and red locusts. Recipes are included for termites, black flying ants, sand crickets, cicadas, the regular shield bug, and the large green shield bug. Green caterpillars are better with the stomach and intestine removed. Then they should be boiled and fried. For variation add one chopped tomato, a chopped onion, and some peanut flour. After drying, caterpillars can be stored for three months.

I am perhaps most amused by the tiny lakefly, *Chaobora edulis,* Livingstone's *kungu,* as an ingredient of the Malaŵi kitchen. Every month at the new moon these gnat-sized flies arise in clouds, billions of them, from the lake. Their mists can be seen from far in the distance, even from the tops of the high scarps overlooking the lake (see Figure 11 in Chapter 2). When they drift ashore at a village, moistened winnowing baskets, usually used for separating chaff from grain, are waved through the swarm. The tiny midges stick to the wet basket. Then they are scraped off and molded into cakes by pressing them into a mass. The cakes are left to dry in the sun.

To prepare, break the lakefly cake into pieces and boil in salted water until soft. Add a chopped tomato, onion, crushed peanuts, and a little oil. Cook gently and serve with rice. Livingstone said it "tasted not unlike caviare, or salted locusts." Sound delicious?

No, I have never eaten Malaŵi sausage or tasted any of the recipes just related.

The drive from Kasungu Park to Ngara camp, past the children selling Malaŵi sausages, was uneventful except for the radiator boiling dry. We arrived at Ngara camp two days ago to find no one. Fidelis and James had begun to set up camp, but had left it unfinished. Where were they? I finally tracked Fidelis down at noon yesterday in Karonga. They were having vehicle trouble and had gone to town for repairs. Then they could not get back to camp. Stuck in town, Fidelis was asleep at the Enikani Rest House where I found him. I took him back to camp with me, leaving James to look after the departmental Land Rover. Vehicle problems are to be expected.

Now, a day later, the camp has taken shape. It is at the village of Ngara, where the M-1 highway runs close to the lake. The village itself is probably larger, but otherwise not much changed since earlier days when Migeod and Parrington visited the Scotsman Maxwell in 1930. A sandy dirt track from the tarmac, paralleling the lakeshore, leads down to African Mr. Maxwell's cotton ginnery. Mr. Maxwell is the official village headman, a very important position in the social and political infrastructure. Because his elder brother is also a village headman, at Nyungwe, this Maxwell has taken on the official title of Village Headman Makonganya. It means "big man," and there could not be a more accurate description of him. On the west side of the dirt track, between it and the tarmac, are Maxwell's five brick houses, stuccoed with concrete and crowned with corrugated iron roofs. He parks his old brown Mercedes off the track next to the first one. His houses are surrounded by chicken coops, children, and his wives' open cooking fires. The area is literally swarming with Maxwell offspring of all ages. At last count he had thirty-two children from six wives, but that was a few years ago. Some of Maxwell's sons have worked for me. He will not allow them to learn skills; even the art of truck driving is prohibited. He does not wish them to be educated. He is very protective of his daughters, who, with their gray eyes, are striking in the extreme.

I have just looked over the camp. It is good. It extends along 165 feet of prime beachfront property, across the track from Mr. Maxwell's houses. The beach is sand with a strand of cobbles. They grind in the surf, adding their percussion to the rhythm of the waves, providing an audible background to all we do at this place. And because this is our home in Malaŵi, we will do a lot at this place. This is where we will return after the day's work, where we will eat, and where we will rest. I want it to be pleasant and comfortable.

The camp sits on a flat, dusty terrace of sandy black soil fifteen feet above the lake. A rank of spindly young blue gums, as *Eucalyptus* trees are called, variable in height but none more than a few feet high, lines the terrace edge along the central part of camp. The north end is bounded by a clump of low-growing palms with fan-shaped, palmettolike fronds. There is also an *Acacia* tree. North of that a few hundred yards is an abandoned, crumbling church building and the cotton ginnery built by the big man's father. During the 1959 civil disturbances the Maxwell home at Nyungwe was razed and the ginnery came under attack. The Maxwell boys were armed and sent to the roof. They were told to shoot to kill if they heard two shots from their father's pistol. One shot was fired over the heads in the crowd. No more were necessary. The ginnery was saved, and it is still operating today.

Kent's blue-domed nylon tent sits under two large, mostly leafless euphorbia trees. The African name for them is *mkomwa*. They have thin, light-colored, peeling bark and large, hairy seeds scattered beneath their branches. South of Kent's tent and the two *mkomwa* trees is my abode, a large green-canvas safari tent, shaded by an *Acacia*. Landward, and next to me, is Dale's and Will's safari tent. A small *Gmelina* tree, a member of the teak family introduced to Africa from tropical Asia, sits to the left of their front flap. Our tents, at right angles, open into a common area crisscrossed with a spiderweb of guy ropes and clotheslines. Our towels and the day's laundry are hung out to dry. Behind their tent is a large *Gmelina* and a clump of fan palms, into which is set a grass-walled shower enclosure.

The focal point of camp is a large tamarind tree, its shade, with typical African hospitality, yielded to us by the local beer drinkers. Drinking is popular in Malaŵi. The intemperate natives of Ngara seem to prefer their own home brew, or else they cannot afford the commercial product. They imbibe glass-bottled beer only infrequently. The only commercial brand available is Carlsberg. It comes in four labels: green, which is a lager, progressing to brown, which is an ale, then gold, which is expensive "special brew" for the Malaŵian yuppie crowd. The fourth label is for black stout. The rallying cry of Malaŵi's Carlsberg drinkers is "Give a guy a green." The brewing company has a tree-planting program to further the greening of the country. It is activated by the appropriate number of green bottle tops.

Maxwell and the boozy men of the village seemingly spend every spare moment imbibing an acrid, cheesy home brew. It is prepared from millet by the wives. Every three or four days a new batch is ready for drinking. The thick, sediment-laden elixir is drunk through a common straw, submerged in a calabash to a depth that provides for maximum alcohol and minimum sludge.

A commercial version, *chibuku,* sold in half-gallon-sized milk-container-type cartons, takes the place of home brew during necessity. *Chibuku,* like home brew but unlike bottled beer, is a dense millet concoction. It continues fermenting after its delivery from the factory. The sides of the carton begin to bulge with the pressure of generating gas. When this happens, the *chibuku* is said to be tough. The millet residue settles to the bottom. At drinking time the top of the carton is grasped and the package vigorously agitated, giving the mixed liquid the correct texture and chewyness. The top of the carton is cut off and the package is passed around the circle of friends. Huge, rickety articulated lorries distribute the brew, touted as "The International Beer," across the length and breadth of the country, their grumbling sides gayly painted with the company motto, Shake, shake *Chibuku!*

Drinking parties can begin at any time of day. They are often loud, accompanied by blaring music when the generator is working or if there are batteries for the radio. We are never bothered by the inebriates, however, and they do not join us in our camp. I think that is very gracious of them considering that their preferred venue is the shade of the tamarind.

Under its thick, spreading branches our three tables are positioned end to end. There we sit, talk, and take our meals. Between the tables and the scraggly line of blue gums at the terrace edge is Fidelis's and James's safari tent, which doubles for field and vehicle supply storage. Outside their tent, under the fly, hundred-pound sacks of plaster of Paris, ten of them, are stacked. Here, too, the gleaming rows of white plaster jackets, each containing its treasure of fossil bones, will be lined in a display for constant inspection and inspiration as the season progresses.

Behind the tamarind is the kitchen. It is a roofless two-room grass enclosure. The first has a makeshift worktable constructed of reeds, four or five buckets of lake water for washing, a trash pit, and two cooking fires. A stack of firewood is replenished daily from the head of a young woman with a baby of a few months old swaddled on her back. She genuflects, in accordance with local custom, when she accepts payment for the wood.

The other enclosure is the pantry and sleeping quarters for Ronald, the cook. It has a long reed table to keep food supplies off the ground. Plastic buckets with tight-fitting lids provide moral support but few tangible results in the continuing struggle to keep our food supplies away from the jaws of marauding ants. We would enjoy the right to dine without them, but they are as much a part of the camp as the tamarind tree. There is also a space for the storage of small fossils, and for crates of beer (greens and browns) and soda bottles. Finally there is a pit, which is actually a show of bush refrigeration technology. It is filled with drinks and covered with wet burlap and sand. The refreshments are kept marginally, but pleasantly, cooler than the ambient temperature.

Next to the pantry enclosure is the 150-gallon water bowser, a tank on a trailer, for storing drinking water. Next to it is the car park for our two Land Rovers. Beyond, at the edge of the terrace, is Elizabeth's blue-domed nylon tent. The south edge of camp is marked by a thicket of prickly pear, where local drinkers pee; a baobab; a pink-flowered desert rose; and a few cashew trees. Then starts the fishing suburb of mud and thatch huts, smoking sheds, and dugout canoes. Beyond the fishing huts are the marshes with mosquitoes, mud, and bilharzia. Discreetly tucked away across the road from our camp in a thicket of fan palm is the grass-walled enclosure for our long drop.

All is in order at camp, and we are ready to begin with the bones tomorrow. It is almost as if we never left Malawî after the field season closed last year. Almost, but not quite. Things are not exactly the same this year. The receptionist at the Department in Lilongwe died, and Village Headman Maxwell lost one of his six wives to cerebral malaria.

14 July, Saturday.

Our first day in the field. It is good to see this again, to let my eyes take it in. The fossil localities of Mwakasyunguti sit high in the Luwonya Hills on the east side of the valley of the Sitwe River. They are perched in the white and pastel-red sands of the Dinosaur Beds. Surrounding the sites and down the valley the scrubby trees are green and yellow, some with leaves daubed red. It is the dry season, and the rains were poor this year. Most of the trees are mercifully without thorns.

The valley on its eastern edge is topped with straight-walled white cliffs capped with hard, red gravel. The terrain is rough and broken from the foot of the cliffs down to the valley floor. Patches of dinosaur-bearing sandstone, white and pink and rust in color, peek through the scrub. Parched, tawny grass patches the ground, growing in tiny hillocks and mounds. It grows as tall as a person in some of the low places. Short fronds of pale-green palm are scattered about in clumps. Along the river the trees are a brilliant dark green. Coarse reeds grow thick and rank along the stream banks. There is one small stand of bamboo with spidery leaves and golden, jointed trunks. Fields cleared for agriculture are dotted white with cotton or infested with spindly cassava. Monstrous gray baobabs lumber out of parched earth, grasping the sky with leafless, tortured branches. The air smells clean, especially in the cool morning.

Across the valley the vegetation is colorless on the dry, crystalline slopes of the opposite hillside. Beyond, to the west, through the African haze, is the Nyika Plateau. Beyond that lies Zambia and its Luangwa Valley, where fossil bones have also been found. The clouds build up daily over the Nyika, but it will not rain—at least it is not likely to at this time of year. The breeze picks up and dies. As the day heats up, the sweat bees emerge, sometimes in droves.

To reach the sites, we must first drive south along the tarmac M-1 lake road from Ngara camp. After ten minutes we reach Nyungwe and turn right onto the dirt road that skirts the ridge of crystalline rocks forming the east side of the valley. After another ten minutes we turn north onto the rough track that leads up the valley to the region called Mwakasyunguti. The jolting track requires four-wheel drive. It steeply fords the Sitwe River—twice.

We wave at potbellied children, naked or in rags, and men languid in the shade. Women, pounding maize with heavy four-foot-long pestles, carry babies tied to their backs. They group together around the mud and thatch huts. After half an hour or so we reach the new Land Rover path constructed in our absence by Mjuda, one of our local Tumbuka labor force. This is all four-wheel drive. We can only go another five minutes before we hit the end. More roadwork is needed. We park and walk the last fifteen minutes on a footpath snaking through the divides and drainages to the quarries.

The total distance from Ngara camp is eleven miles. The whole trip takes just over an hour. We would save a lot of time if we camped here at Mwakasyunguti, but we would give up some important creature comforts. The camp would be much more difficult to supply. The monotony would play on our minds. There would not be enough clean water for bathing. Resorting to the river would invite bilharzia. It is worth the extra drive to stay at Ngara. The afternoon dip in the lake is good for the soul. It picks up the spirits and relaxes the body. It is good for morale. Better to camp there.

Once we have turned onto the dirt track into the valley, we never see any vehicles besides our own Land Rovers. We are told the track is also used by the Water Department for periodic checks on a borehole and by a medical team that cares for lepers in remote places.

There are no stores or shops in the valley. There is a school and there is a clearing used for a soccer field. Virtually all the food that is eaten in the valley is raised here. All along the river bottom, interspersed with cotton, the cash crop, are fields of cassava, maize, ground nuts, a few beans and cowpeas, tomatoes and squash, and a bit of sugarcane. Around the huts and villages are dark-green mango trees, now in flower, and the odd pawpaw tree. Luxuriant banana groves thrive in low, well-watered earth along the river.

There are cattle, a few black-and-white-spotted hogs, and chickens around every hut. Some dwellings sport round pigeon roosts of reeds woven into a four-foot-long cylinder, roofed with thatch. The roosts sit on stilts and are closed off at night to protect the furry-footed pigeons from interlopers such as genets and civet cats. Storage granaries are also perched on stilts to keep vermin out of the grain as much as possible.

Life appears idyllic in the valley, but it is not. It is a difficult existence, fraught with disease and hardship. Yet the people have quick, bright smiles, abundant laughter, and a radiant, endearing warmth.

This is the dry season and winter below the equator. For the people of the Sitwe Valley it is the slow time of year. There is little to do in the fields, save a bit of cotton harvesting. Much of their time is taken up with dancing. Women dance the *ndola,* and men the *malipenga.* Different drums and rhythms characterize each. We will hear them practicing most every day, at most any time of day. The sound of the drum, the quintessential sound of Africa, will sublimate our minds while we quarry, and we will never forget it.

The *malipenga* dances are big events. Each village has a team of dancers and musicians that competes with neighboring villages. The only instruments used besides the drums are kazoos made of calabashes with mats of spiderweb, or occasionally bits of plastic bag, for reverberation.

The *malipenga* conjures visions of the Chinese martial art tai chi, danced in synchrony to an African beat. The men arrange themselves in a line, dancing in unison while playing their kazoos. Drums and a primary kazoo ensemble are just off to the side. Legs are kicked, arms snaked, heel to ground, then toe pointed, and spin, all in slow motion, or at most half speed. It is said that the *malipenga* is derived in part from World War I prisoner-of-war camps and from the South African mining camps of transient workers in the 1920s.

The women's *ndola* dance is more animate. For them, movement is in counter-circles, with feet moving and shuffling, round buttocks gyrating, and chests heaving to the shrill soprano voice characteristic of African women in song.

THE OBJECTIVES FOR our first day of work at the fossil localities are simple. The state of the last year's quarries must be evaluated, a preliminary strategy for excavation must be devised, the size of the needed labor force must be estimated, and the local crew must be assembled. Our first day went well with regard to all of these. In our absence over the past year, Mjuda, our former employee, has shown greatly appreciated initiative. He not only worked on the road, laying out a path all the way to the quarry, but he bushwhacked the right-of-way for a large part of it single-handedly. He also maintained a watchful, protective vigil over the sites, making certain that drainage channels trenched around important areas diverted rain and runoff, shielding unexcavated fossils from erosion and weather. No cattle hooves were allowed access to the bones still in the ground.

There are three good quarry sites strung out along seventy yards of west-facing hill slope. CD-9 was worked last year and a bit the previous field season. It will be our main quarry. CD-10 was found by Alisa in 1987. It has a very important stegosaur pelvis, fragile but large and heavy. We have protected it for three years because of the difficulty in removing it. This year, events permitting, we will get it out. The third quarry site, CD-11, is at a slightly higher level in the Dinosaur Beds than the other two. It has some interesting bones sticking out and it looks to have a chance of some small animals as well as dinosaurs.

We assembled a crew and set them to clearing off the overburden at CD-9. We know how much to remove because we can already see the fossils of the productive bone layer—the sweet zone.

18 July, Wednesday.

The excavation of bones has begun. Fossils are coming fast and furious. It is fun to work like this, with excitement running at a paleontological fever pitch. The whole excavation crew is assembled, both foreign and domestic components. All three quarries have been opened. The generator works, but it can handle only one of the two roto-hammers we brought at a time. However, that one cuts through the overburden as if it were cheese. Thick chunks slump off. The roto-hammer cuts rapidly through the soft sandstone, more slowly but still effectively through the stony, heavily cemented, concretelike sand. The crew likes to use it; it is like a toy, noisy and powerful. The protective soil and enough overburden has been stripped from each quarry to allow the excavation to start. A large bamboo and grass shade has been erected over CD-9, the main quarry. A smaller one covers CD-11. Later, when we can expend more effort there, I will have one built over CD-10.

The bone, when it is freshly exposed by excavation and not weathered on the surface of the ground, is in good shape. It is not petrified fully to stone. Although it is fragile, it is well preserved and not particularly distorted, even after 100 million years under the ground. Fresh bone is pale, creamy white with an iron-red stain on the surface. With the abundance of fossils we can see now, there is no sign that they will give out, but how do we know what will happen a few feet farther under the ground?

Last year we left a number of good specimens in place. At CD-9 the sauropod tail we have been excavating for two seasons is continuing into the hillside. There are also three or four ribs and a few vertebrae. At CD-10 Kent's first assignment is to outline the stegosaur pelvis. What a beauty it is! The small sliver of bone next to it led into most of a sauropod femur, a thighbone. CD-11 has some limb bones, arms or legs, but it also appears rich in small bone fragments. Dale has begun mapping the first bones to get uncovered. Kent has plastered a few. Fidelis and Elizabeth are clearing new specimens they just found. This is really good. There are as many bones as we can handle—more even. We hit the ground running this year and it feels great.

I have a fine crew. For now there are four Americans including me. Will Downs is the *mnyako mwembe,* the bearded friend. He is animated, unconventional, and foulmouthed. His face is hidden behind a full, bushy beard, starting to gray. His piercing eyes are quick behind metal-rimmed spectacles. His dark pelage is thin on top with a few unkempt strands remaining. The back and sides of his head are fringed with a disheveled shock of not especially long, but wild and unruly swept-back hair. He had it trimmed before he came here with me in 1984. I do not think it has grown longer since. Energetic and quick to laugh, he is a unique individual in the good sense. We met when I moved to the Museum of Northern Arizona after I got my Ph.D. in 1977. He was already employed there. We have worked together consistently ever since.

Will has a degree in humanities, but he is loathe to follow standard patterns of social systems. He inherited a tremendous respect for the truth and an admirable disrespect for authority from his dad. His father was a big newsman in the days of Edward R. Murrow. He is exceptionally well read, proficient in Mandarin Chinese, and hates television (there is none yet in Malaŵi). His mind is creative and perpetually active, springing from subject to subject. He fires off questions and ideas like a Gatling gun. Life is never dull around him.

He knows fieldwork. His eye is keen for finding fossils. Once they are found, he can get them out of the ground. His excavation tools are custom machined, the paleontological equivalent of pearl-handled six-guns. He is patient. He is good with his steady hands. His knowledge of field geology is first-rate and all self-taught. His experience is broad: the United States, China, Africa, Greenland, the Punjab, and Baluchistan. Now he works as a free lance with me, Harvard, the University of Arizona, the American Museum of Natural History, and I do not know who else, but he is based at Northern Arizona University in Flagstaff. Besides fieldwork, he prepares fossils in the laboratory and translates Chinese technical reports into English.

Dale Winkler is as methodical as Will is impetuous. He is clean-cut with curly blond hair and sideburns. His pelage is as fair as Will's is dark. The only similarity is a thinning on top. Quiet, deliberate, and precise, Dale is responsible for all the mapping and measuring. Dale has been with me for five years now. He's originally from Michigan. I hired him after I saw his presentation at a scientific meeting on fossils from the Texas Panhandle. His quality was immediately obvious. He brings expertise in understanding the ecological implications of rocks and sediments and the patterns in which bones are scattered. He is an absolutely essential member of the team.

Kent Newman, a tall, big Texan with blond hair, came to work for me nearly four years ago on what was to be a six-month stint preparing fossils in the laboratory. He has been with me ever since, but after this field season he will begin teaching in public schools. He is proud and has a good sense of humor. His memory holds a wealth of the right facts, stored for use at just the right moment. I will be sorry to lose him, but the job I can offer simply will not provide for a secure future. My loss is the Plano Independent School District's gain. He will be the kind of teacher a school system always needs, a good one. I hope he, or someone very like him, teaches my kids. At the very least he will have good stories of Africa and dinosaurs to enliven his classroom. Kent and I will be the first to leave the field this year.

The final member of the American suite is Alisa Winkler. She was my first Ph.D. student. Because she is so deeply interested in science and so without pretense, she is truly a pleasure to work with. Now she has a postdoc and teaches anatomy at the medical school. She will not arrive until Kent and I have departed. Then she will join Dale and Will on the reconnaissance of the south. She is piggybacking a trip to Kenya on this one. She will examine the dinosaur specimens in the National Museum in Nairobi. They only have a few, but they might be important. She will also continue her studies of small-mammal fossils from the Rift Valley, eighty (and more) million years younger than the Dinosaur Beds here in Malaŵi. She may want to stock up on Malaŵi sausages for their bones. Alisa and Dale are married to each other.

OUR AFRICAN COLLEAGUES have a very different approach to life from that of the American contingent. It is characterized by the pervasive fatalism so common in the impoverished world. There is a quiet resignation to, if not an acceptance of, events and conflagrations that are, or appear to be, beyond immediate control. Things like high infant mortality, or failed rainy seasons, or no spare parts, or the bus showing up three hours late or not at all, or, if you have the few *tambala* in coin, your order of a cold Coke being filled with a warm Fanta, an orange drink. The lack of reliability, the unpredictability, and the fatalism suffuse the atmosphere, blanketing everything, every action, with the façade of calmness. It is a peaceful veneer over a pitiless resignation. Entering this system from the West can be frustrating, nerve-wracking. But it is their country and their lives. Things are done their way in Africa. Of course people of the Developing World have the same basic desires, the same feelings, the same emotions, the same anxieties that are common to all people. They are just more resigned.

The obverse of the fatalism is a kind of ingenuity that accompanies material inadequacies. The symbol of this ingenuity is, for me, a spirit lamp Dale bought in the Karonga market (Figure 22). It is made from a light bulb and a tin can. Many remote areas of Malaŵi are not yet supplied with electricity. But a light bulb still has its use. With the metal base removed, leaving only the globe, and turned upside down, it makes a perfectly functional reservoir for spirit. A string hanging down into the globe is the wick. The tin can is cut and bent to form a stand and holder, complete with handles on either side. How very clever. What a good example of making do.

FIGURE 22: An ingenious spirit lamp. People make their own light where electricity does not reach. A light bulb is inverted and used as a reservoir into which a wick dangles. A tin can is cut and fashioned into a base—complete with handles—for the lamp.

My Malawian colleagues are indispensable to the project. They are as much a part of it as any of the Americans. We all have our responsibilities. They, like all Malawians I have met, are kind, friendly, soft-spoken, and exceedingly polite. Fidelis Morocco has worked with me since the first expedition. A longtime employee of the Department of Antiquities, he sports a university T-shirt purchased during his three-month training period in my Dallas labs last year. He learned to prepare fossils and has since set up a preparation lab in Malawi. James Khomu is the departmental Land Rover driver. His hands are full trying to coax yet another kilometer out of the tired gray machine. Occasionally he does, but it is so old that every effort, even if the battle is won, is a futile gesture toward a lost war. Twice already the vehicle has been in for repairs and we only just got here. I anticipate a long convalescence for it. We will be lucky to have it as a backup to the rental vehicle if (when?) we really need it.

Elizabeth Gomani is recently graduated from the University of Malaŵi with a strong background in Earth sciences, chemistry, and computers. Her voice is so soft, it can barely be heard. Last year she joined us as a student. This year she was hired by the Department of Antiquities to take on this project. If all goes well, as anticipated, she will undertake graduate studies with me in the United States, then return to her permanent professional position at the department.

It is hard to handicap the odds of success for Elizabeth. There is no pool of aspiring paleontologists to sort through to find the best person for foreign training. Only one person can be selected, in this case Elizabeth. All the eggs are in one basket. That is the general case in the Developing World. Only a few have the opportunity for advanced study abroad, and by the time they are selected, their futures are locked—and so is that of the sponsoring agency.

Certainly Elizabeth has the ability. And she has had enough experience with me and my crew in the field that she should know by now if she can stomach it. She says she enjoys the work and will dedicate her professional life to the study of fossils. Okay. Let's go with it.

At the site we have five permanent assistants during the field season. Four or five others are hired as day laborers for roadwork or when there is an extra-heavy load of pick-and-shovel work. The Dinosaur Project is the only source of employment in the valley. Because we work through a government agency, the Department of Antiquities, I pay government wages, about two *kwacha* per day, less than one dollar. That is beefed up with a few perks and a bonus at the end, but still field labor remains one of the smaller expenses of the expedition.

All but one of the five permanent staff have worked for me before. Mjuda is the man who watched over the sites in our absence and who laid out the new road from the track to the quarry. He works for us digging bones during the day. At night he sleeps in the canvas storage tent at CD-9 to keep an eye on the supplies. He is thin and spare, missing a few teeth. His high voice is characteristic, but his quick, Woody Woodpecker giggle is his trademark. Some of the locals say he is a witch doctor and can turn people invisible, but no examples can be cited. He has a command of medicinal plants, taught him by his father and which he is passing on to his son. Like Mjuda, Wellington, Joseph, and Yasaki are good guys. They like to joke around.

Wellington smiled and asked Kent, "What is the capital of New Zealand?"

"Wellington, I think," Kent replied, and Wellington beamed with pride.

Joseph is the most quiet of the lot. Yasaki is the least industrious and just a bit surly. Finishing off the crew is Dyson Mkwala, the brother of Lightwell, the former employee, now schoolteacher, who taught me Malaŵi history at the site during the first field season. Dyson spent most of the afternoon today singing *"Frère Jacques"* in English. All of the others have run through most of their English vocabularies.

"One, two, three, four, five, six, seven, eight." Then the counting stops. "This is my nose, this is my eye, this is my ear"—all phrases from their childhood schooling.

They get into their work. Their eyes are keen to *mafupa,* bone, and some of them are becoming skilled excavators. They appear to be at ease, laughing and joking, even though they work hard. That is how I prefer it to be. It makes the days fun.

23 July, Monday.

Camp life has become a steady routine, ably managed by Mr. Ronald Mwagomba. Ronald is the cook, and a very good one, especially with *chambo* fish and curry. Now in his mid-sixties, he spent years working in government rest houses, which are a kind of official hotel. He started in 1946, serving a couple of two-year stints in South Africa. Malaŵi, itself being chiefly agricultural, has traditionally been a source of industrial and support labor for the southern part of the continent, mainly, in Mr. Mwagomba's early days, for the mines of the Rhodesias and South Africa. He is now retired and reasonably well off, relatively speaking, although not so well off as he might have been. Up to a couple of years ago he had forty cattle. All but two have died of hoof-and-mouth disease. He supplements his pension by working for us. This is his second year.

Mr. Mwagomba is a dapper fellow and he runs a tight kitchen. His stove burners are beds of coals from two open fires. He has three helpers. One of them, Gresham, clean and smartly dressed at dinnertime, has been taught by Mr. Mwagomba to serve meals with British decorum in strict adherence to the protocol of etiquette: Serve from the right, remove from the left; Elizabeth, the lady, must be served first, then me as expedition leader.

The day starts early, before dawn. Ronald and his assistants are up before five. The rest of us get up later, awakening in our tents to the nearby sound of the lake with its sleepy morning waves lapping the shore. I am usually the last one out of the bag. At this early hour the sun is an incandescent orange-red sphere rising from the lake. Pans of warm water are brought to the tent for the morning's wash. Around six the crew begins to gather at the breakfast table. Maxwell's wives and daughters are already filling water buckets at the lake and trudging back to their cooking fires with the full vessels balanced on their heads.

Breakfast, usually served by six-fifteen, is toast, cereal, fresh fruit, tinned juice, coffee or tea, and boiled eggs if we have them. Accompanying breakfast is malaria prophylaxis: one Paludrine tablet every day and two chloroquine tablets on Mondays. The American Embassy reminded us to take both; they lost one of their people last year. By seven we are on the road to the quarry, each and all tumbled into one of our two Land Rovers. It is usually the rented one because it seems to be the more reliable. We take turns driving, rotating to a different driver each day. When we arrive at our parking spot, plaster or whatever other supplies are needed at the quarries are carried up by the local crew and we set to work.

During the day, while we are out, Mr. Mwagomba oversees the cleaning of tents and washing of laundry. He irons all the clothes, including under-wear, with a heavy metal iron filled with coals from the fire. He sets the program for running the camp, in his fashion, with little direction from me. As long as he is doing such a good job, the best thing I can do to help him is to stay out of the way.

Some supplies for the kitchen can be obtained at Ngara. Fresh fish, chickens, ducks, and a bit of milk are available around camp, regularly brought in by our neighbors. The word has spread that we are in the market for such things. Every four or five days a Land Rover must drive the forty-mile round-trip to Karonga for dry goods and other supplies. Drinking water, held in the 150-gallon bowser, must be replenished at the Karonga Teacher's College, but it does not often require refilling.

Once we took a busman's holiday to give Ronald and the camp crew a day off. It also gave us a change of scenery and provided the opportunity for me to visit 250 million-year-old Karroo rocks at a spectacular locality overlooking the lake near the village of Chiweta. Karroo rocks are most abundant in South Africa and are important in paleontology because they contain in massive abundance an extensive fossil record of mammalian relatives as they existed before they can really be deemed mammals in the modern sense. They are more primitive than all the animals we commonly and easily recognize as mammals today. They used to be called mammallike reptiles. I had long wanted to see this site, also visited by the Britisher Migeod in his 1930 trek to Nyasaland. The locality is incredibly rich in bone preserved in tough concretions. We found three skulls and lots of other fossils. The sky was blue, the breeze was cool, the foam was white on the crests of the waves dancing on the lake—and the fossils stampeded from the ground. It was just the kind of day off I like.

In previous years we used to take our day-off dinners in the first-class dining cabin of the *Ilala* when it docked at Chilumba. This year it is being refurbished. We took our meal at a small but pleasant attempt at a tourist camp on the lake.

WE ARE MAKING good progress at the quarries. Our daily ritual is an obsession to get the fossil bones out of the ground in good shape, ready to transport, and with all the necessary data accompanying them to maximize their significance. Dale continues the mapping, quarrying when he is not measuring. The rest of us are either scratching away at a specimen, awling through sediment to find new ones, sacking up matrix, plastering a bone, or removing overburden. The musty smell of damp earth is always in our nostrils, the rat-a-tat sound of the roto-hammer constantly rings in our ears.

Gray clouds off the Nyika have been threatening the past couple of days. The sky has spit rain, but not enough to cause any damage. It keeps the weather cool. I doubt it has reached much over ninety, if that, since we have been here. Overburden is becoming a problem, but we each have a little spot, a choice area, in which to work. I want it to stay that way. The roto-hammer is running full-tilt and full-time to cut through the steadily increasing thickness of rock covering the pay layer as we quarry farther into the hillside. Bones, mostly sauropod, are coming as fast as we can handle them. They are so jack-strawed that we cannot get one out without running into another. Which should be removed first? New specimens are found every day. With every new bone, someone on the crew, the discoverer, has the intoxicating honor of being the first person ever to lay eyes on that bit of the Earth's treasures.

Will found what looks to be part of a sauropod skull. That is quite a find because skull bones are especially interesting and important. Who wants to see a dinosaur without a head? But Will's specimen is so small, no larger than a size-ten shoe. It is almost cute, if such things can be. So now we have skull bones, claws, tail vertebrae, and some of the bones in between. What more could we want? The excitement of discovery persists through the mornings, provides the subject for lunchtime conversations, and propels us through the sunny afternoons.

Lunch at the site is arranged individually from stocks of pilchards and sardines, fresh and dried fruits, macadamias and peanuts, corned beef, and assorted biscuits. The villagers cook *nsima* for our local laborers. Elizabeth, Fidelis, and James join them. *Nsima* is the staple dish of Malaŵi. It is ground maize meal, sort of like grits. Some form of it is eaten all over Africa. The project provides *nsima* to the local crew just as it does pilchards to the rest.

At three we begin to clean up the quarry and put away our tools. The bones and jackets removed during the day are transported back to the Land Rover on the heads of the crew. We get back to camp between four-thirty and five. Then the lake.

How refreshing it is—the lake. Cool water washes away the sweat and grime and dust, the sore backs and aching muscles of the day, leaving the euphoria of our pleasant surroundings and our good fortune. There is plenty of time for unwinding, sundowners, and sodas with fresh roasted peanuts. Kerosene lanterns are lighted at dusk. We prefer them to pressure lamps because they cast a softer light and they have no sound to permeate the evening.

Sunset is a very special time in Africa. The tropical sun drops rapidly, cataclysmically, from the sky, leaving almost no time for twilight. The fading light through the African haze, in whichever hue has been chosen for the night, has a thick, palpable quality, like a pleasant taste that is just on the verge of being too sweet. It flows viscously and bathes and consumes. The jagged branches of the trees take on a vivid blacker-than-black color against the sky. Concealed by the roaring silence is the sound of the lake, and the birds taking roost.

The evening meal is served around six-thirty. It begins with soup. Then comes ample, maybe too ample, quantities of rice or *nsima,* a main course of chicken, duck, or fish, sometimes beef, with cabbage and tomato salad, and tinned vegetables. Ronald makes a mean stuffing to go with duck. Dessert is usually tinned or fresh fruit with cream, also tinned.

After dinner there is brandy and light conversation, or perhaps deep philosophy, a discussion of chaos theory, or who knows what else. The day's results and tomorrow's plans are mulled over. Problems are anticipated and solutions discussed.

The skies of moonless nights are illuminated by incredible numbers of incredibly bright shining stars. The Southern Cross hangs over the fishing village. The plane of the ecliptic crosses diagonally over camp, spraying the skies with misty drops of light. Fireflies dance along the line of breaking waves, a segue from the Earth to the heavens.

On most nights, everyone is ready to retire to the tents by eight, read a few pages by flashlight under the mosquito net, and drift off to sleep, lulled once more by the waves. The sounds of the lake, its seiche and cycles in waking and sleeping, provide a symmetry to the day.

25 July, Wednesday.

Yesterday we had a few equipment problems. First the generator failed. We could be handicapped in the extreme without the roto-hammer to knock off overburden. We also had a bit of a vehicle problem. We had come to the site in the departmental Land Rover with James driving. Usually we park at the top of the big hill at the fault cutting through the Dinosaur Beds. Because the generator is heavy and we needed to load it into the Land Rover to take it for repairs, an attempt was made to motor along Mjuda's road to get closer to the quarry. That way the generator would not have to be hauled so far by hand. The plan worked well except for one thing: The Land Rover got stuck in a steep hollow between two hills. The drive shaft broke, knocking out power to the rear wheels. With no power at the back, the front wheels could not pull the Land Rover up the incline and out of the bush. At the moment of this writing it is sitting along the gully where it stopped, at the converging bottom of two steep hills, in the middle of the badlands, unable to go anywhere.

There we were, stuck at the site, with no easy way of getting back to camp. Will, a cross-country cycling enthusiast, scrounged a teetery bicycle from who knows where with the help of Mjuda. It had nearly flat tires, a bent sprocket, a chain with the annoying habit of popping off, and no brakes. But it was a bicycle.

Down the dirt track went Will, bouncing and waggling, bound for camp to fetch the other Land Rover. The rest of us walked down to a big tamarind tree in the valley. It was a leisurely walk, and at that time of day, quitting time, we were able to appreciate a portion of the vast and colorful array of birdlife in Africa: iridescent sunbirds, green bee eaters, red fire finches, blue cordon bleus, black drongos. Casque-headed hornbills chattered in the tops of trees (Figure 23).

Under the tamarind were the *malipenga* dances. We watched, mesmerized by the drum beat, as the synchronous rows of dancers performed with precision under the eyes of their elderly coach. Tiny children, stationed at the edge of the adult sphere, mimicked their dancing role models. The village headman, drunk on local brew, as village headmen sometimes are, came to extend his greetings, have his photograph taken, and join in the dance the way that drunks often do.

In the meantime Will had made it safely back to camp, although the chain on the bicycle had begun to fail every hundred yards. He drove the Land Rover back and picked up the rest of us where we waited under the tamarind.

TODAY WAS THE day to begin repairing the damage. I had to make a trip to Karonga. At seven, as usual, we left camp in the functioning Country Car Hire Land Rover. At the site I picked up the defunct generator and, leaving the crew at Mwakasyunguti, headed back for camp with Fidelis. It was windy and the lake was rough, like the Gulf of Mexico. In camp we picked up James and the expected gaggle of neighbors needing a lift to town. Then we headed for Karonga. Since I had to go to town to get the generator repaired anyway, this was a good opportunity to restock our supplies. The drive to Karonga is long enough, loud enough, and shaky enough to induce a trance.

The M-1 highway is always littered with pedestrians on both shoulders, north and south, coming and going, for the entire twenty miles to Karonga. That is usual. Most people in Malaŵi do not have cars, so most people walk. Most people in this part of Malaŵi live near the lake, which is where the road lies. They walk along the road.

In contrast, there were few vehicles on the road to Karonga. There were some oxcarts and bicycles. And there were a few odd cars, a handful of overloaded lorries, belching *chibuku* transports, a tractor, and one or two broken-down trucks. Mostly there were people.

Almost all the women along the road had a load of some sort, if only a baby slung on behind. African women have a certain grace and poise. As they

FIGURE 23: Birds of the African bush: a casque-headed hornbill (left), a bee eater (upper right), and a sunbird. Birds have an illustrious evolutionary history inextricably linked with that of dinosaurs.

walk, they carry their inanimate burdens on their heads. They carry almost anything you can imagine: amorphous bundles wrapped in cloth, firewood, a full pail of water, shocks of long grass, baskets of maize, calabashes of home brew, and who knows what else. One lady, barefooted, balanced a single shoe on her head and held the other in her hand. This is not so uncommon as you would probably think. The shoes are for show on dressy occasions. If they are uncomfortable on broad feet used to being unfettered, why not carry them to the ultimate destination, then put them on?

With their loads balanced on boldly erect heads, the women glide along the road on thin-calved legs. Their posture is accentuated by their striking *kitenge*s, a long sheet of cloth wrapped around like a skirt. The *kitenge*s come in many designs. Some are vibrant geometrical patterns or brilliant floral prints. One popular motif is political. All over Africa, heads of state are immortalized, their pictures woven into *kitenge*s, then strategically placed over the round bottoms of women. Even the pope has his holy likeness gracing one. Most, however, are not political, but rather they depict visions of everyday life and nature, things like antelope, or perhaps a village scene. Those that have made their way down from Tanzania have a quaint moral or cliché written in Swahili underneath the picture. Once in Kenya I saw a *kitenge* with the picture of a large insect being sprayed symmetrically by four cans of insecticide arranged about it. Here in Malaŵi, the two-humped bactrian camel is particularly popular. Camels do not inhabit this part of Africa. Those in the desert north are one-humped dromedaries. *Kitenge*s are fun clothes that provide a splash of verve to hard lives. Dinosaurs would look good on them (Figure 24).

IT IS TOO loud to talk inside the Land Rover, so it is a good time for reflection. What a different perspective of the world one has from inside a screaming vehicle compared to the vantage of walking along the road. Inside is a cacophony of noise and petrol fumes. Outside, anonymous people—they might as well be trees—zip by the windows, unnoticed, taken for granted. It is a distorted relativity of time and space. Everything glimpsed is gone in an instant, but nothing changes, because more of the same replaces that which has been passed by. Inside the Land Rover life is loud and fast.

Outside the Land Rover, on this road with few vehicles, the walk is mostly quiet, punctuated with the odd Doppler roar and a cloud of dust. Then it is gone, and it is as if it never happened. Periodically the process repeats, but it has no relevance to the side of the road. Like the passengers in the Land Rover, the pedestrians get where they are going. It just takes longer. The ride has speed, but the quiet of the walk has something to offer that the ride cannot give. Some people cannot afford the effort to walk, others do not have the resources to do otherwise. The perspectives of the riders and the walkers are

FIGURE 24: *A woman walking along the road. She is wearing a* KITENGE, *a sort of wraparound skirt decorated with colorful patterns or pictures. The design shown here is not one I have seen, but it looks good, doesn't it?*

different, but they are interchangeable. After all, pedestrians may one day ride, and riders might one day walk again.

AT THE END of the ride is Karonga. It is a grubby commercial center in northern Malaŵi, but not without its own brand of rustic African charm. It lies alongside the lake, south of the Tanzanian border. To the outsider there appears to be a chronic shortage of sugar and varying acute shortages depending on the demands of the bustling smuggler trade with the north. There is little motor traffic, but lots of pedestrians. And lots of dust.

I motored past the turnoff to the airport, served by Air Malaŵi on Mondays and Fridays, past the transplanted World War I graves, past the new post office and the traditional court. All over Africa, villages govern themselves democratically with *barazas*. These are open to all who wish to attend. The people meet with the village headman in the shade of a tree to work out acceptable solutions to problems. Both accuser and accused, transgressor and victim, are present. All the facts are laid bare. Options are discussed. Everyone has a say. Everything is in the open. A consensus is reached. Usually conflicts are resolved. Miscreants are dealt with. Last year Mjuda's brother, Brighton, was brought before a *baraza* for beating one of his wives. He suffered the ostracism of his neighbors and remained an outcast for some time. That is a strong punishment in rural Africa, where extended families are the center of social life. The traditional court in Karonga is a formal extension of the *baraza* system on those occasions when difficulties cannot be sorted out at the village level and when they take on greater legal significance. However, the process is not much different, even in the traditional court, from a village *baraza*.

Each year at the digs we hold a *baraza* with the area schoolteachers, political-party representatives, and village headmen of Mwakasyunguti present. Our purposes in being there, strange foreigners that we are, digging in the ground, are explained so that they do not misunderstand our intentions. Everyone makes a speech. Mutual friendship is expressed. Blessings are heaped upon us. Once, after we had presented the school with a soccer ball, the headmaster thanked us profusely because, he said, with the ball "more children will be drawn to school." I was given a chicken.

THE ROAD TO downtown Karonga leads up to the T-junction across from the New Apostolic Church (In Malaŵi). Straight ahead, the Northern Corridor, an ambitious road-building project to allow Malaŵi's goods to be transported across Tanzania to the port of Dar es Salaam, is under construction by Germans. Just a few miles due north of here Germany and Britain fought a battle during World War I. It has not gotten much attention, as battles go. German forces marched south in two columns from the border with German East Africa into Nyasaland. At the same time a British force was headed north, toward German territory. As it happened, the British marched between the two German columns undetected. Neither the British nor the German forces were aware of the other's proximity. They were like ships passing in the night.

The German force continued its march and attacked the British garrison at Karonga. They were repelled. As they retreated, they ran squarely into the British column. German casualties were high, British losses were less. Most of the dead were blacks. White Germans and British who died—there were not many—were buried in Karonga. Their graves have been moved so as not to be destroyed by a rising lake, but they are still preserved to this day. They are maintained by the Department of Antiquities.

The loss of African lives in this skirmish, the lives of black men conscripted against their will, was one of the factors that played on John Chilembwe, an African missionary trained at Lynchburg, Virginia. He led his followers in a rebellion in 1915, precipitated by the Battle of Karonga, that cost him his life at the hands of the British. This was the first major colonial uprising in what was to become Malaŵi.

I NEEDED TO get my errands done. I turned right past the Home of Sofas Furniture store, the Chipiku General Store, and the Tikhalenao Grocery and Bottle Store, its painted walls showing Coca-Cola and screaming CAFENOL STOPS PAIN FAST! I drove past the squalid *chibuku* bars with rancid early-morning clientele lounging in the lurid shade, drinking or slumped over in septic corners.

I left Fidelis and James at the PVHO (the acronym for Plant and Vehicle Hire Organization, I found out later; it is the government mechanical work-shop) to arrange for the extrication of the stuck Land Rover and to see to generator repairs. Then I went to my first stop, the National Bank of Malaŵi, to change dollars to *kwacha*. The bank is a small block building with manicured lawns next to the National Library Service, Karonga Branch. Bank transactions are not simple in Africa. I stopped in at the library while some required signatures were being obtained at the bank. It is a small reading room. I was surprised, although I do not know why, to find it full of young people perusing books, newspapers, and magazines. It is, after all, a library.

The library is next to Southern Bottlers Limited, the soft-drink and beer distributor. I exchanged empties for three crates of sodas, three crates of green, and a crate of brown. Up the street is the police station, whitewashed a gleaming white and trimmed in blue. The Malâŵi Police insignia, a white-headed fish eagle, very much like the American bald eagle, flies high on the wall. Rows of whitewashed stones spell out:

WELCOME

TOKARONGAPOLICE

SUBDIVISION

Down the street is the Marina Club on the lake, the hub of upper-crust social life in Karonga. It has a one-room bar, a dart board, a few cable spools for tables scattered outside, and some hotel rooms under construction. Past that is the Government Rest House, where my group stayed in 1987.

The center of town is the market and bus station. I parked next to a tree across from the Corner Tarven (*sic*) Chibuku Welcome bar. On the *Gmelina* tree in front was tacked a notice for a traveling movie theater. It was showing an old Tarzan film.

The market in Karonga is lean; it lacks the excessive color and vibrance, not to mention the foodstuffs, of one better stocked. I continue to be surprised at the lack of vegetable diversity and abundance in this tropical market. Bright tomatoes, pale-green cabbages, and shiny dried beans provide some color in the marketplace, breaking the monotonous earth tones of peanuts, rice, tiny onions, shriveled sweet potatoes, and sometimes eggs. Cabbage is a a wonderful field vegetable because it keeps. It can last a couple of weeks without going bad or losing its flavor. Fish—dried, smoked, or fresh—is the main protein source. Meat is available early in the mornings, but it is usually sold out before we arrive. The butchery stalls are great charnel houses thronged with customers. The butchers smash the beef carcasses mercilessly with axes, more like woodsmen than the spattered butchers they are.

Each vendor in the market has goods aligned in small piles on the ground or on tables, each pile worth a few *tambala*. The camp requires so much more than the average household that merchants ought to enjoy my coming. I go by, scooping up pile after pile into my plastic market bag to what I would suppose might be their delight. Some are happy and fun to joke around with. Others are resigned and fatalistic, expressing little satisfaction over a big sale. To them, either I will buy or I will not, and it seems to have little consequence to them either way.

Outside the market are the fruit vendors. Bananas, of course, are cheap and abundant. Pawpaws are less common and more expensive. There are plenty of oranges, tangerines, and occasionally avocados brought down from Tanzania.

My next errand was to check the progress on the generator repair. It was now in working order. For the Land Rover, James and Fidelis had arranged through the district commissioner for a PVHO road-service vehicle to fix our ailing steed—sometime. Now it was approaching lunch. I still needed to call Yusuf in Lilongwe to check in with headquarters. That could be done later. The water bowser needed filling. The petrol needed topping off as well. And then I had to purchase canned goods. I decided on lunch.

The culinary delicacy of Karonga is *susa,* which is small cubes of beef and fat skewered on a bicycle spoke, rubbed in salt and crushed red pepper, then grilled over a charcoal bucket. It is delicious. Its only accompaniment is roasted green unripe banana, which is not sweet, but serves as a starchy "bread." Fidelis, James, and I sauntered across the street to a grimy *susa* man whose stand was under a shade made of long grass. On either side, under the trees and out of the tropical midday sun, were greasy bicycle repairmen working in the dust at the edge of the road. Lightwell Mkwala, in town from his school, popped up and joined us. He looked sharp in his brown tie, a respectable teacher. We arranged a visit to the camp for him after the school term ends on Friday. Lunch was topped off with some cold buttermilk.

The water bowser was filled at the Karonga Teacher's College, where we were also able to phone headquarters. After buying pilchards and tinned fruit at the PTC (which stands for People's Trading Center), we crossed over to the petrol station to fill up. I had two jerry cans to carry fuel for the generator. They also needed filling. Both had holes, so I left them—empty—at the PVHO to be welded. The afternoon wore on. Finally all was done that could be done. The generator was repaired. We drove out of town, past the Enikani Rest House, the Safari Lodge, and the Kampunga Entertainment Center. For the twenty miles back to Ngara I drove past the unbroken line of pedestrians.

After unloading at camp I jostled hurriedly back to Mwakasyunguti to get the gang. They had had a good day. Four bones were plastered, and they found some new ones. Best of all, no days will be lost due to the departmental Land Rover or the broken generator. The work will go on uninterrupted.

Back again to Ngara and into the evening routine. At sundown a group of fishermen pulled their big net near our camp. Ronald's youngest son and his grandson, both the same age, early teenagers I suppose, are working with them. Fresh fish will be on the table. The lake is exceptionally calm tonight. The soft, lapping waves are good music for sleeping.

28 July, Saturday.

We are making good progress at the quarries. Bones are *still* coming thick and fast. Each day brings new discoveries. There is no sign of it letting up. We have only been working CD-9. That one quarry is more than we can handle for the time being. It does not look like it will play out before we leave.

Elizabeth found a lower jaw of the sauropod yesterday. It is so tiny, smaller than the one Will found last Saturday. If that one was cute, this one is dainty. Strange, but all the sauropod bones seem small. The stegosaur pelvis does not strike me as being particularly diminutive, but the sauropod bones are unusual in their uncharacteristically small size. Sauropods, after all, include the largest of all dinosaurs, the largest of all land-dwelling animals ever. Is this a small species, or are they just youngsters?

There are carnivorous dinosaur teeth, too, but no limb bones or vertebrae that we have recognized, other than the sharp, hooked claw Kent found last year. Certainly there are no skulls of a meat-eater yet. Where are they hiding?

Clouds have been gray and heavy for the past few days, but thus far only bluster, no rain. The PVHO road-service vehicle came out yesterday to repair the drive train of the departmental Land Rover, which had been awaiting the arrival of first aid, nestled in the hollow where it was stranded. I had provided it with its own watchman for company so that it would not get too lonely. The PVHO mechanics finally got it functioning by cannibalizing their own vehicle, then without four-wheel drive themselves, they got stuck for two hours while crossing the river. They chewed up the riverbed, spinning their wheels, trying to get out, which made the conditions dicey for us to pass through when our turn came. But all is well that ends well. James was able to limp the departmental Land Rover into Karonga for a thorough going over. Fidelis went with him. The PVHO does not work on Saturdays (today) or Sundays, so I expect James and Fidelis back no earlier than Monday night, if then. We could sure use them at the site. There are a lot of bones to get out, and time is getting short. Oh, well, so long as the rented Land Rover is in working order, knock on wood, we can manage.

A more immediate problem is the generator. The motor runs fine now, this minute, but there is a loose connection in the wiring system preventing the juice from getting out. It must be repaired—again. We do not have the tools to work on it, so I have instructed Fidelis to try to find an electrician in Karonga. The thickness of the rock overlying the payload is now a real difficulty. The local labor is attacking it with hammers and chisels, but that is inefficient, and they cannot clear enough to give each of the excavators room to quarry. We have opened CD-10 in earnest to sidestep the overburden problem. It, too, is packed with bone, and not just the stegosaur pelvis and sauropod femur we found earlier. Parts of two articulated tails have turned up, some stegosaur plates, and some unidentifieds.

THERE WAS A labor problem when I was in town last Wednesday. One of my employees, Yasaki, the surly one, apparently did not wish to shovel with the others. He was rude in explaining to Elizabeth that he was not going to do it. This certainly is not the atmosphere I want. I sacked Yasaki. Fidelis gathered all the Tumbuka crew around in a mini-*baraza* under the tree near the supply shed. He explained in excruciating detail why the sacking was taking place. He reiterated to them the government's sanction of this project and its interest in it. He expostulated on the fame it was bringing to their region. The men of the local crew, their faces stern, reminded Yasaki that they themselves, his neighbors and relatives, had scolded him for his behavior. They told him he should not have been arguing about the work. He should not have been rude to Elizabeth. Fidelis said Yasaki seemed humbled by the experience, which is what *baraza*s are supposed to do if someone misbehaves. It is the mechanism for maintaining social harmony. Yasaki was paid for his time. He absently sauntered off to join the *malipenga* dance. I hired Joseph's brother, Alfred, to fill the gap. Alfred is a nice fellow, blind in one eye. He worked for me in 1987.

Fidelis used the *baraza* for something else since he had everyone's attention. He made the point, in a nice way, that overly helpful children living in these parts, or adults looking for a quick profit that they will not make from me, should not pick up bones and bring them to us. This has increasingly become a problem, but it is not unexpected. We know there are bones all over this valley, but it is unwise to pick them up until their geological context and their exact location can be properly evaluated. If children, or anyone else, no matter how well-meaning, picks up the fragments, the original context is lost, plus clues are removed that might have helped us to find more bone. But more immediately important, the government of Malaŵi, through the Department of Antiquities, has strict rules protecting fossils and other such objects. They are not to be disturbed without authorization. The department is quite serious about enforcing its policies. It is equally serious about educating the local people so that they understand what they ought and what they ought not do. Many Western countries could stand to be so enlightened. Fossils in Malaŵi are recognized to be for the public good—long term.

LIGHTWELL SHOWED UP at breakfast this morning. He has joined us at Mwakasyunguti, his home area, but only for the day. At the site, Mjuda, his legs bowed ricketslike, had our tools laid out as usual. He maintains a written inventory, not on my instruction, but by his own volition and desire to do a good, responsible job. We have not lost so much as an awl. His mother and father were there. You could see the pride, theirs and his, as he showed them around the digs with a flourish.

I noticed a ring of ashes around the supply tent where Mjuda sleeps. They were for *siafu*. *Siafu* are the safari ants of legendary ferocity. They travel in roving columns, devouring hapless victims of any animal persuasion. When they enter a hut, snakes and lizards leave their safe havens in the walls. I used to pull the clinging bodies and clamped jaws of these fearless insects from between the toes of my dogs in Kenya. Human babies have succumbed to their vicious attacks. There is a story that Mary Leakey once set the legs of one of her son's cribs in dishes of kerosene to prevent *siafu* from getting at the sleeping child. Mjuda saw some on the march near the site yesterday. Kent came across a regiment on the trail this morning. Mjuda says they will not cross ashes. I have heard that before, and I believe it. *Siafu* are too painful not to find some protection from them.

2 August, Thursday.

Today was the last day of quarry work for Kent and me. It was hard to concentrate on excavating even when I had the chance. After leaving camp tomorrow I will be spending a few days in Lilongwe tying up loose ends. Will and Dale will spend another week or so here, then seal the quarries and head south, way down the country. Alisa will join them for a reconnaissance of the southern equivalent of the Dinosaur Beds.

The bones have not played out in the quarries at Mwakasyunguti. They show no signs of doing so. If our experience is any indication, and I think it is, there are bones to dig here for many seasons to come. There are clearly enough specimens to do a thorough scientific study. But the fossils are better than that. There are enough to make a display available to all the people of Malaŵi. That would be exciting for everyone, not just scientists. Hooray!

The generator has not been working well, just barely or not at all, for the past couple of days. It has not been much help during that time. Never mind. We are beyond the critical point. Two days ago the departmental Land Rover returned from the shop. Yesterday it went back for starter repairs. Today it is with us again.

Still the work goes on. Now we have the enviable problem of setting priorities for which of the bones can realistically be removed and which will have to be protected, buried, and left for seed until the next field season. It is almost like too much of a good thing. CD-10 is every bit as good as CD-9. If we had time to find out, I bet CD-11 would be as well.

After a fast-paced excavating season, the crew has grown together. They move like clockwork. Senses are acute, attuned to the subtle nuances of each exhumed bone. Skills are honed sharp. The camp is full, littered with heavy, treasure-laden plaster jackets carried from the quarries on the heads and shoulders of straining laborers, wrestled into the vehicles, and chauffeured to the lake. A camaraderie has built up. It is hard to leave.

A couple of days ago a fellow with a homemade guitar showed up at the site. He makes guitars himself, but he appears deaf and dumb, an autistic savant. He struck a good chord. Spontaneously, as the guitar strummed, hammers tapped chisels and awls drummed shovels in a paleontological symphony, culminating in a crescendo of exuberant laughter. It is a good crew.

We had visitors in camp at six-fifteen this morning. We do not get many visitors anyway, but these would have been noteworthy at any time. It was a group of villagers, maybe a dozen people, all singing and dancing. The rhythm came from an aluminum cooking *suffria* filled with a bit of uncooked rice and shaken to the beat. One particularly animated and overweight woman danced with a two-pound plastic bag of salt balanced on her head, her jiggling contours outlined by her soiled dress. Everything together was a strange sight to see so early in the morning, when our eyes were still dusted with sleep. I wonder if it would have seemed less strange later in the day. This was the

African equivalent of an Irish wake. Someone in the neighboring village had died during the night. Now this group of dancers was going around soliciting money for the funeral expenses and food to feed the bereaved, who would be arriving shortly from all over Malaŵi, from wherever the extended family had dispersed. I donated.

THIS BEING THE last day for Kent and me, it was the time for a photo session at the quarry. All of the local crew were dressed in their best. Mjuda had on a military hat with a Maria Theresa medallion pinned to it. He had a big leather belt around his waist and across his shoulder. He wore boots and high knee socks, but he was disappointed that he did not have short pants like an official guard and watchman. The guys brought up all their wives and children. They were pretty women and plump babies, done up in their best. One of Wellington's wives could not negotiate the rocky path to the site in her thick-soled, high-heeled shoes, so naturally she carried them on her head and walked barefoot up and down the hills. We all took turns in various permutations of picture taking and posing. Will, the bearded friend, was in big demand. Alfred, self-conscious of his bad eye, wore dark glasses for his photographs. Everyone felt close. It was really a very touching event. When it was over, the ladies left and the men changed into their workaday rags, with the exception of Wellington, who continued to wear a new makeshift hat of bright yellow cloth with embroidery saying, "I re member."

Then the press arrived. Yusuf came up from Lilongwe, bringing with him half a dozen newspaper and magazine reporters and photographers. I particularly wanted Yusuf, a Berkeley-trained Ph.D. archaeologist, to see our digs. I had been urging him to come up and pay a visit for some time. He is the man in authority at the Department of Antiquities and he would be able to evaluate, and hopefully appreciate, our efforts. A few minutes of his viewing the sites would do more for the project than all the final reports I could write. Not that there was any problem; Yusuf has always been more a member of the team than a governmental administrator. I wanted him to see because he would like it.

And he did. So did the press. They photographed and questioned and wrote and taped. How it will turn out I do not know, but they seemed impressed. As usual, they were first of all impressed at seeing the resurrection of these bones from the Earth.

"How did they get there?" they wondered.

Next they wondered at how I ever came to this exact spot to find these bones, halfway around the world from where I live.

"How did you know where to dig?"

Finally they were overwhelmed with the pride that these dinosaurs are a part of little Malaŵi.

"Will you put them on display?"

THEY LEFT IN the middle of the afternoon, and I tried to go back to work.

4

THE
ROAMING TITAN
LIZARDS

W ITH SO MANY bones coming out of the ground in Malaŵi, there was little question that they would have an interesting and important story to tell about life in the Age of Reptiles. The most common, but by no means all, of the fossils that have been excavated so far are the bones of sauropod dinosaurs. We assigned around 150 field numbers to jackets and wrapped specimens of sauropods already taken out of the ground. Not all were single, isolated bones. Some were articulated sets found as they were arranged in life, most notably a section of tail with twenty-two vertebrae in a row and a set of breastbones placed just as if the dinosaur had lain down on its belly. There were also two lower jaws, parts of skulls, assorted vertebrae from various positions along the body, arm bones, toes, a claw, a thighbone and other parts of the hind leg, and a spaghetti bowl of ribs. The next step, now that these specimens had been removed from the ground, was to make sense of them. We already knew more than when we started out simply from seeing the bones as we excavated them, but that is not enough. Some of the fossils, at least the more important ones, obviously needed to be prepared from their jackets before we could get any reliable, if preliminary, understanding of the animals they represent. Information from the prepared specimens could be supplemented with photographs and measurements of other bones recorded in the quarries while they were being excavated, and the pieces of the puzzle would begin to fall into place. Dale and I, along with Will and Elizabeth, jointly undertook to study the sauropods.

Sauropod dinosaurs are familiar to most everyone. It is the group commonly called brontosaurs, and with such creatures as *Brachiosaurus* (see Figure 4 in Chapter 1), it includes the largest animals that have ever lived on land. Like most all really huge animals inhabiting the landscape at a given time, the sauropods were herbivorous. They ate plants and only plants. They were big, and they were not necessarily friendly, but they were not necessarily ferocious either.

Larger size often conveys certain advantages. It stacks the deck in favor of bigger individuals in the competition with other members of the same species. Larger individuals can obtain the best space, resources, mates, and they may be better able to defend themselves. Thus increasing size through a biological lineage is a common trend in evolutionary history. This trend to evolve larger descendant species from smaller ancestors is known as Cope's rule.

The best-known sauropods are of gigantic proportions. The largest of the sauropods might have weighed as much as fifty, sixty, maybe even eighty tons. Most were probably in the twenty-to-thirty-ton range, still highly respectable. Early in sauropod evolution there had to be even smaller ones, presumably, if the evolution of larger species followed Cope's rule. The dinosaurian ancestors of the known sauropods, the hypothetical first true sauropod, if we had a complete fossil record, would have been much smaller than the giants. Some or all of the evolutionary lineages leading to different species of sauropod giants became larger with geologic time until they went extinct.

The only animals that have ever surpassed the sauropod size record are the blue whales. They, of course, have an advantage because they live in seawater, which is a dense fluid that buoys up their massive bodies. If stranded on land, whales, even the smaller ones, will suffocate from being crushed under their own weight. The structure of their bodies cannot keep their weight off of their lungs.

The problems of supporting weight for any animal are much greater on land than those encountered in an aqueous medium, such as whales inhabit, but the problems are particularly difficult for those land-dwelling animals of exceptionally large size. Being such large animals as most of the sauropods are, shear bulk places a tremendous strain on them. One reason contributing to why sauropod dinosaurs were able to evolve into such large and heavy forms is that at some time in their early history they began to walk on four legs rather than two. Strange as it seems, dinosaurs started out walking, running, and standing on two legs. Bipedal locomotion is primitive for the group as a whole (and for many of the more familiar dinosaurs, such as *Tyrannosaurus rex*). In sauropods, dinosaurs specialized in obtaining large size, four legs provide a more stable foundation for body mass and double the number of pillars supporting the animal.

There are big ancillary problems associated with Cope's rule. The mass of an animal's body increases at a greater rate than the simple increase in a linear dimension. That means that an animal twice as long as another of the same shape and physical appearance will weigh more than twice the second animal's weight. Larger animals weigh proportionately, as well as absolutely, more than smaller animals. Therefore, if a sauropod lineage is to become gigantic, it must be able to support a spiraling increase in weight with each moderate increment in size. The strength of the bones must be great enough to hold up all that bulk, but if the bones are made bigger to be stronger, they will reach a point where they increase in weight faster than they increase in strength. There is the dilemma.

The solution is to evolve structural modifications in the shape and construction of bones so that they are both light and strong. Birds do it by having thin-walled, hollow bones. Pterodactyls do it the same way. From a paleontological point of view, such bones are fragile. That is why both these groups of flying reptiles are uncommonly preserved as fossils, and when they are, they are usually crushed.

Of course, sauropods do not fly, but their bulk necessitates modification of their supporting bones. Not surprisingly, they do it in a rather different sort of way from birds and pterosaurs—one that reminded the great American vertebrate paleontologist and dinosaur expert Edwin H. Colbert of a ship. A ship, if laden with more than it can safely hold, will founder. In nineteenth-century Britain a law was enacted against the overloading of seagoing vessels. It was decided to place a line on the outside of British merchant ships to indicate the lawful level of submergence of the hull. The ship could be loaded until it rode in the water at the level of the line and no more. The mark was called a Plimsoll line, after Samuel Plimsoll, the statesman who championed the legislation. Sauropods no more ply through the water than they fly through the air, but that is not what the analogy with the Plimsoll line is based on. It is based on the fact that the limbs of sauropods are heavy and rather dense, while the vertebrae and skull are light with many weight-saving modifications. If you were to draw a line along the base of the backbone in a sauropod skeleton from the shoulder girdle to the hips, the bones below the line—the paleontological Plimsoll line—would be heavier in construction, and the bones above would be lighter (Figure 25). Such a distribution of weight provides for a low center of gravity and therefore greater stability.

This has some interesting evolutionary implications. Above the Plimsoll line the evolutionary modifications for making the skeleton in sauropods lighter are profound. The outer, superficial layer of each bone is extremely thin, not all that much thicker than that in a bird. Inside the bone the osseus tissue takes on an appearance rather like soap bubbles, the curved surfaces of fragile bone providing internal strength to the whole. The vertebrae of the back and neck, and the head, do not have the dense internal structure of the bones below the Plimsoll line, but they are not hollow either. The bubbly internal bony structure is a good and apparently very effective compromise. However, it creates practical problems for the paleontologist. Such thin-walled bone with wispy internal structure is easily damaged or destroyed

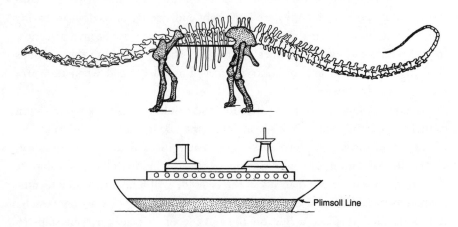

FIGURE 25: The paleontological Plimsoll line. The bones of the limbs that support the body of a sauropod are heavily constructed and dense relative to the vertebrae, which are light and have evolved a number of weight-reducing features. In a ship the heavy ballast, which gives stability, is placed well below the Plimsoll line, the level above which a ship cannot safely float. Neither ships nor sauropod dinosaurs are top-heavy.

unless the conditions of fossilization are just right. The bones in Malaŵi have not been completely petrified into stone, so excavating them and even preparing them in the laboratory is a tedious job if the delicate surface is not to be damaged. If the lightness of sauropod bones above the Plimsoll line presents practical field and laboratory problems to the paleontologist, other structural adaptations for making bone lighter while still supporting weight provide a wealth of features for analyzing the family relationships among sauropod species. One obvious modification for bearing weight is the altera-tion of vertebral structure. Vertebrae of any land-dwelling animal are compli-cated, but especially those of sauropods. The vertebrae must be strongly enough linked together to provide for their support function, yet they must retain the capability to bend at the joints so that the backbone can retain flexibility. On top of that, they must be light. The way this is achieved in different sauropods is a clue to their relationships.

All sauropods have long necks. In some species the neck vertebrae and the adjacent vertebrae at the front end of the back are modified in a special way. If you tilt your chin down toward your chest and feel the back of your neck, you will notice the tight nuchal ligament that attaches from your head to your back vertebrae. The hard, bony projections in your back at the base of your neck and down are called the neural spines of your vertebrae. These are quite long in animals that must hold up a large head and neck. Think of the hump on a buffalo's back. The hump, beneath the hide, gets its shape from long spines of the vertebrae and the muscles and ligaments that run toward the head. The spines must also be long in sauropods, not so much because they have big heavy heads but because the cranium is so far away from the body on such a long neck. In some, but not all, sauropod species the spines appear to be forked, bifurcated, in the neck and adjacent back, forming a trough or channel in which the neck muscles lie (Figure 26). In general, among those species that show this feature, the shorter the front legs are, relatively, the deeper the trough. Sauropods such as *Diplodocus* with a trough apparently formed by their vertebral spines have their long necks cantilevered out in front of the body. The neck held out in that way provides a long radius through which the head can move while the animal is feeding. It could browse a large area while standing in one spot. In sauropods such as *Brachiosaurus* the head is held atop an erect, giraffelike neck and there is no trough at all formed by the spines of the vertebrae. It was better suited for feeding off higher foliage in the tops of trees.

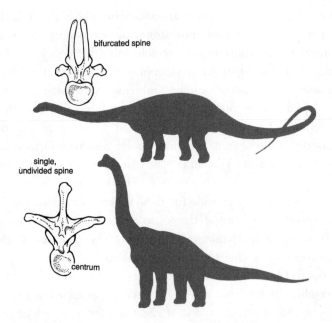

FIGURE 26: Cantilevered-versus-erect posture in the necks of sauropod dinosaurs. One suggestion of the meaning of differing vertebral shape in sauropod necks is that vertebrae with divided spines support cantilevered necks (top) while vertebrae with undivided spines support necks held in a more erect posture (bottom).

There are a great many vertebrae in a spinal column, so it makes sense that if something could be done to make each of them lighter, it would have a relatively big effect when totaled up along the entire backbone. The main body of a vertebra, to which the spine and other bony processes attach, is called a centrum. The centrum is the biggest single component of a vertebra. Centra are basically cylindrical in shape, and in the backbone they line up one after the other lengthwise. (In humans a slipped disk is a cartilage plate between two vertebral centra that has shifted.) Some sauropods have lightened the centra in ingenious ways. Large pockets, called pleurocoels, are excavated in the sides of the centra, rearranging the primitive cylindrical shape into a form that is lighter yet still provides adequate strength and retains appropriate length. Not all sauropods have pleurocoels, and not all those that do have them developed on the same vertebrae or in the same way. It seems that once the evolutionary potential for producing pleurocoels was achieved, natural selection and chance could mold the specific shape of the pleurocoels in a number of directions depending on the species. And since the lightening of vertebrae through the development of pleurocoels is obviously related to the attainment of gigantic size, pleurocoels may have evolved more than once in separate sauropod lineages as grand size was approached.

It seems pretty clear that huge animals must have a large intake of food to keep themselves alive. Even a low estimate of food requirements would have to be large in real terms for such animals as sauropods. Therefore, it is all the more astounding to take a look at a sauropod head. No species of sauropod has a large head; all are small considering the total size of the body. Yet all the food that is ever eaten must enter the tiny pinhead and pass down the gullet.

Sauropod heads have a particularly nasty habit so far as field paleontologists are concerned. They are not often found. In life they must have been weakly attached to the end of the neck, because in death the head is quickly separated from the body. I cannot shake the image of a sauropod head rolling off like a soccer ball, but of course it was not like that. The light, thin bones of the head are as lightly built and as thin-walled as the vertebrae are. They are insecurely fastened to each other. As a dead sauropod rotted or was dismembered, the head separated from the neck, and the delicate bones became scattered and destroyed. The problem this makes for paleontologists is that many species of sauropods are known only from bones that come from the neck or farther back in the skeleton, and we have no idea what the head was actually like. Heads are known in only a fraction of the named sauropod species. In fact *Apatosaurus,* the real name of brontosaurus, suffered for decades with the wrong head until the mistake was caught and corrected.

Sauropod skulls that are known show quite a bit of diversity in their shapes (Figure 27). In all, the bony holes through which the nasal passages go appear excessively large. In life these accommodated, in addition to the air passages, tissue and blood vessels that have been considered speculatively at one time or another to control the temperature of blood flowing to the brain, to resonate the sounds uttered by the beast, or to facilitate a flexible proboscis. The issue is still open.

Some sauropods have long heads, others have heads that are almost incredibly blunt. Elongation of sauropod skulls seems to have evolved in at least two different ways. *Brachiosaurus* was described in Chapter 1 as having an absurd, toothy duck's bill. The front of the head is long because the bones that hold

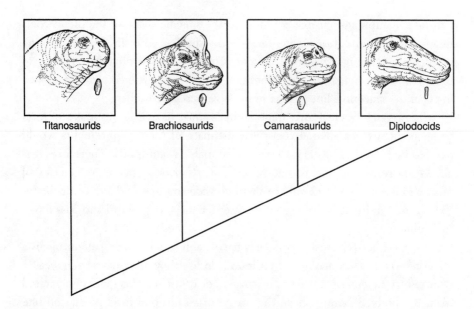

Titanosaurids   Brachiosaurids   Camarasaurids   Diplodocids

FIGURE 27: *The head shape, tooth shape, and family relationships of sauropod dinosaurs. This cladogram suggests the pattern of evolutionary branching within the sauropods. Two of the less well known families, the vulcanodontids and cetiosaurids, are not included, but they may fit to the left of titanosaurids. This is only one of many possible evolutionary trees. It is an hypothesis that seeks to explain where titanosaurid relationships lie among the sauropods and provides a focus for discussion.*

the teeth, called maxilla and premaxilla, are exaggerated into the shape of a duck's bill. The nasal bones, which support the nostrils, are looped high up and back, doming the skull. Other sauropods, such as *Camarasaurus*, have high heads, but the jaws are not drawn nearly so far forward as in *Brachiosaurus* and the nostrils are not so far back and up. Sauropods such as the familiar *Apatosaurus* and *Diplodocus* are different. Their nostrils are back and on the top of their heads, but the nasal bones are not looped and the bony opening in the skull for the nasal passage is much smaller. The skulls in *Diplodocus* and *Apatosaurus* are oblong-shaped, somewhat like lozenges. The jaws are long, but taper from the back of the skull to the snout gradually, rather than being drawn out into a duck's bill. And the teeth are restricted to the front part of the upper and lower jaws instead of continuing back along the sides of the mouth. In addition, the front of the jaws is squared off and blunt, rather than curving more gently to meet at the midline.

Jaws and teeth are particularly important when considering how the sauropod giants managed to obtain sufficient nourishment. Besides the variation in jaw shape discussed above, there is also variation among sauropod species in the shape of the teeth (see Figure 27). Some sauropods, such as *Brachiosaurus* and *Camarasaurus,* have teeth with spoon-shaped crowns. Others, such as *Diplodocus,* have teeth that are shaped like pencils. They are little round cylinders. Both of these shapes of sauropod teeth, when multiplied by a mouthful of them, are adequate for plucking and nipping sprigs, twigs, fronds, and leaves, but they are not good for chewing them up. In addition, they are not held very strongly in their sockets, and they were replaced in life at frequent intervals by replacement teeth growing in from the roots. After a sauropod dies, the teeth very quickly fall out. Since neither tooth shape is adequate for a good, thorough chewing of the food, the teeth were used primarily to obtain food. The processing of it was done by gizzard stones, called gastroliths, that ground foodstuffs into a mash, after which it was most likely fermented by the action of microbes. The gastroliths are rocks that were selectively swallowed for the purpose. Birds and crocodiles do that now. It is not all that unusual in the world of animal digestion.

There can be variation in the shape of teeth within certain species of sauropods. In *Brachiosaurus,* for instance, the teeth in the front of the mouth are more broadly spoon-shaped than those farther back. Still, even in the back of the mouth they are different from the pencil-shaped teeth found in *Diplodocus,* a shape that is much more simple and less variable because it is basically an uncomplicated cylinder. By comparison with other, more primitive dinosaurs, it seems most likely that the spoon-shaped teeth are less evolved and more akin to the shape of teeth in hypothetical ancestral sauropods. Pencil-shaped teeth evolved from the more primitive spoon-shaped form, but since one simple cylindrical shape looks pretty much like any other simple cylindrical shape, the possession of pencillike teeth alone, when considered among all the species of sauropods, does not necessarily reflect a common ancestry. In other words, simple teeth may have evolved from more complex teeth more than once. That idea plays an important role in understanding the evolutionary history of the sauropod bones from Malaŵi.

The heavier bones of the limbs, those that lie below the sauropod Plimsoll line, are designed for transmitting the total weight of the animal to the ground. Now, for a dog or a horse or a lizard, walking on four legs is the primitive way of doing things. But, as I said before, for dinosaurs, the style of locomotion that characterizes the group as a whole is bipedal progression— walking on two hind legs. The common ancestor of all dinosaurs, the hypo- thetical first true dinosaur, was bipedal. Sauropods and some other plant- eaters, such as stegosaurs and ceratopsians, have secondarily resorted to walking on all fours. Evidence of their two-legged heritage is reflected in the length of the back legs compared with those of the front. They are generally quite a bit longer and more massive than the front legs, showing that the distribution of the weight in a sauropod body is shifted toward the back end. In bison or horses or camels, good self-respecting quadrupeds who never had a bipedal ancestry, the front limb bones are more massive than the hind, reflecting a different distribution of the weight, a different build, if you will (Figure 28).

Such evolutionary modifications as occur in sauropod limbs are in large part graviportal—adaptations for carrying great weight, as in elephants. The

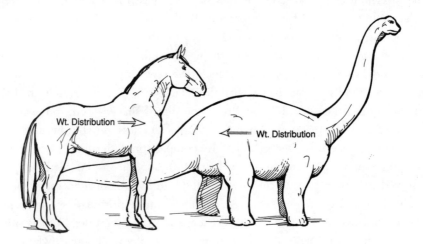

FIGURE 28: Weight distribution in a horse and in a sauropod dinosaur. Horses and their ancestors have always been quadrupedal, with the front end of their bodies more massive than the rear. Quadrupedal dinosaurs evolved from bipedal ancestors. As a consequence of their evolving four-legged locomotion from ancestors anatomically suited to moving about on hind limbs only, their weight is distributed more toward the rear of their bodies.

legs of graviportal animals are always heavily built, like the columns of a Greek temple. Large graviportal animals cannot lift all four feet off the ground at the same time. Sauropods, like elephants, were not jumpers. Nevertheless graviportal animals such as elephants can rear up on their hind limbs, and they do so occasionally, rather than habitually, in their natural state. At Amboseli Park in southern Kenya, where the herd is large, I have witnessed two elephants in the wild rear up facing each other and engage in a bit of a wrestling match.

If it is true that some quadrupedal mammals have a weight distribution different from sauropods, and with more massive forelimbs than hind, then an interesting analogy, with regard to their repertoire of movements anyway, might be the rearing up of sauropods on their hind legs, compared with the tilting of horses or buffalo onto their forelegs. Horses, of course, can do just that whenever they choose to kick the hell out of someone. Bulls can as well; just go to a rodeo if you want to see them do it. Even elephants, which are much more sauropodlike than horses in their general body shape, because both elephants and sauropods are graviportal, can do it. I saw them do it last year when I took my children to the circus. Elephants can tilt up on their front legs into a pachyderm handstand. I do not believe they do it in the wild, except perhaps in the strangest of circumstances, but they certainly could do it if the mood so struck them. There is obviously nothing in their anatomy that physically prevents them from doing handstands.

As quadrupedal animals that reverted to quadrupedalism in their evolutionary history, it is not unthinkable that even the largest of the sauropod species maintained the anatomical capacity to rear up on their hind limbs. In fact, it has become quite popular to reconstruct them that way even to the point of going overboard. In the tails of all sauropods there are bones, called chevrons, that articulate with the vertebral centra and hang down. A blood vessel flows along the underside of the vertebrae, and the chevrons branch around and protect it, then either they progress downward and backward, providing areas for muscle attachment, or they fork into a sled shape pointing forward up the tail to the hip and backward toward the tip of the tail. *Diplodocus* and its relatives, perhaps uniquely among sauropods, possess the sled-shaped chevrons. The strange shape of the chevrons, which occur only on vertebrae in the middle of the tail, not the base, has suggested to some that they formed a protective shield on the underside of the tail, allowing the dinosaur to use it as a brace when rearing up on its hind legs. The chevrons protected the blood vessel in the underside of the tail from being damaged, and with the tail acting as a third leg, the animal could stand and graze from the tops of trees for as long as it desired. Further evidence for the suggestion comes from the height of the spines in the diplodocid rear end and the massive size of the pelvic bones. None of the evidence has been quantitatively analyzed, but nevertheless, that is the way the story goes.

I do not buy it. It seems a bit too Hollywood for me. The conclusion that huge graviportal animals had such an habitual behavior should follow detailed analysis of functional reality based on a thorough review of the evidence from the bones. I will concede, anecdotally, that sauropods could rear up, and if they could, I see no reason why they should not grab a few snacks every now and then that way. But the thought of tripodal dinosaurs, especially diplodocids, the sauropods with the shortest forelimbs relative to the hind limbs, and with the longest tails, disrupts my sense of symmetry.

When sauropods did rear up, it very likely would not have been to walk about in any extended way. Rather, it might have been only for a second or two, or a little longer, perhaps to nip a leaf, or to intimidate another sauropod of its own species, maybe to wrestle like the elephants I saw at Amboseli. It seems rather unlikely that a huge animal like a sauropod would habitually rear up on its hind legs to feed off the tops of trees or as a defensive posture against threatening carnivores, as they are sometimes shown. Rearing up would do little more than expose the vital belly to the scimitar claws and rapier teeth of predators. Animals, whether elephants or sauropods, are capable of a greater range of locomotion and movement than they utilize as a regular part of their natural behavior. The fact that they are able to rise onto two legs, whether the front or the rear, does not mean they do so at every feeding, every attack by a predator, or every social encounter.

Sauropods show little in the way of defensive structures except large size. Some sauropods, like *Diplodocus* and *Apatosaurus,* have long, thin tails, drawn out at the tip to resemble a whiplash. Even more strangely, two Chinese sauropods, *Shunosaurus* and *Omeisaurus,* are reported to sport bony clubs on the ends of their tails. Defense has been suggested as the function of both the clubs and the whiplash. But a whip is a weapon of finesse, a trait not generally associated with graviportal animals, and a club or a whiplash swung at the end of a tail several yards long could cause a lot of unnecessary injury to the tail's owner when it made contact. Sauropods may have used their tails to communicate with their own kind, much the way that wolves communicate, by changing postures and holding the tail in different positions. Tails may well have been used for signaling, for touching and caressing, rather than as whips or bludgeons. The variation in the shape of the ends of tails may reflect this kind of use among different sauropod species.

So how did sauropods protect themselves from fierce predators if not by rearing up to squash their attackers or swatting them with their tails? Adult sauropods, because of their size, were fully able to walk over any animals attempting to subdue them. Certainly young would be vulnerable, and even large individuals might succumb to a coordinated attack by a pack of theropods, but basically I imagine sauropods just tried to get away. In escaping, they might go in any direction, away from the predator or directly over it. Their behavior while under attack may have had no more motivation than the urge to flee. One of the selective factors leading to the operation of Cope's rule in sauropods may have been the fine defense that gigantism in and of itself provides. In fact, it is possible that the reason sauropods got so large was behaviorally no more complicated than the evolution of a passive defense mechanism.

IF ALL THIS talk of different features in the tails, teeth, limbs, skulls, and vertebrae of different species of sauropods is confusing to you, you are not alone. It has often been lamented by top paleontologists that sauropods are evolutionarily very complex. Their relationships are difficult to unravel with the very good but limited sample of their fossils that is known. The sample is limited because it is spotty. Some species are better known, some continents are more thoroughly searched, and some times, geologically speaking, are much better represented in collections. And that is why the sauropods from Malaŵi are so important. It is a new batch of fossils, a whole new set of data, to throw into the argument. It gives better material on a poorly known species, from a continent that has not been thoroughly sampled and a time that is poorly represented.

Somewhere around 150 species of sauropods have been named; however, not nearly that many are really valid. Some names have been applied to fragments of bone so incomplete that their true owners are completely unknowable. They do not tell us much about anything. The good, recognizable species are grouped into six families, some of which are more familiar than others. The diplodocids contain such genera as *Diplodocus,* obviously,

Apatosaurus, and some others like *Dicraeosaurus* from Africa and *Barosaurus* from both Africa and North America. (All the names of families end here in "-id," the vernacular for the scientific ending of family names "-idae.") Diplodocids have long, whiplash tails, pencillike teeth limited to the front of the mouth, long heads, and a trough formed by their vertebrae to house the muscles and ligaments that control movements of the neck and head.

Brachiosaurids are the giraffe-necked sauropods with long front legs. Their tails are short compared with diplodocids, and they do not end in a long, thin whiplash. Camarasaurids are similar to brachiosaurids in having spoon-shaped teeth, but the spines on the neck vertebrae are divided into the beginnings of a trough, like diplodocids. The vulcanodontids are the most primitive of the sauropods. They have an extra bump on the thighbone near where it slips into the hip socket. The bump is for muscle attachment, and it is present in most other dinosaurs, but not the other families of sauropods—that is one good reason why vulcanodontids are considered so primitive. One family, the group called cetiosaurids, is basically a wastebasket full of names, some of which represent apparently primitive species and some that represent other species that are obviously not primitive. None of them has been adequately studied. The final family, the titanosaurids, is the one that will concern us most. The bones from Malaŵi enable us to graft its branch onto the evolutionary tree of sauropods (see Figure 27).

Sauropods have been known from Malaŵi for a long time, since the 1920s in fact. The specimens in the British Museum collected by Migeod in 1930 have never, even now, been studied in detail, but two years before Migeod, the South African Britisher S. H. Haughton named *Gigantosaurus dixeyi* from the Dinosaur Beds. He named it for Frank Dixey, the British head of the Geological Survey in Nyasaland, to whom a planter named Holt had first reported fossils. Dixey investigated, collected some bones, which he sent to Haughton, and later guided Migeod around the fossil beds, showing him all the localities he knew. Among the fossils Dixey sent to Haughton were a vertebra from the front part of the tail, part of a hipbone, a breastbone, and part of a shoulder blade. It was those specimens to which Haughton applied the name *Gigantosaurus dixeyi.* No firsthand study of sauropods from Malaŵi was undertaken after Haughton's in 1928 until my project started in 1984. It has taken six years to develop the sauropod bones found by my group to the point where they make sense and can say something of real value in understanding the dinosaurs.

Nevertheless it was known early on, since 1911 in fact, that the name *Gigantosaurus* was not valid for African sauropods; it had been used before for another fossil in Victorian England, so it could not be used again for a different species in which a relationship to the original was not demonstrable. The naming legalities of *Gigantosaurus dixeyi* are even more complex than what I have written, but you get the picture, I am sure. It boils down to this: The species *dixeyi* is a good species, but it does not belong to *Gigantosaurus*.

Haughton named only one species of sauropod from the Dinosaur Beds. My project has shown that there are two at least. The evidence proving the existence of two species came most conclusively from the two lower jaws we collected from CD-9. They are clearly not the same. Both of them are small, as sauropod jaws go, the larger being only about a foot long, although the specimen is not complete in the back. The second specimen is only a little more than half the size of the first. Therefore we needed to rule out the possibility that the differences we could see in shape and form between the two were a result of the age of the individuals, baby versus adult. Neither of the jaws has functional teeth protruding from their sockets, but the tips of a number of replacement teeth are still there. From what can be seen of the replacement teeth, the tooth shape is different in the two jaws. The tooth sockets extend in a row back to near the end of the jaw in the larger specimen, but in the smaller of the two the tooth sockets stop much farther forward. Moreover, the front end of the smaller jaw seems to curve more sharply toward the "chin."

Even before we found the jaws, there was evidence from teeth that two kinds of sauropods are present. In quarrying, two different kinds of sauropod teeth were found isolated and scattered about through the sediment. One group had a rounder cross-section, the other was flattened, but narrow, and also a bit larger in length and breadth than the first. The larger-sized teeth matched with the replacement teeth of the larger jaw, and the rounder teeth matched with the smaller jaw. It then became clear. The smaller jaw, regardless of being a very young animal, has pencillike teeth limited to the front of the jaw, which curves more or less sharply toward the chin. Therefore it is a diplodocid. However, there was one additional feature of the small lower jaw that seemed strange and puzzling. The front end flares in a way not seen in other diplodocids. Based on that, it is very likely that the little diplodocid jaw from Malaŵi represents a brand-new species.

But what of the larger jaw? If the smaller is a diplodocid, and the larger is different from it, to which family should the larger be assigned? Frankly it is easier to say what it is not than to say what it is. So we proceeded to find out what the rest of the sauropod bones could tell us. One interesting pattern is that of all the other bones diagnostic enough to be assigned to a family, none seemed to be diplodocid, even though we knew from the tiny lower jaw that that family was there. Moreover, of all the specimens that have been prepared, none is small enough to go with the smaller lower jaw. From measurements taken while excavation was under way there seemed to be one vertebra that might go with it, but since it has not been prepared and because our photographs at home are inconclusive, we have no way of knowing for sure. All the rest of the sauropod bones seem to belong to one nondiplodocid family. They are titanosaurid.

The titanosaurid family has a long, complicated history. Its first member was named in 1877 when Richard Lydekker called some tail vertebrae and a few other bones from the Cretaceous of India *Titanosaurus indicus.* The name *Titanosaurus,* the "titan lizard," was just too clever and too good to pass up for nineteenth-century paleontologists in a frenzy to name giant reptiles never before seen. The legendary feuding paleontologists O. C. Marsh of Yale University and E. D. Cope of Philadelphia had one of their many episodes when Marsh, quite independently from Lydekker, named an American dinosaur *Titanosaurus.* To his glee, Cope was able to reprimand Marsh by pointing out the preoccupation of the name.

Since the time that Lydekker named the first one, titanosaurids have been found all over the place. They are in Europe, Africa, Madagascar, South America, and even North America. Their occurrences outside of Africa are restricted to the Cretaceous Period, and mostly the Late Cretaceous at that, well after the reign of the diplodocids and brachiosaurids that occurred forty million years—and more—prior to the heyday of the titanosaurids. The roots of the family can be traced back to their first generally accepted record at Tendaguru in the same area with *Brachiosaurus* and diplodocids. Making the connection between the later titanosaurids, spread all over the world, and the rather poorly known and confused titanosaurid from Tendaguru was a difficult task for paleontologists. In fact, it could not be done satisfactorily until the Malaŵi specimens came out of the ground.

Titanosaurids have one feature that was known to Lydekker, which set them apart from all other sauropods. The vertebrae of the tail have an extremely peculiar shape (Figure 29). The centrum has a deep cup at the front

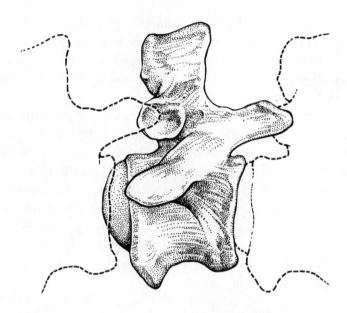

FIGURE 29: Ball-and-socket tail vertebrae of the titanosaurid sauropod Malaŵi-saurus. The rounded surface toward the bottom left (the back side of the vertebra) is characteristic of titanosaurids and allows them to be recognized wherever they may be found.

end, into which a large ball at the back of the preceding centrum fits. Vertebrae of this shape are called procoelous. It is a ball-and-socket joint unlike that seen in any other group of sauropods. Because that feature is so characteristic and so obvious, and because tail vertebrae are more massive and therefore more readily preserved as fossils than other vertebrae, the titanosaurs can be recognized and identified with only a small amount of very lousy material. Even though they are known from many places, the bones from most of them do not tell us much more than that titanosaurids were there. That state of affairs led to titanosaurids being looked upon as the bad boys of the sauropod clan, not telling all they could and not seeming to fit in anywhere.

As it turns out, there are a number of diagnostic features that help to make sense of titanosaurids. First of all, the ball-and-socket tail vertebrae really are a unique feature that the family shares with no other sauropods. Haughton knew that when he described and named *Gigantosaurus dixeyi* in 1928. That is why he called his new species *Gigantosaurus* to begin with, because that is what the titanosaurid from Tendaguru had first been called. (The name of the Tendaguru titanosaurid has since been changed to *Janenschia* after passing through another iteration on the way from *Gigantosaurus*. Will the confusion never cease?)

When I went into Malaŵi, I knew that titanosaurid bones had been found there, and now my project had verified it. One thing about it, though: Neither Dixey nor Haughton nor my project ever found any truly gigantic bones at all. Not one. The name *Gigantosaurus* certainly does not fit, if for nothing but esthetic reasons. It is hard to accept that all of the collections made over the years by Holt, Dixey, Migeod, and my group represent only juvenile sauropods. Rather, I think we have a picture of near-average-sized individuals. I think the Malaŵi titanosaurid is just small for a sauropod, primitive in size relative to the giants, probably about thirty feet long, and perhaps ten tons in weight. Not bad for a pip-squeak.

In addition to the ball-and-socket tail vertebrae, there are other features unique to titanosaurids. For instance, one of the bones of the hip, the ischium, the bone in humans on which you sit, is greatly expanded and uncommonly wide in most titanosaurids. None of those had ever been found in Malaŵi before us, but we got one. We also found a set of breastbones laid out as in life. Their shape, and the way they were arranged was exactly like that of the titanosaurid *Alamosaurus* as it was laid out in the hills of Utah. Haughton had reported a breastbone from Malaŵi, but the one he had was in bad shape. It had to be pieced back together and patched with plaster. The reconstruction was a tad iffy. What it looks like most is a breastbone, yes, but it appears that Haughton's specimen needs to be rotated ninety degrees clockwise from the way he put it in his original picture to get the proper orientation for joining with its companion bone.

Titanosaurids have another feature that is the most odd of the lot. They have bony armor in their skin. That is not unheard of among vertebrate animals. After all, crocodiles and alligators have bones in their skins. (That is why the fashion industry utilizes only the belly leather of crocodiles for belts and purses and shoes.) Armadillos have a bony shell made up of many dermal plates. Some other dinosaurs, notably the ankylosaurs, are well armored. Why not sauropods? There is no reason why not, but there is also only one family of sauropods known to be armored, and that is the titanosaurids.

Surprisingly enough, the suggestion of armored sauropods was made long ago. The French paleontologist Charles Depéret, while studying dinosaurs from Madagascar, found characteristic pieces of dermal armor that he suggested belonged to titanosaurids. That was in 1896. Depéret's claim was considered interesting but it did not make a real splash because titanosaurids have been for so long back-burner sauropods, and at the time the concept of armored dinosaurs was just too foreign. The confirmation of Depéret's assertion came not from more work in Madagascar or Africa. It came from South America. In 1980 two Argentinian paleontologists, José Bonaparte and Jaime Powell, working with the excellent titanosaurid material they had been excavating—excellent except for missing the heads—published a paper illustrating scutes of dermal bone and proving unambiguously that at least some titanosaurids were armored. There are a number of different shapes of armor plates, but basically they have a round base with a ridge or crest rising up from its surface. The exact arrangement of the different variations of this form on the body is currently unknown, and the purpose, whether for decoration or defense or some other reason, is also unknown. But the titanosaurids are armored.

If titanosaurids are armored, and if we were digging up titanosaurids in the Luwonya Hills of Malaŵi, then why were we not digging up dermal ossicles along with the other bones? We never have, even to this day. However, we were finding a number of strangely shaped objects composed entirely of crystals of the mineral calcite. The same mineral also grew in the marrow cavities of some of the fossil bones in Malaŵi. Looking at those calcite objects carefully, we concluded that they had to represent some shape of biological origin. It is not all that rare in geology for a structure to be dissolved away and its shape to be filled with a different mineral. The resulting forms are called pseudomorphs. Inorganic substances such as salt crystals, the mineral halite, can be dissolved away from rock, but their original cubic form left behind. It can also happen with biological structures in the same way. The calcite pseudomorphs from Malaŵi resemble nothing so much as dermal armor. They are not shaped exactly the same as the armor from South America or Madagascar, but they are similar. There is no bone left, so if they are pseudomorphs of dermal ossicles, all the bone was dissolved away and calcite grew in its place. The pseudomorphs have a circular base with a dozen or so projections sticking out from the edge. There is a tall spine that slants backward—at least to what we consider to be the backward direction. So in Malaŵi we have ball-and-socket tail vertebrae, a hip with a wide ischium, articulated breastbones, and very possibly the remnants of dermal armor. A good case for titanosaurids indeed.

You may have noticed that I have not mentioned the larger of the two lower jaws from Malaŵi by name, or the flattened teeth. That is because they do not necessarily fit the mold of what titanosaurid jaws and teeth are supposed to look like. But they are almost certainly titanosaurid. We came to that conclusion through a circuitous investigation.

In 1929 Friedrich Baron von Huene named the sauropod *Antarctosaurus wichmannianus* from the Cretaceous of Argentina. The specimen consists of skull parts, the front end of a lower jaw, some teeth, part of an ischium, and a few other odds and ends, but no tail vertebrae. At that time there was no way to recognize titanosaurids other than by the presence of ball-and-socket caudal vertebrae. So why did von Huene call *Antarctosaurus* a titanosaurid if he did not have even one ball-and-socket tail vertebra among the material that he did have of it?

There was probably no place better for him to assign it than to the titanosaurid family, judging from the perspective of hindsight. It was not a bad hypothesis (and there is still the chance that it may turn out to be substantially correct, in which case the evolutionary history of titanosaurids will be even more complicated than it seems to be now). Plenty of good titanosaurid vertebrae were known from the Cretaceous of South America, it is just that none belonged to *Antarctosaurus*. And besides, it was not like he knew that *Antarctosaurus* had tail vertebrae different from titanosaurids. There were no tail vertebrae of *Antarctosaurus* known at all from South America. That is still the case today. One other thing: No other families of sauropods, none but the titanosaurids, were known from the Cretaceous of South America in von Huene's day.

None of this would make any difference to the story in Malaŵi were it not for the jaw and the teeth of *Antarctosaurus* that von Huene described. The teeth are pencillike, and they are limited to the front of the jaw, which itself curves sharply toward the chin. It is on the basis of that jaw and those teeth that every reconstruction of titanosaurid skulls until now has been modeled after *Diplodocus*—long, with nostrils at the top and teeth limited to the front.

The features of *Antarctosaurus* are the same ones we used to identify the smaller of the two jaws from Malaŵi as a diplodocid. Those are the same characters that we use now to suggest that, given the lack of positive evidence to the contrary, *Antarctosaurus* is not a titanosaurid at all, but rather a South

American Cretaceous diplodocid. For over sixty years titanosaurids have been taking a bum rap over what their heads look like.

The reconstruction may have also caused some problems for von Huene in his later studies. In 1933 he published a monograph on Indian dinosaurs with Charles Alfred Matley. In it they recognized a new species of *Antarctosaurus*, which they called *Antarctosaurus septentrionalis*. The Indian specimen included the back of the skull, thought by von Huene and Matley to be similar to that from South America. They were led to the conclusion, based on that similarity, that the animals from which those bones from the back of the skull were derived belonged to the same close-knit group of sauropod species. Thus the genus came to be known from both Argentina and India. The Indian specimen also included a ball-and-socket tail vertebra, which was therefore obviously titanosaurid (but of course, as we have seen, the first place from which titanosaurids were known was India, so it is not surprising that more of them should be found). Unfortunately the back ends of skulls are often very conservative in evolution. In this case, while the Indian *"Antarctosaurus"* material is definitely titanosaurid (we know that from the tail vertebra), the South American *Antarctosaurus,* the true *Antarctosaurus,* may not be. It is more likely to be diplodocid. The resemblance between the South American and Indian bones from the back of the skull may ultimately prove to indicate nothing more than that both belong to sauropods.

Von Huene and Matley also described a sauropod upper jaw bone, or maxilla, in their monograph. Now, this is an interesting specimen. It was described by them as coming from a beast with a short and very high snout, so they concluded that it could not have come from *Antarctosaurus,* which they thought to be a titanosaurid, but which we now know may involve sauropods of two different families anyway. Von Huene had reconstructed *Antarctosaurus* as having a long *Diplodocus*-like snout based on the *Antarctosaurus* jaw from South America that he had described four years earlier. As we shall see, the upper jaw from India fits with nothing so well as a titanosaurid, short snout and all, based on what has been found in Malaŵi.

There was one other complication. Some more or less pencillike teeth, not spoon-shaped, had been found with good titanosaurid bones. As I have said before, it is not unlikely that simple teeth may have evolved from spoon-shaped teeth more than once in different sauropod evolutionary lineages. The larger sauropod teeth from Malaŵi demonstrate that possibility because they are not of either shape. They are intermediate, more derived than spoon-shaped teeth and more primitive than pencillike teeth. In most features no two families of sauropods are more unlike each other than titanosaurids and diplodocids. That some titanosaurid species may have pencillike teeth superficially resembling diplodocids merely shows that cylindrical teeth evolved separately more than once in sauropods.

Simply stated, there is no reason to accept that titanosaurids had heads like diplodocids. Since that is the case, there is no particular reason to lump the small diplodocid jaw from Malaŵi with the ball-and-socket tail vertebrae and the other bones that are definitely titanosaurid. The other jaw, the larger one, with its long tooth row and flattened teeth, fits better with the titanosaurid bones because it is the right size. From that reasoning, we can say that we know what the lower jaw of the Malaŵi titanosaurid looks like. Moreover, the teeth, which are flattened, not pencillike, and have the edge formed like that in brachiosaurids and camarasaurids, show clearly that the common ancestor of diplodocids and titanosaurids did not have pencillike teeth.

Once it was decided that the larger of the two lower jaws from Malaŵi was titanosaurid, it became relatively easy to identify as titanosaurid a premaxillary bone, the tooth-bearing bone right at the front of the skull, found in Malaŵi. Four replacement teeth are still in the sockets. They are of the flattened variety, proving that this premaxilla belongs to the same species as the larger lower jaw. In fact the two could have belonged to the very same animal. Now we could show for the first time with reasonable certainty what the lower jaw and the snout of a titanosaurid really looked like.

The premaxilla is very strange as sauropod premaxillaries go. It is not so long as in diplodocids or drawn out into a toothy duck's bill as in *Brachiosaurus*. The hole for the nasal passage is large. A thin piece of the premaxilla stands up nearly vertically to form the front edge of the nose. The premaxilla shows conclusively by its structure that the snout was blunt—very, very blunt. Weirdly blunt. The back end of the premaxilla ends in a more or less straight edge that runs from the bottom of the nose opening in a downward direction, perpendicular to the tooth row. That edge is where a maxilla, the other tooth-bearing bone of the upper jaw, would fit.

The premaxilla from Malaŵi is the only titanosaurid premaxilla that has ever been found anywhere. In addition to showing how blunt the face was, it shows that the front end of the maxillary bone ends below the nasal opening where it abuts against the premaxilla. None of it extends in front of the nose holes. That, too, is strange for sauropods. In fact no sauropods known, except titanosaurids, have this feature. Some other dinosaurs do, such as prosauropods for instance, and that suggests that the position of the nose at the very front of the head is where, evolutionarily, it started out in sauropods. Those sauropods in which the nasal openings are farther back evolved from sauropod ancestors that were more like titanosaurids in the position of the nose. As I said, there is only one titanosaurid premaxilla known in all the world as of this moment—that is, known to me anyway. There is also only one maxilla known, and that is the one described by von Huene and Matley from India in 1933, but which they could not identify because of the *Antarctosaurus* confusion. You can tell it is a titanosaurid because its front edge ends completely below the nose hole. It would fit nicely against a premaxilla shaped like the one from Malaŵi. Both of these bones show important features of the titanosaurid skull: It is short but very high, and very narrow. From the side these guys had heads that looked like the front ends of giant worms (Figure 30).

Obviously the next step in the study of the titanosaurid from Malaŵi was to figure out what to call it. Haughton had called it *Gigantosaurus dixeyi,* but for the legalities of nomenclature, the name *Gigantosaurus* was not good. The way to start the next step was to decide if *dixeyi* was a good species based on its biological merit, unique in the animal kingdom, or if it was simply a patronym for a sauropod that was known more commonly under another name. The way to begin finding that out was to compare it with the titanosaurid from Tendaguru.

Janenschia robusta was described in 1908 (under a different name). It is known from a tail and some other bones that may or may not really belong to the same species of animal as the tail. It does not matter for our purposes because all we really need in this case is to show that the tail is, or is not, the same as that of *dixeyi*. We can show that it is not because the spines of the vertebrae, and the bony processes by which they attach to their neighbors, are different. Those in *Janenschia* are more like other sauropods. But there is one big similarity between *Janenschia* and *dixeyi*. While the vertebrae in the front of the tail are procoelous—they have big balls on the back end of the centra—the vertebrae toward the middle and in the back of the tail are not. The species *dixeyi* is distinct from but similar to *Janenschia robusta*. *Janenschia* is geologically older and anatomically more primitive.

All the other titanosaurids scattered around the world with only a couple of exceptions have ball-and-socket caudal vertebrae all the way to the end of

FIGURE 30: *A family group of Malaŵi-saurus in a gallery forest. Swift-flowing braided streams and rivers drain nearby hills and mountains. The climate is seasonal. The vegetation—with ferns, horsetails, cycads, and conifer trees and shrubs—is generally similar to that at Tendaguru except that by 100 million*

years ago, the time of the Dinosaur Beds and 45 million years after Tendaguru, flowering plants (angiosperms) were starting to come onto the scene. Vegetation grew luxuriantly in the galleries along the watercourses, but away from the streams and rivers vegetation was much less dense.

the tail. Therefore *dixeyi* cannot belong to any of those species groups either. We will soon give it its own scientifically valid first name. For now I will informally refer to it as Malaŵi-saurus. Nevertheless Malaŵi-saurus is similar to the titanosaurids of South America, and even North America, in the shape of the neural spines and other bony processes on the vertebrae. It is particularly close to *Andesaurus* from South America. That means it is intermediate in both anatomy and in age to the older titanosaurid of Africa and the younger titanosaurids of the Western Hemisphere. With that bit of knowledge, we are able to devise a geographic scenario for the evolution of titanosaurids.

The oldest known titanosaurid is *Janenschia* from Tendaguru, approximately 145 million years old. Titanosaurids were definitely in Africa then, nearby other sauropods including *Brachiosaurus* and diplodocids. They are not currently unambiguously known from that time interval in any other continents, but that may be misleading. At that time the dinosaurs show a great deal of similarity between North America and Africa as a holdover from the Pangaean geography, when landmasses were broadly connected and animals could roam widely. Of the six families of sauropods, all are in existence by the time interval represented at Tendaguru. All six are known from Africa, and five, all but the titanosaurids, are known from North America way back then. *Brachiosaurus* and *Barosaurus,* both sauropods, are known, albeit from different species, in both North America and Africa. The similarities in those dinosaur faunas is pretty amazing. Therefore, it would not be surprising if a North American titanosaurid of the same vintage surfaced. Moreover, a Chinese paleontologist, Dong Zhiming, has only recently named the new sauropod *Bellusaurus,* which has tail vertebrae suspiciously like titanosaurids. But *Bellusaurus* is from China, and so far no one who has studied it firsthand has called it a titanosaurid. The point of this is to say that the early fossil record of titanosaurids is so poorly known at this time that it is quite impossible to say with any degree of certainty where they originated, but with every degree of certainty that they were in Africa by Tendaguru times.

Then, after Tendaguru, through plate tectonics and continental drift, South America and Africa began to separate as the South Atlantic opened. This, the Early Cretaceous, is the time represented by Malaŵi-saurus. During the Early Cretaceous, the more familiar sauropods were on the decline. Whereas they used to dominate the landscape in earlier times, they now became rare, in the Northern Hemisphere at least. Toward the end of the Early Cretaceous to the beginning of the Late Cretaceous, about ninety million years ago, sauropods apparently became extinct in North America.

Meanwhile they persisted in the Southern Hemisphere. Between Tendaguru times and Malawî-saurus the characteristic features of the anatomy evolved that link Malawî-saurus with *Andesaurus* and the other South American titanosaurids.

After the South Atlantic opened, the South American titanosaurid fauna, and most everything else that was there, evolved in isolation. The South American continent was separated by the sea from Africa and North America, and by the rigors of Antarctica, to which it was still attached, from Australia. The isolation lasted for about the next thirty million years. It was not until around seventy million years ago, near the end of the Age of Reptiles, that North and South America became once more connected by dry land, a cycle that was to repeat again at a later time during the Age of Mammals. With the connection of the Americas, animals from one continent, but new to the other, were able to spread. The bipedal hadrosaurian dinosaur *Kritosaurus* came south. So did the horned ceratopsians. So, too, did marsupial mammals, the opossums. And from south to north across the bridge went the titanosaurids. After twenty million years or so without sauropods, North America was invaded by titanosaurids. The last North American sauropod is the titanosaurid *Alamosaurus sanjuanensis,* named for the old Ojo Alamo trading post, Spanish for cottonwood spring, now gone, just like the water, in the San Juan Basin of New Mexico. *Alamosaurus* is also known from Utah and southern Wyoming, but not from farther north, and from the Big Bend of the Rio Grande in Texas. *Alamosaurus,* possibly the last of all the sauropods, died out near the end of the Age of the Reptiles, a part of the Great Dying that decimated the Mesozoic world and brought it to a close.

WHAT A HISTORY!
Titanosaurids traced from 145 million years ago until their extinction at 66 million years ago—79 million years of family genealogy leading from the shorelands of ancient Tendaguru, through the heart of Africa, across South America, then over the land bridge linking South with North America. There was one reason, and one reason only, why this history could be completed: the titanosaurian missing link, Malawî-saurus, had been recognized.

WHO SAYS STUDYING dinosaurs in Africa does not tell you about things closer to home?

5

AFRICAN
DINOSAURS,
BEFORE AND
AFTER

T HE SAUROPOD Malaŵi-saurus is apparently the most abundant animal in the Dinosaur Beds, but it is by no means the only one. There is its sauropod cousin, the new, unnamed species of diplodocid. There are at least three more kinds of dinosaurs besides the titanosaurid and diplodocid sauropods. Besides dinosaurs there are crustaceans, snails, fish, frogs, and crocodiles. But dinosaurs make up the bulk of the collection, in mass and in numbers of specimens.

Dinosaurs, by definition, are nothing more nor less than a particular group of genetically related reptiles. They are more closely related to each other than they are to any other reptiles because they all share a common ancestor. That common ancestor had specific characteristics and features that can be recognized in its descendants, but not in other reptiles, and that is why they deserve to be lumped together under the dinosaur rubric. Quite fortunately many of the diagnostic features of reptiles are in the bones; therefore they can be seen in fossils and we can interpret reptilian genealogy from bones dug out of the ground.

Some of the diagnostic features of reptiles are in the skull. The arrangement of bony arches in the cheek region, and the gaps and spaces that separate them, show similarities among such seemingly disparate groups as lizards, snakes, crocodiles, dinosaurs, and even birds, each of these groups exhibiting the same fundamental pattern of reptilian anatomy. Dinosaurs have an additional structure in front of the eye that separates them from snakes and lizards, and marks them as members of the Ruling Reptiles, the Archosauria.

You might think that it is overkill to use such features as the structure of the face and snout to sort out relationships between, say, snakes and dinosaurs, but there are a great many kinds of reptiles, and the characteristic used to make genealogical sense out of them must reflect fundamental relationships, not adaptations to specific kinds of life-styles and ecological niches. To make a light analogy with our own species, we would not expect members of the same trade union to be related by blood necessarily, even though in the same community many of them might be. More fundamental relationships would be obvious from observing family reunions when cousins and uncles and the rest, all of whom have been out in the world to make their livings in their own ways, come together. The family portrait shows the family resemblance, regardless of the differences in work clothes. Many of the most obvious skeletal differences among animals reflect adaptations to their ways of life, and conversely, animals with similar ways of life may exhibit similar adaptations and skeletal features. One must look deeper for characteristics of genealogical significance.

Dinosaurs are not the only members of the Archosauria, and there are, of course, several branches to the dinosaur tree. All of the dinosaurs, however, are united by the possession of certain characteristic features of the skull, pelvis, and limbs. Dinosaurs, with all their diversity, have traditionally been divided into only two fundamental groups.

The bones from Malaŵi represent both of the classical divisions of dinosaurs, the "lizard-hipped" saurischians and the "bird-hipped" ornithischians. The sauropods are examples of lizard-hipped dinosaurs, and so are the bipedal carnivores, of which we have found a few bones and teeth (Figure 31). The stegosaur that Kent was working on at CD-10 is an example of a bird-hipped dinosaur (Figure 32). The recognition that the shape of the pelvis is important in determining the evolutionary relationships of dinosaurs goes back to near the beginnings of their study. Harry Govier Seeley, a Britisher, devised this classification in 1887, at the time the slaver Mlozi was being battled by the British in northern Malaŵi. The differences in anatomy between bird-hipped and lizard-hipped dinosaurs are real, but more recent discoveries, not in Malaŵi but elsewhere, have suggested to some investigators that the twofold division may be too simple to account for all the diversity seen in dinosaurs. Nevertheless, in discussing African dinosaurs, the twofold division is convenient and adequate.

There is a good reason why the pelvis should be so important in the study of dinosaurs. Because dinosaurs are primitively bipedal, walking about on their two hind legs, there had to be structural changes in the skeleton to carry the weight in a way different from their quadrupedal ancestors. Walking on the back legs involves tilting the body backward, with the consequent transmission of all the weight down the hind legs to the ground. It makes sense that the joint connecting the legs to the hip would be modified, as well as the muscles controlling the legs and back. There are two major ways in which that has been done in dinosaurs. The resulting skeletal changes are obvious in the

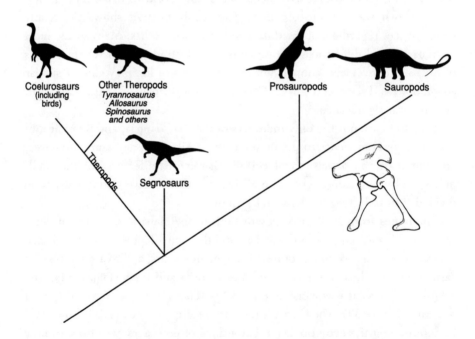

FIGURE 31: Relationships of lizard-hipped dinosaurs. This cladogram is one possible evolutionary tree of these dinosaurs. It provides a logical arrangement that facilitates discussion and investigation. The bones of the lizard-hipped pelvis are shown in the lower right. Compare this saurischian pelvis with the bird-hipped pelvis shown in Figure 32.

three bones that make up the pelvis. Those features are what have become termed lizard-hipped or bird-hipped. Both groups contain some species that are bipedal and others that are quadrupedal. Given that bipedalism is primitive for dinosaurs in general, it seems that in both the lizard-hipped and bird-hipped categories some of the species have, through evolution, eased their forequarters back down to the ground and reverted to walking on all fours.

Generally speaking, the dinosaurs can be viewed as being either carnivorous or herbivorous with regard to their role in the ecological community. As we have seen, with regard to their locomotion, they are either bipedal or quadrupedal. All of the carnivorous dinosaurs belong to the lizard-hipped group (see Figure 31), as do the quadrupedal herbivorous sauropods and their plant-eating relatives, the bipedal prosauropods. While there are many species of bipedal herbivorous dinosaurs, both lizard-hipped and bird-hipped, there are no quadrupedal carnivorous dinosaurs. All of the carnivorous dinosaurs together are called theropods. This is the group that includes *Tyrannosaurus rex,* the giant meat-eater at the end of the Age of Reptiles. *T. rex* was enormous, with a huge head armed with serrated daggerlike teeth. The hind

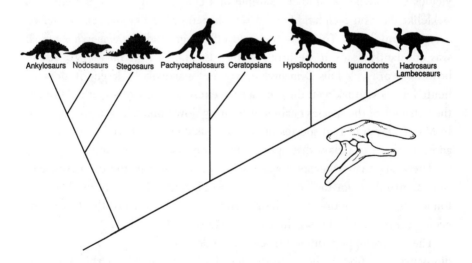

Ankylosaurs Nodosaurs Stegosaurs Pachycephalosaurs Ceratopsians Hypsilophodonts Iguanodonts Hadrosaurs
Lambeosaurs

FIGURE 32: *Relationships of bird-hipped dinosaurs. This cladogram is one possible evolutionary tree of these dinosaurs. It provides a logical arrangement that facilitates discussion and investigation. The bones of the ornithischian pelvis are shown in the lower right.*

limbs were large, but the forelimbs, while strong, were relatively minute and had only two fingers. Other theropods are not quite so much like the tyrannosaurid mold. *Allosaurus,* for instance, known from North America and Tendaguru in Africa, had larger forelimbs, with three fingers, rather than two, on the hand. *Spinosaurus aegyptiacus,* shown in Figure 2 in Chapter 1, is also known from Africa, but from Egypt and from rocks much younger than those at Tendaguru. It is one of the strangest of the theropods. It had a narrow, crocodilelike snout, and on its back was a sail or hump supported by very long spines from the vertebrae. The spines and the sail are enigmatic.

All of the theropods are interesting, but one rather confused jumble of theropods, the coelurosaurs, I find particularly interesting. Evolutionary relationships within the group are very imperfectly deciphered, and it is likely that a major reorganization of the group will occur as its evolutionary tree is more realistically resolved. For now it is convenient to discuss them as one set of dinosaurs.

Coelurosaurs are lightly built, active animals. There is an enormous variety of them, even some that have lost all their teeth. *Elaphrosaurus bambergi* from Tendaguru is an African coelurosaur. Its skull is unknown. The small but vicious *Deinonychus* is another example of a coelurosaur. It has one enlarged sicklelike claw on each hind foot. It was shaped rather like the can opener on a Swiss army knife. The claw was held off the ground as *Deinonychus* ran. It was constantly ready to be brought into use, like a switchblade, to disembowel its prey. While *Deinonychus* was not particularly large, it possibly hunted in packs, making it the dinosaurian equivalent of wolves, and therefore the behavior of the species enabled it to bring down much larger prey species. In Malaŵi teeth of two species of carnivorous dinosaurs have been found. In addition there is a claw that appears to belong to a coelurosaur.

There are many theropod species known other than those I have mentioned, mainly from the continents of the Northern Hemisphere. They are found on every continent, including Antarctica. They were the top of the ecological pyramid, the last link in the Mesozoic food chain.

The lizard-hipped dinosaurs also include three groups of plant-eating dinosaurs. The first of these are the very large quadrupedal herbivores—the sauropods—like Malaŵi-saurus, *Brachiosaurus, Apatosaurus, Diplodocus,* and *Camarasaurus,* which were discussed in Chapter 4. There is a large number of lesser-known species to complement the range of the more familiar giants. African sauropods, besides Malaŵi-saurus, include *Brachiosaurus, Barosaurus,* and *Dicraeosaurus,* known from Tendaguru, the first two from North America as well. Other African sauropods include *Vulcanodon* from Zimbabwe, *Cetiosaurus* and *Rebbachisaurus* from North Africa, *Algoasaurus* from South Africa, and *Bothriospondylus* and *Titanosaurus* from the island of Madagascar (which was not an island for a good part of the time sauropods lived in Africa). Not only were sauropods widely distributed across the continent, but they were there, apparently, for as long as sauropods existed on Earth, so far as we can tell.

All the sauropods can be easily recognized as sauropods, regardless of the differences between separate species. Although distinct in shape, all the sauropods have ridiculously small heads for their body size. Their teeth are simple pegs, or sometimes spoon shapes. They are loosely set in the jaws, and seemingly not good for much of anything, but obviously, if surprisingly, they were functional. The teeth of sauropods are as unlikely for their giant owners as a meat-eating dinosaur's teeth are blatantly like steak knives. Both existed, so the tiny teeth of sauropods clearly did their job as an integral component of the sauropod food-processing system. The most giant of the sauropods were the height of the herbivore guild, literally and figuratively. They derived protection from predators simply by virtue of their size. A herd of sauropods must have had quite an effect on the landscape as it passed through, browsing and trampling with unworried ease.

The second group of lizard-hipped plant-eating herbivores are the bipedal prosauropods (see Figure 31). This group occurs earlier in time than the sauropods, and it is from something like them that the sauropods evolved. They are quite widespread across the globe in the early part of the Age of Reptiles. Several species are known from Africa.

The final group of the lizard-hipped dinosaurs, the segnosaurs, are very poorly known, their major feature being a strange pelvic anatomy that mimics that of a bird-hipped dinosaur to some extent. How confusing! Nevertheless, those who have most studied the segnosaurs think they are an odd bunch of lizard-hipped dinosaurs, not belonging with the theropods yet not quite a sauropod or prosauropod either. The consensus is that they are plant-eaters. Their forelimbs are robust, and they may have spent about as much, or more, time in the quadrupedal position as they did bipedally. None is known from Africa as yet.

All of the bird-hipped dinosaurs (see Figure 32), whether bipedal or quadrupedal, are herbivores. There are no bird-hipped meat-eaters. Their teeth, except in the more primitive forms, are much more sophisticated than the simple pegs and spoons of sauropods. Primitively leaf-shaped, the teeth become modified into elaborate chopping and grinding batteries. Food is held in the mouth by fleshy cheeks. While all ornithischians are plant-eaters, this group contains a startling and amazing diversity of body forms, although none obtains the truly gigantic size of the biggest sauropods.

Just as in the lizard-hipped group, the bird-hipped dinosaurs can be divided into those that walk on their two hind feet and those that reverted back to four. The geologically oldest bird-hipped dinosaurs are small, bipedal, and have simple leaf-shaped teeth. Small *Hypsilophodon* and *Dryosaurus* are examples of primitive bipedal bird-hipped dinosaurs. They and their relatives bounded and gamboled goatlike across the Mesozoic landscape. The latter is known from Tendaguru and North America. However, bipedal bird-hipped dinosaurs as a group are anatomically varied, especially those that lived toward the end of the Age of Reptiles. Many of them achieved quite a respectable size. *Iguanodon*, the first dinosaur named in the nineteenth century, was called "iguana tooth" because its teeth look like those of an iguana lizard. Its thumb was a stiff spike directed upward. Its relatives were the duck-billed hadrosaurian dinosaurs, so common near the end of the Cretaceous in North America. Unlike the iguanodonts, which have a row of relatively large plant-eating teeth, the hadrosaurs have many teeth forming dental batteries that slice and shred vegetation. Each of the teeth in a dental battery is small, and there are many of them, continuously growing out from the roots and replacing older teeth that have become worn down from chewing. The worn teeth are shed and spit out. Cheeks imprison the food in the mouth while it is being masticated and tortured. Closely related to the hadrosaurs are the lambeosaurs. They developed ornate crests on their skulls. These were probably for interactions with members of their own species, including both display and resonating sound through the greatly lengthened nasal passages, which coursed through enlarged cranial crests. Their trumpeting was common in North America.

Ouranosaurus (shown in Figure 3 of Chapter 1) is a bipedal plant-eater from Africa related to lambeosaurs, duck-billed dinosaurs, and iguanodonts. It is unique in having a sail or hump on its back supported by the spines of the vertebrae and superficially very similar to the African theropod *Spinosaurus*, to which it is not closely related. These sails are intriguing. I suspect that they functioned to control body temperature, perhaps by engorging the large surface area they provided with hot blood in order to dissipate heat.

Two other groups of bird-hipped dinosaurs developed special bony arrangements around the skull. These are the bone-headed pachycephalosaurs and the horned dinosaurs or ceratopsians (see Figure 32). In their extreme development the pachycephalosaurs have a very thick dome of bone enlarging the head. The head is reminiscent of a bald-headed man with a long face. The thick skull roof was behaviorally functional. The pachycephalosaurs apparently butted heads, slamming their bone domes together the way bighorn sheep slam their horns. Pachycephalosaurs are mostly known from the Northern Hemisphere, but one specimen is known from Madagascar.

The horned dinosaurs, or ceratopsians, beasts such as *Triceratops,* are four-footed plant-eaters. Their teeth, like those of advanced bipedal herbivores, also evolved into an efficient shredding machine, which they used for chewing up low-growing plants close to the ground. There is good evidence that at least some horned dinosaurs lived in herds and migrated seasonally, just as the great herds of wildebeest do today on the Serengeti Plains of Africa. There are fossil localities with immense concentrations of ceratopsian bones entombed in sediments deposited by rushing rivers, apparently the victims of flooding, again similar to the fate of a portion of the Serengeti herds.

Some of the early bipedal bird-hipped dinosaurs had small bony plates in their skin. These species are apparently close to the ancestry of geologically later, and larger, dinosaurs that had bony plates or armor and that walked about on all fours. Included here are the familiar stegosaurs, with plates and spikes of bone running down the middle of the back from the neck to the tip of the tail, and on the other hand, the nodosaurids and ankylosaurids, which were covered with bony armor and spines (see Figure 32). Like the horned ceratopsians, the armored and plated dinosaurs fed on low-growing vegetation. Unlike horned dinosaurs, the armored and plated dinosaurs did not have an evolved battery of teeth to chew their fodder; rather, they had simple, leaf-shaped teeth quite similar to those of the oldest and most primitive bird-hipped dinosaurs. The heads of plated dinosaurs were small with long jaws to hold the teeth. In the armored dinosaurs the skull was covered over with secondary growths of bone, but they were still relatively small, unlike the ceratopsians.

North American *Stegosaurus* is the best known of the plated dinosaurs, but the group is widespread and also known from Africa. The best-known African form is *Kentrosaurus* from Tendaguru. It is very much like *Stegosaurus,* but a bit smaller and with spikes instead of plates down the tail end of the back.

There is a stegosaur in the Dinosaur Beds of Malaŵi—the one Kent was digging on. We have not yet found the skull, but it is clearly a stegosaur because of the shape of the pelvis. Moreover, there are some unique features on one of the bones that we do have that demonstrates that either the Malaŵi stegosaur is a new, unnamed species or it is one of the scrappy African stegosaurs named on material that does not include the pelvis. More fieldwork will sort out that problem.

The nodosaurids and ankylosaurids are covered with a mail of armor. They are four-footed minibus-sized (or smaller) dinosaurs that fed on plants growing close to the ground, using teeth that retain the primitive leaflike shape. They probably resembled giant armadillos as much as anything else. In North America the nodosaurids are rather commonly, so it seems, found floated out into rocks that were deposited in the sea, so they must have enjoyed the seashore as well as any other environments they may have inhabited. Ankylosaurids have a particularly rich record in Asia. No reliable records of nodosaurids or ankylosaurids are known from Africa.

The thumbnail sketches just provided present a taste of the dizzying array of dinosaurian species that inhabited the Mesozoic world. There are many more than were mentioned by name above. The grand panoply seems infinite. Ornate lambeosaurs, spike-thumbed iguanodonts, duck-billed hadrosaurs, giant sauropods, tiny hypsilophodonts, and all the other plain, decorated, horned, or armored herbivores fed on ancient greenery. The carnivores fed on them or, depending on the species, other fare, such as eggs or small reptiles or insects. Dinosaur species, all of them, must have had elaborate social-structure and behavioral repertoires equal to the sophistication seen in birds and mammals. How could they not? Together among themselves, and with all the other species of plants and animals living at the time, they comprised viable, working natural communities, webs of life different from today but suited to their times.

The Mesozoic Era, the Age of Reptiles, lasted from about 220 million to 66 million years ago. It was an interval of 154 million years of dinosaur dominance over the ecosystem. During that time the continents rearranged from the confluent landmass called Pangaea to end up, in most essentials, as they are now. There were profound changes in the physical world, in the geography of continents and oceans, and in climate. All this vast dynamism in the physical world invoked changes in the biological world through natural selection, which in turn affected the physical world through the influence that plants and animals have on their environments. The Mesozoic was a long expanse of time, but it was ever changing.

No dinosaur species lived for the entire duration of the Mesozoic. None even came close to doing that. There was tremendous faunal succession among the dinosaurs. Those species alive at the end of the era did not exist at the beginning, and those inhabiting the landscape at the beginning were long extinct by the end. As the sands of the Age of Reptiles passed through the hourglass, life was not still. There was a sort of continuous turnover, a conveyor belt exhibiting older species to be replaced by newer models through time.

During the Mesozoic Era, as in any extensive interval of time, the species of life were changing, and the physical world was changing, and they were both influencing each other. From this we can make certain predictions. First, we would expect the inhabitants of the land to be more uniform if all the landmasses are joined, as in Pangaea, subject, of course, to regional differences that may affect the distribution of animals. Regional effects, if there are no absolute mountain barriers or other such obstacles, should be at a lower level of significance than the opportunities for interbreeding provided by broad and more-or-less easy access throughout a confluent supercontinent. We should see a similar pattern of faunal succession all across the landmass as time progressed. Next, we should see increasing differences develop in terrestrial faunas as the continents drift apart from one another. Greater periods of isolation should produce greater differences among the faunas. If land connections between continents become reestablished, even if for a brief period, we should expect to see the dispersal of species, and new competition between species, in the connected faunas. Africa should be an ideal continent to test these predictions during the Mesozoic because of its early inclusion in Pangaea and its subsequent isolation from South America during the Early Cretaceous.

Speaking specifically of dinosaurs, in Africa they go back to the time when the world's landmasses were coalesced into Pangaea (see Figure 9 in Chapter 1), over 200 million years ago. That was at the the very beginnings of the dinosaurs, when they first evolved. With all the continental areas broadly connected at that time, it is expected that the animal inhabitants would be substantially alike across the land, a certain amount of geographic variation in the fauna notwithstanding. That is what is seen in the dinosaurs. The earliest known dinosaurs of over 200 million years ago were not-so-large, carnivorous creatures that walked upright on their hind legs, freeing their hands for manipulation and other functions. Those features characterize the origin of dinosaurs. Later, but not much later, plant-eaters evolved. At this early stage lizard-hipped and bird-hipped dinosaurs looked very much alike. However, they soon began to develop their obvious distinctions of body form. The lizard-hipped and large prosauropods became the conspicuous plant-eaters.

There was an interval of roughly 30 to 40 million years between the evolutionary beginnings of the dinosaurs and the first major breakup of Pangaea. In that time period the sedimentary record shows significant changes in the environment, and the fossil record shows considerable changes in the vertebrate life. The interior of what is now North America went from a more mesic, wetter, climatic regime to one that was more arid and dominated by vast sand dunes. Rift-valley lakes began forming in eastern North America, expressing the tensions about to rip the continents apart. Then, around 180 million years ago, the North Atlantic began forming, shallow seas covered much of Europe, and northwestern Africa split away from southeastern North America. Africa and South America were still conjoined with each other and the other Gondwana continents, but the relationship to North America was less clear. One thing is certain: Arid conditions in the heart of North America were replaced by more pleasant climates, seasonal, but with a reasonably abundant water supply. All this time life continued to evolve. Now the environment had a much greater carrying capacity than the preceding time of deserts and sand dunes. That set the stage for the Late Jurassic, 145 million years ago, the golden age of the dinosaurs.

The Late Jurassic is most notable for having the greatest diversity of the largest creatures that ever lived on land—the sauropods. Surprisingly, even though the breakup of Pangaea had begun, big sauropods are found all over the place. They are in Europe, South America, China, Australia, India, Africa, and North America. Virtually everywhere. Part of this is simply a legacy, a holdover from earlier times when Pangaea was together. Broad connections still remained intact between the Gondwana continents. But it must also mean that temporary or otherwise minor connections existed between close-lying landmasses that were no longer permanently connected and had embarked on their drifting courses. True, there are regional differences across the globe, and some fairly strong ones, even in the sauropod fauna, especially in China. Still, one cannot help but be impressed with the amazing, almost uncanny similarities between the dinosaurs of Tendaguru and Colorado, Utah, and

Wyoming. And not just the sauropods; the theropods and hypsilophodonts are also similar. And not just in Africa and North America. *Apatosaurus* and *Brachiosaurus* are also reported from Portugal.

With the close of the Jurassic, the heyday of the sauropods was over. Their numbers dwindled in North America, where they had been so common. The last period of the Mesozoic Era, the Cretaceous, saw the final dismantling of Gondwana and the development of familiar continental positions, not quite modern of course, but nearly so. With the Cretaceous came more changes in climate, more areas of isolation, and more transient connections that allowed dinosaurs to migrate from continent to continent.

Sauropods, specifically titanosaurids, were reintroduced to North America from South America near the end of the Cretaceous. Stegosaurs, like sauropods, have their most abundant fossil record from the Late Jurassic in the middle portion of the Age of Reptiles, around 145 million years ago. They are known from Europe, North America, China, and Africa in the Jurassic, but not from South America or Australia, then or ever. They decline after the Jurassic. North American ankylosaurids and nodosaurids are more abundant and diverse after the decline of the stegosaurs than they were before. At the time sauropods begin their decline in North America, so do stegosaurs. Elsewhere, stegosaurs continue on into the Cretaceous in China, India, Europe, and Africa, notably in Malaŵi.

The diversity of North American ankylosaurids in the Late Cretaceous is due to the intermittent establishment of a connection across the Bering Straits. The more primitive of the two armored bird-hipped dinosaur families, the nodosaurids, apparently had a broader geographical distribution than their scions, the ankylosaurids. Ankylosaurids underwent a great deal of isolated evolution in Asia. Then, when the straits afforded the opportunity, they came across. They were not alone either. There has been a suggestion that the newly named sauropod, *Dyslocosaurus,* may have come from Asia. Other groups used the straits as well—duck-billed dinosaurs and lambeosaurs and big ferocious tyrannosaurids—and they have a complicated history of migration between Asia and North America. The horned ceratopsians, so characteristic of North American fossil fields, trace their roots back to Asia. They kept moving south through the continent and, along with one of the duck-billed species and a few others, crossed the Central American land bridge from North America to South America as titanosaurids were crossing the other way.

The fossil record in Africa covers much of dinosaurian history, but in a spotty, incomplete, and not very adequate way. There is a good record of the early Pangaean fauna. There are a few reports from the middle of the Age of Reptiles prior to the excellent and astounding suite of fossils from Tendaguru. Throughout the Cretaceous, Early and Late, there are scattered occurrences of dinosaurs in Africa. Few of them have been adequately worked and studied. Two stand out more than the others: Gadoufaoua in Niger, and the Dinosaur Beds of Malaŵi. Gadoufaoua is important because it has relatively complete skeletons of a number of species. The most famous dinosaur from there is the ornithischian *Ouranosaurus,* the two-footed, plant-eating, sail-backed creature related to the crested lambeosaurs. Dating of Gadoufaoua is imprecise, but it is Early Cretaceous.

Ouranosaurus is not found in the Dinosaur Beds of Malaŵi. Nor is anything like it. There are some similarities between the two spots, for instance in the common occurrence of the small crocodile *Araripesuchus,* first described from South America. But no *Ouranosaurus.* Is that because Gadoufaoua is younger? Maybe dinosaurs like *Ouranosaurus* had not entered Africa from the north until after the Dinosaur Beds were deposited? Or is it because the ecology of the two areas was different, even though they were about the same age? Or is it just the chance of collecting? We do not know yet, although as you will see in Chapter 6, there were significant regional differences across Africa at the time it was breaking away from South America.

AT THE CLOSE of the Cretaceous, 66 million years ago, after an immense history of domination and change, origination and extirpation, the same thing happened in Africa as happened everywhere else: Dinosaurs, in the traditional sense, went extinct. During their tenure on Earth, dinosaurs had a long and distinguished record. They inhabited every continent, including Antarctica, essentially covering the Earth's entire range of latitude, from within the Arctic Circle, over the temperate zones, through the tropics, to near the South Polar region. Their time on Earth lasted over 150 million years. The conspicuous giant and not-so-giant denizens of the Age of Reptiles played major ecological roles in the communities of the Mesozoic world. Those beasts—*Diplodocus, Allosaurus,* and the rest—were the obvious dominant vertebrate herbivores and carnivores of the Mesozoic community. Nowadays mammals dominate. Therefore a basic rearrangement in the lineup of players in terrestrial ecosystems has occurred since the end of the Age of Reptiles. The dinosaurs, which ruled the land, are no longer here.

Of course, as we have seen, nothing about the Earth or the life on it remains static for such an immense span of time as that represented by the Age of Reptiles. Dinosaurs underwent a great deal of evolution during that interval. The species that lived at the beginning of their reign were quite different from those at the end, or even in the middle. Thus, besides the Great Dying at the end of the Age of Reptiles, there were numerous extinctions of lesser impact to the group as a whole throughout their time on Earth. There were also times of origination of new species. Many of the details of this evolutionary puzzle remain to be deciphered because, contrary to the common popularity of dinosaurs and despite the impression you may have received from this summary, dinosaurs are on the whole less thoroughly collected, more poorly dated, and less intensively studied than mammalian fossils from the succeeding era. They are more popular because of the size of their giant members, which also makes them harder to collect, and the ambivalent fear instilled in some of us by the more ferocious species.

Regardless of the fact that many dinosaur species originated and went extinct at various times during the Age of Reptiles, there is an undeniable trauma in their history at the end of the Cretaceous. The Great Dying of the dinosaurs is one of the most challenging of questions because so many species went extinct. That, too, instills an ambivalent fear in us. However, our view of it should be tempered to some degree by having seen the complicated patterns of origination and extinction that operated throughout their reign. But there are still overpowering questions. Why, and how, did dinosaurs go extinct? How could these vast behemoths, around for so long, yet that no one has ever or ever will see in the flesh, the rulers of the land for millions and millions of years, how could they go extinct? The answers we have so far are not completely satisfying. It is hardly surprising that there are many unresolved issues about extinction. The end of species is nearly as enigmatic as their origin.

The Great Dying affected more than just dinosaurs. Monstrous marine lizards, flying pterosaurs, a number of invertebrates, many of them tiny, and some plants went extinct at the same time. Other groups survived, most notably crocodiles, birds, and mammals. Why this selectivity? Whatever ideas may be put forward to account for the extinction, in order to be realistic, they must also account for the species that did not go extinct because, for whatever reason, they were able to resist the cause of the dying.

Many theories have been advanced for the cause of the terminal Cretaceous extinction event. Collective constipation, for instance. Or disease. Changing climates and environments very often are attributed a role in the process. Some of these ideas make more sense than others, and the extinction could have involved a train of events and circumstances that operated synergistically, together culminating in a result that none of them alone might have caused. That seems reasonable, if not probable, but it is also reasonable to search for a catalyst, some constellation of circumstances or events that precipitated the mass extinction.

There is mounting evidence and a growing consensus that extraterrestrial events, ultimately or immediately, may have contributed to the demise of the dinosaurs in the calamity that marks the end of the Age of Reptiles. The fundamental evidence for an extraterrestrial-extinction hypothesis is the presence of a thin layer of clay at the boundary between the Cretaceous and overlying rocks. This layer has been found in many places all over the world. On the face of it the mere presence of such a widespread clay layer appears to be reflecting some global event that occurred right at the end of Cretaceous time, and that of course is the time of the dinosaur-extinction event. Is there a meaningful connection between these two observable phenomena?

Chemical analyses of the boundary clay layer have yielded some very interesting results. The most interesting is the anomalously high concentration of iridium, a metallic element of the platinum family. Usually the rocks of the Earth contain very, very small amounts of it. However, iridium is many times more abundant in the boundary clay layer than it ought to be. Where on Earth could all that iridium have come from? There is no good explanation.

It can be assumed that all of the chemical elements making up the solid Earth were originally present when it was first formed billions of years ago in the cosmic proportions of the solar system. If that is so, then the concentration of iridium in the Earth should be the same, or at least comparable, to that measured in meteorites that come into our world from outer space and strike the Earth. That is because meteorites and the Earth all had the same cosmic origin, along with the rest of the solar system. On the Earth's surface, however, the iridium concentration does not reflect cosmic abundance. Iridium is many times less rich than the primordial concentration measured in meteorites, except in one instance—the boundary clay at the terminal Cretaceous extinction event. This raises two fundamental questions. Where has all the original iridium in the Earth gone, and why are the concentrations in the boundary clay more like cosmic proportions?

Iridium is what is called a siderophile; it is an element that loves to combine chemically with iron. In the early formation of the Earth, billions of years ago, before life existed, heavy elements like iron concentrated in the planet's core, leaving lighter elements to make up the crust. Siderophilic iridium presumably accompanied iron as the core and surrounding mantle were formed, migrating to the center of the Earth, enriching its center while depleting the crust. The result is the observation that concentrations of iridium measurable today on the surface of the Earth are much less than that in meteorites.

But what about the boundary clay? Either the concentration of elements was restored to that more nearly resembling meteoric amounts by forces bringing rock from deep in the bowels of the Earth up to the surface, or iridium was brought to the Earth from somewhere else. There are no other realistic options. Which was it?

The only mechanism for bringing rock from deep down in the Earth to the surface of the crust is through volcanic processes. There are in fact large volcanic fields of about the right age in India. But there are some problems with the volcano hypothesis that make it not completely satisfactory. For instance, why are there not many more layers high in iridium commonly associated with volcanic events throughout Earth time? On the other hand, a volcanic mechanism has not been ruled out completely.

As for the second option, how could iridium be brought from outside the Earth to end up in the boundary clay layer? The answer is simple: Through the collision of the Earth with a meteorite. Meteorites have the right composition. Small ones enter the Earth's atmosphere all the time. There is ample evidence, such as Meteor Crater in Arizona or the Steinheim Crater in Bavaria, that larger ones can also strike the surface.

When a meteorite slams into the Earth, it plows into the ground, vaporizing rock and itself and creating a massive explosion. The magnitude of the explosion depends on the size of the meteorite and the speed of the collision. The size of the hypothesized meteorite that may have caused the Great Dying was over one-half mile in diameter. The amount of ejecta thrown up into the atmosphere by its impact would have been of enormous proportions. As the dust resulting from the explosion settled out of the sky, the boundary clay layer, enriched in iridium compared with the usual composition of the Earth's crust, formed in depositional environments, such as in ocean basins, where the layer is most easily found.

There is a great deal of supporting evidence to suggest that the impact hypothesis is more probable than the Earthbound volcanic hypothesis. Chicxulub Crater on the northwestern margin of the Yucatán Peninsula of Mexico has even been suggested as the site of impact. Furthermore, a suggestion of the timing of the impact has been made based on fossil plants found in Wyoming. Damage, apparently caused by freezing, can be observed in aquatic, water-dwelling, species that were subsequently fossilized. The fossil deposit is of the appropriate geologic age and occurs in a stratigraphic section that also contains impact debris. The reproductive stage of the fossil plants when they died suggests that the freeze that killed them occurred in June— early June no less. Such precision must be very critically examined. A certain amount of skepticism is healthy. Concordance of data may be more apparent than real. Even if there is concordance, there may be a better or an equally tenable explanation. Nonetheless he suggestions are plausible.

In either hypothesis, however, Earthbound or asteroid, the immediate physical effects of collision or volcanic explosion must be analyzed in relation to the selective extinctions at the end of the Age of Reptiles In either scenario, the immense amounts of dust and vapor thrown up into the atmosphere would block the sun, casting the Earth into an eerie daytime darkness. It would persist for months. Temperatures would plummet drastically, remaining below freezing, like an endless winter night, until the sun could fight its way through the dusty atmosphere to warm the Earth. Plant productivity, which depends directly on the sun's rays, would drop precipitously. The effect on photosynthetic organisms, plants, would depend somewhat on the season in which the impact occurred, but in any case, on a global scale it would be devastating. That is the basis of estimating the timing of the unseasonable early June "winter" mentioned above.

Those organisms not killed by the immediate effects of the blast would suffer long, agonizing, torturous years of ecological readjustment. Some species could not, would not, survive it. Herbivores left without fodder would starve. Predators would be deprived of prey. Only those species that could survive the cold and dark with the integrity of their populations intact would endure through what was to become the Cretaceous-Tertiary boundary, defined by the death of so many species. Small, secretive mammals survived. Crocodiles and turtles survived. Frogs survived. And so did warm-blooded birds. But not, for whatever dismal reasons, the dinosaurs.

DOES THIS SCENARIO of an atmosphere full of dust, shrouding the Earth from the life-giving energy rays of the sun, sound uncomfortably familiar? Is it an apocalyptic tale? In fact some of the stimulation for the directions taken in assessing the less immediate effects on life of thermonuclear war, and in developing the concept of nuclear winter, comes from just this recognition of the effects of dust in the atmosphere. It does not matter whether the dust is put there by volcanic eruptions or meteorite impacts or the irresponsibility of humans. The calculations are done the same way in each case, and the predicted outcome is the same. The demise of the dinosaurs, in a very real sense, displays the fragility of life. Once something like an impact happens, there is absolutely nothing that can be done to stop uncaring, insensitive, amoral physical processes from running their course and taking their toll. The lesson of dinosaur extinction is apocalyptic to that extent.

Even with the similarities, there are some important differences between the Great Dying at the end of the Age of Reptiles and the most realistic models of thermonuclear war. The effects of intense radioactivity due to atomic explosion and fallout must be added to the equation. That would render the destruction of life far greater and far more horrific than the loss caused simply by darkness and cold and their associated havoc. The second fundamental difference, of even greater significance, is that in thermonuclear war we are not speaking of the extinction of dinosaurs. We are talking about people. People do not cause meteorites; they do cause wars.

We do not need to examine the effects of nuclear war to derive insights from dinosaur extinction. How long, for instance, do you think a catastrophic extinction like one of the magnitude of the Great Dying takes to occur? How long is a geological instant? The answers to both those questions vary, but think of this: We are now in the midst of the greatest episode of extinction that the world has ever seen, all brought about by the effects of humans, not through nuclear war but through our efforts to build better lives for ourselves, by stealing a kiss from the Earth when we might be building a lasting ecological relationship. With our current tools for unraveling geologic time, the extinction period in which we now live would appear but an instant on the Earth's scale of things if it were viewed from sixty-six million years in the future. There must be a better way.

ALL THAT SORT of talk is depressing. We are fortunate to be at the end of the Cold War when the threat of nuclear confrontation appears less imminent. Also, as a society we are more fully aware of the ecological consequences of our actions if we choose to care. Careful as we ought to be in the future, this is not the place to dwell on the thought. Ideas of nuclear winter may derive in some way from the study of dinosaurs, and incongruously we may be enthralled more by the extinction of dinosaurs than by the species going extinct today, but there is one thing for certain that dinosaurs are not supposed to be—depressing. Happily there are relationships between some living animals and dinosaurs that give a more positive view of life. In fact, looking at the issue of dinosaur extinction from the point of view of genealogical relationships, rather than the fate of the commonly depicted dinosaurian species, they have not really gone extinct at all. Some are still alive. In fact, they comprise one of the most common, diverse, and familiar of all the vertebrate groups. They are the birds. The common ancestor of birds and the traditional dinosaurs was a dinosaur. Therefore birds are too. And while dinosaurs in the common sense did not pass through the Great Dying at the end of the Age of Reptiles, birds did.

To understand the origin of birds from their dinosaurian roots, and therefore to understand the "nonextinction" of dinosaurs, we must go back for another look at the twofold division of the dinosaurs. Recall that there are the lizard-hipped saurischians and the bird-hipped ornithischians as proposed by Seeley in the latter part of the nineteenth century. He proposed those names for the very simple reason that the pelvis of some dinosaurs reminded him of lizards, and the others reminded him of birds. This has been a surprisingly resilient way to divide up the dinosaurs, later discoveries notwithstanding. However, the naming of bird-hipped or ornithischian dinosaurs has turned into a strange sort of historical accident. The resemblance to birds is superficial. There is a bony process that points backward from the fused and stiff pelvis of modern birds that recalled a backwardly projected dinosaurian pubic bone to Seeley. It turns out not to be the same structure at all, so the bird-hipped dinosaurs do not resemble birds in the way they were supposed to. Moreover, to make the story a bit more interesting, as you will see, the birds evolved from the lizard-hipped saurischians, not the bird-hipped orni-thischians.

One feature that living birds have that no other group of organisms has is feathers. Feathers are a body covering, evolutionarily derived from reptil-ian scales, that shape the wings and body for flight and insulate the bird's warm-blooded body, protecting it from heat loss. Living birds have other features, too, and the ones most important for paleontologists are those of the skeleton. Living birds generally have thin-walled and hollow bones, a factor that is thought to contribute to their dismal fossil record. Much more often than not, the light, fragile bones get destroyed before they are pre-served. Most modern birds have a large breastbone and a curvy wishbone, to which the muscles of flight attach. The forelimbs of modern birds are unique, and the number of fingers and their claws are reduced. Several of the arm bones have fused together, as have some in the leg. The pelvis has become a solid, rigid structure, and the spinal column is short. There are no teeth to weight down the skull, nor do living species have long, bony tails. This description does not sound very much like a dinosaur, so why are birds thought to be a dinosaur scion, an evolutionary shoot from the most famous of all fossils?

The biggest and most important clue comes from feathers. You would not think that feathers would preserve in the fossil record, yet some of the most worthwhile fossils known in the world are the impressions of feathers sur-rounding the bones of a crow-sized species called *Archaeopteryx lithographica* (Figure 33). The feather imprints owe their existence to a particular set of geological circumstances that culminated in their preservation. *Archaeopteryx* is about 150 million years old, Late Jurassic. It is found only in the Solnhofen Limestone of Bavaria. This limestone was deposited in a shallow sea covering much of western Europe and was probably related to continental movements following the initial breakup of Pangaea in the Northern Hemisphere. The sea was broad, shallow, and quiet. It was so quiet, and the water so still, that very fine grains of lime, calcium carbonate, were deposited undisturbed on the seabed. The fine lime blanketed the bodies of many kinds of vertebrates, including *Archaeopteryx,* small dinosaurs, and pterosaurs, among other species. The extremely small size of the sedimentary particles, slowly filtering onto the carcasses, encased the bodies without any subsequent disturbance to speak of. The lime was left to lithify into limestone, preserving in exquisite detail the skeletons of the animals contained within it, sometimes even retaining the shapes and impressions of tissue that would normally vanish. That is why the feathers of *Archaeopteryx* are preserved.

The Solnhofen Limestone today lies in thin, hard layers that have been quarried for building and flagstone for hundreds of years. Because it is so fine-grained, in earlier days it was used to make lithographic illustrations. Basically the process involves drawing a picture on a polished surface of the stone with a wax pencil. The block is then submerged in an acid that etches away the surface where it is not protected by the wax. Then the stone is washed and cleaned of the wax. The result is a raised surface where the wax was and a lowered surface, eaten down by the acid, where the wax was not. The stone is then ready for inking, and the image is pressed onto paper. Although it is no longer practical to use stone lithography, some of the most beautiful illustrations ever made of fossil bones were done with this technique. The use of the Solnhofen Limestone for lithographic plates gave *Archaeopteryx* its specific epithet, *lithographica*.

FIGURE 33: ARCHAEOPTERYX, *the most primitive, and at 150 million years, the oldest unquestionable bird.*

Archaeopteryx has true feathers, as is clear from the impressions in the Solnhofen Limestone, and from that we can conclude that it is a bird. What other features does it have? It has teeth, which seems unbirdlike, but it turns out that some birds from the Cretaceous have teeth. The presence of teeth, therefore, is only a primitive characteristic, lost in modern birds but present in some extinct birds and also in most all dinosaurs, predictably including the ancestor of birds. *Archaeopteryx* resembles the ancestral condition in a number of important ways. None of the wing bones is fused. There are three fingers. The breastbone is poorly developed. There is a long tail supported by a string of vertebrae. The bones of the legs have fused in a specific kind of way. There are other characteristics as well, and they all seem to point in the same direction. *Archaeopteryx* is a dinosaur. It is a special one, but it is one neverthe-less. It is also a bird because it has feathers. It is often said that if *Archaeopteryx* had been preserved without the feather impressions, it would have been called a dinosaur and much of the interest and controversy surrounding it would not have materialized or would at least have been forestalled. But the feathers were preserved, and *Archaeopteryx* is undeniably a paleontological missing link. Thank goodness for those feather impressions!

If *Archaeopteryx* and all other birds are dinosaurs, to which of the traditional dinosaurs are they most closely related? Surely not the stegosaurs, or ceratop-sians, or duck-billed dinosaurs. Those are ornithischians, and we know that the pelvis of *Archaeopteryx,* strange as it may seem, is not "bird-hipped" in Seeley's sense of the term. It is lizard-hipped, and the boxlike pelvis of modern birds is evolved from that.

But there are many kinds of saurischians. Birds surely are not most closely related to Malaŵi-saurus or the other sauropods. Those giants are quadru-pedal, and everyone can see from the sparrows hopping about at the window that birds are not. We must look to the bipedal theropods. Meat-eating giants like *Tyrannosaurus rex,* which in many ways are primitive theropods, are too specialized to have given rise to *Archaeopteryx* because, among other things, *T. rex* has only two fingers in the hand and *Archaeopteryx* still has three. Some other theropods have three fingers, plus the same kind of leg structure, plus a similar kind of wishbone. This distribution of characters among species (and some others I have not gone into), all taken together, indicates that *Archaeop-teryx*—and therefore the primitive state of all birds—has the defining features of coelurosaurian dinosaurs.

Another way of stating the same thing is to say birds are coelurosaurian dinosaurs (see Figure 31). You could say that all birds are coelurosaurs but not all coelurosaurs are birds. That is the relationship. All coelurosaurs share a common ancestry with each other that other groups of dinosaurs do not share. *T. rex* and *Allosaurus* join the genealogical tree farther back. They branched off the main theropod trunk before the coelurosaurs, including birds, formed their own branch. After that branch was formed, the birds, separate from other coelurosaurs, split and split in an adaptive radiation leading to the huge diversity of feathered splendor that brightens our world today, with color and song, each living species its own twig on the tree of life.

There are many species of coelurosaurs that evolved birdlike features in parallel with birds, yet they are not true birds. The ostrich dinosaurs, for example, have a build more or less like an ostrich, and they have no teeth, as in modern birds. But the ostrich dinosaurs are their own evolutionary lineage, a separate branch within the coelurosaurs, to be sure, but not part of the bird branch of coelurosaurs. Ostrich dinosaurs are not the only ones with birdlike characteristics. Interestingly, the most birdlike of the nonbird coelurosaurs, the group that includes sickle-clawed *Deinonychus,* occur relatively late in time, long after *Archaeopteryx,* by tens of millions of years, and even after some other fossil birds were on the scene.

If we look at the fossil record of coelurosaurs and their distribution through time, we find that one of the oldest-known coelurosaurs is *Archaeopteryx lithographica.* Famous *Archaeopteryx.* It has feathers. Only birds have feathers. *Archaeopteryx* is already a bird. There are some older coelurosaurs going back toward the very beginning of dinosaurs, but they are poorly known and confusingly difficult with respect to early dinosaur, much less bird, evolution. Coelurosaurs start to become better known at about the time of *Archaeopteryx.* In fact, I mentioned above a nonbird coelurosaur from Tendaguru called *Elaphrosaurus bambergi.*

How can it be that the fossil record of bird origins is so topsy-turvy? Where are the older, nonfeathered coelurosaur ancestors of birds? This is a bother for those, like me, who would prefer the fossil record to reflect the sequence, species by species, of the evolution of major groups of animals. Unfortunately that is an ideal that the fossil record has been unable to live up to in many cases. If it already did that, there would be less reason to search for fossils. The true ancestral species may never be found, but so what? We cannot even say for sure that the species ancestral to birds was fossilized. In this case, rocks of the appropriate age—that is, immediately preceding *Archaeopteryx*—and representing the necessary depositional environment to preserve bird ancestors are rare. Nevertheless the hypothesis, based on the anatomy of birds, dinosaurs, and all other animals, remains that all birds, not just *Archaeopteryx*, are coelurosaurs, and that they evolved specifically from an older, as yet unknown ancestor. This provides a prediction, as good hypotheses do, that such an animal may be found. The hypothesis does not depend on such a discovery. It could, in principle, be falsified, that is, it could be shown to be impossible, strictly from anatomical data derived from known species. That would not be intellectually devastating so long as realistic models of bird evolution can be reconstructed from what we have in the fossil record and in living species, constrained in time to some extent and tested by future discoveries.

If new discoveries can be expected to test hypotheses, they can also be expected to throw a few wrenches into the gears. That is what has happened with *Archaeopteryx* and the origin of birds. New fossils found only a few years ago in West Texas appear very birdlike to their discoverer, so much so that a new genus and species name, *Protoavis texensis,* was given to them. In fact, the pheasant-sized *Protoavis* is reported to be more like modern birds than is *Archaeopteryx.* This is not impossible, but what makes the report so fascinating is that *Protoavis* is older than *Archaeopteryx* by seventy-five million years! That would move the fossil record of birds back to a time comparable with the origin of dinosaurs, a position that is not unreasonable. It would mean that birds split off early in dinosaur history, and it would imply that all coelurosaurs, if they actually have any meaning as a natural grouping of dinosaurs, did so as well. The issue, however, boils down to the anatomical features of the skeleton of *Protoavis.* No feathers of it are known.

Like *Archaeopteryx, Protoavis* has a long tail. It also has teeth, but they are limited to the front end of the jaw rather than extending farther back, as in *Archaeopteryx.* The entire skull architecture is more like that of modern birds. The eye sockets are large, providing for binocular, three-dimensional vision. The brain, judging from the bones that house it, was built for balance and the acuity necessary in a flying bird. *Protoavis* does appear from the description to have been more "birdlike" than *Archaeopteryx*—really.

Protoavis has not gone unchallenged. Suggestions have been made that *Protoavis* is not a bird at all, just a composite of bones of several different species thrown together in a paleontological potpourri. But what if *Protoavis* withstands the scrutiny and turns out to be a bird after all? What does that do to *Archaeopteryx?*

The answer is that it does absolutely nothing to the role of *Archaeopteryx* in the evolution of birds. The fact remains, whether *Protoavis* is a bird or not, that *Archaeopteryx* is primitive, the most primitive of known birds. It may be geologically younger than *Protoavis*, but it still resembles traditional dinosaurs more than *Protoavis* does. Species living today invariably exhibit a mosaic of primitive and advanced features in their anatomy. Lampreys have no jaws, for example. That is one of the most primitive features that any vertebrate could have, because vertebrates evolved from jawless ancestors, yet lampreys are alive today. That makes them a sort of living fossil, at least with respect to their lack of jaws. If birds had been around flying, happily flittering, for 75 million years before *Archaeopteryx* lived, it means that *Archaeopteryx* was a living fossil in its own day. From that we can make a prediction: The common ancestor of *Protoavis,* if it is truly a bird, and *Archaeopteryx* must have lived prior to *Protoavis,* around 220 million years ago.

That means there are still good fossils to find.

6

THE
CROCODILE OF
CARNIVAL

WHEN WE STEPPED from the Land Rover into the tall grass on the way to prospect the Dinosaur Beds for the first time, we met a snake. It could have been a bad omen. In Kenya, in the Tugen Hills, I once saw a spitting cobra spit at paleontologists walking along a path back to camp. It gave me the creeps. Bonnie once almost peed on a saw-scaled viper. That gave her the creeps. It is bad luck to have cobras and puff adders and vipers around.

The second thing we saw in the field in Malaŵi was a good omen. It was dinosaur bone—lots of it. That was exciting. Snakes or not, we were on the right track.

Just which fossil species might be found weathering out of the ground on any particular field trip is tough to say in advance, regardless of what one really wants to find. There are some things that are simply unpredictable. Sometimes what is found, while unexpected, is just as important as what is being sought. I guess it could be called the luck of the draw.

In the early stages of the Malaŵi Project my consuming goal was to find primitive mammals, contemporaries of the dinosaurs. Therefore the prime objective in the field was to locate concentrations of small bones in the rock that could then be sieved to obtain mammals, if they were there. Most of the fossils we were finding in the Dinosaur Beds at first were bone fragments of no value except as clues that we were in the right area. The smaller pieces of bone that were present in the rock did not come from small animals; rather they were only the fragmentary remains of a once-larger bone of a large animal. That is better than nothing.

The rainy seasons and the porous sandstone of the Dinosaur Beds were obviously unkind to fossils, particularly once they lay exposed on the surface of the ground through erosion. Occasionally one of the more durable fragments we found would be recognizable. These specimens, while not spectacular, were of some scientific value. We did not find more than one bone in a spot, and even when we dug down, we did not find better bones. It was getting to be discouraging.

Then on June 5 of the first field expedition, I needed to go to the bush. Seeking privacy, I searched the hidden nooks and crannies of the dinosaur-infested badlands until I found a tiny canyon with just the right ambience. A glint of white in the gully wall caught my eye. You never know when you might find something good. It can happen at the most awkward times.

What is that? I asked myself.

It's probably one of those damned weathered metamorphic pebbles, I thought, *but maybe not. Oh, hell, this can wait.*

Pants buttoned.

I reached over with my pick-mattock and hammered the powdery stone from the wall. I picked up the half that fell out.

It had teeth.

Oops!

Will Downs heard my whoops. He came at a run. I was overjoyed with the find of a skull, but mildly embarrassed, at least a little sheepish, at my lack of finesse.

"Okay, Jacobs. I'll take over from here."

I expected him to. He has good, sure hands, well adapted for salvaging and repairing broken fossils.

Will removed the remaining fragments from the wall. We began to look around. There was a piece of turtle. And there was another skull! It was about three inches long, the same size as the first, but not broken. Fantastic!

Over all it had been a great morning. I broke the first specimen, but I also found it. And clearly it was not damaged beyond repair. Moreover, we had a second skull. These were our first really good finds. The locality was designated CD-1. (The CD stands for "Cretaceous Dinosaur Beds." That is how geologic maps label the rocks.)

From what we could see in the field, we knew the two skulls were good specimens. But to heighten our anxiety, we could not tell exactly what they were. We were not even sure if they were the same kind of animal. They certainly were not dinosaurian. Even though they were only the size of a Chihuahua dog, they seemed a bit large for an early mammal, but who knew how big Cretaceous mammals were supposed to be in Africa?

We just could not see the skulls well enough to judge what they were because both were covered in a red crust. Only occasionally did white, friable bone peek through. They would have to be prepared in the laboratory, not fiddled with in the field. We would only be able to see them really well, free from their rock covering, in a few months. Nevertheless we knew we had a winner. These would be enough to make the project a success in its first year. That we knew even from what little we could see. No comparable skulls, and therefore no comparable animals, had ever been found in Africa before. These were unique. The only casualty of the day was my regularity.

The season continued another few weeks after the skulls were found. We stayed with the fieldwork and continued prospecting for a spot worth sieving. We continued the tedious exercise of examining every square inch of exposed rock for a pocket that might yield tiny bones. We continued to pick up fragments of dinosaurs. Two days after the skulls were found, Will came through. His eagle eye spotted part of a lizardlike thighbone, about half an inch long, weathered from a sandstone originally placed there as an old stream channel. The thighbone was not of a mammal, but it showed that small animal remains were preserved right there in that ancient streambed. And there was more bone still in the ground. We were elated again.

Carefully we began quarrying the channel, which we designated locality CD-4. We began to find the serrated steak-knife teeth of meat-eating dinosaurs. There were also lots of rounded hunks of bone, tumbled and smoothed by the river that had deposited the channel sands we were excavating. The sands were so coarse, and most of the bone so tumbled, that we began to wonder about the probability of finding the really small bones and teeth we were after. Perhaps they had been destroyed before they could be preserved. Luckily, about ten feet above us there were more bones, and in a muddier matrix. This we called CD-5. We bagged gunnysacks full of the fossiliferous sediments from both spots, eager to take it to water, where we could sieve for tiny bones with the eagerness, enthusiasm, and apprehension of forty-niners panning for gold.

Our first task was to get the bags of matrix back to the Land Rover. For this I wanted to hire some of the local villagers. The only positive response to our inquiries was from some of the village women. They were quite happy to balance the heavy bags on their heads, tote them to the vehicle, a distance of a couple of hundred yards over rough and broken ground, then return for another load. I paid by the bag.

When the men saw the women turn to, and that their industry really was being rewarded reasonably well considering the work involved, they wanted a piece of the action. The women, however, had already formed a monopoly and would admit no men. Although all the chatter was in Tumbuka, there seemed to be a lot of good-natured ribbing taking place.

Never since that day have women been available to work for us in the field. They do not seem to be allowed. Tradition insures that the men may do this sort of labor if they choose. Women work incredibly hard in Malaŵi, but now, perhaps because it is for wages, only men work for my project.

The gunnysacks full of sediment that the women carried to the Land Rover were driven to the Government Veterinary Farm in Karonga. We needed an appropriate place to sieve our samples because we did not want to contaminate the lake with the residue of kerosene-soaked dirt. We made arrangements with the farm to do the work where it could do no damage using a large sheet-metal fish tank, borrowed from the Government Fisheries Department, as a sieving trough. Chris Daborn, the expatriate veterinarian, agreed to let us have water from the farm at no charge. That was important because of the state of the Karonga Water Works in 1984. Water was not reliably delivered, so large storage cisterns were necessary for a consistent flow. The cistern we used at the farm was the residence of a large monitor lizard, a foot or so in length, which I discovered only after I filled the cistern and took a drink from the nozzle leading from it. The monitor scrambled out of the end of the hose where only a few seconds before I had had my mouth.

We had one problem with the sieving. There was no kerosene, or paraffin as it is called in Malaŵi, in which to soak our dirt. There was none whatsoever in all of northern Malaŵi. We needed to find a substitute. This we did in the form of diesel oil. It is an extremely unpleasant substance to work with in this way. We used plastic gloves to protect our hands, but after a few minutes they would begin to dissolve into a gummy wad. Despite that, we could get the job done.

So we set to the task of sieving. As sediment was screened and dried, we passed casual moments sorting through the coarser fraction of residue left in the screen-bottomed boxes. Jerry Britt, a graduate student, found a strange tooth. It was about an eighth of an inch long, with a big central cone and a ridge coming down from the tip. It looked a bit like early mammals known from elsewhere in the world, but not enough like them to demonstrate that it really was a mammal tooth. There was no indication of a good root on it, like mammals have, but then again, the base was broken. We finally concluded it came from a fish.

Other than that tooth and a few dinosaur-tooth scraps, we did not pick anything particularly good out of the wash while we were in the field. Patience is a virtue in paleontology. We shipped all our concentrate back to the States at the end of the field season, where Will separated the bone from the sand using heavy liquid chemicals. Then he picked through the bones and scraps. We got no mammals, but we did get several of those "fish" teeth, some frog bones, bits and pieces of other tiny bones, little crustaceans, and curiously enough a couple of seedlike structures—our only plant remains. The first screening campaign in the Dinosaur Beds was not a complete bust, but it was down at the bottom of the barrel for a guy who wanted mammals. Still, it provided a more complete first glance of the life of the Dinosaur Beds than we had gotten from picking bones off the surface of the ground.

When we returned home from the 1984 field season, Will not only sorted the concentrate but he began to prepare the skulls we had found at CD-1. He was working in his lab, in Arizona. Each day he sat staring through his microscope, scraping, gluing, cleaning with a variety of tools. I was in Dallas. As the skulls emerged from their shrouds of iron-stained crust, Will fed me blow-by-blow reports over the phone.

"Jacobs, this is weird. I can see part of another tooth. It has lots of cusps. This could be a mammal."

Next call: "Jacobs, the roots are all wrong. This is a fish."

Next call: "Jacobs, this is a reptile."

We were a bit like blind men trying to describe an elephant from the parts we were familiar with, but not really making much sense. As each little hunk of obscuring crust was scraped away to reveal the details of hidden bone, it became more obvious that whatever we had, it was bizarre. These were the skulls of the animals with the odd teeth we had found in the sieving. Of course we were pleased. We knew all along that searching an unknown time in Africa's past would very likely yield unpredictable finds. Here we had the first of them, and they were more strange than anything we could have expected.

Both skulls from that first season are little more than three inches long, so the animals themselves were not very large, maybe a foot in length. One skull is in better shape than the other, owing to the way I had found the first. The muzzle is short and deep, the back of the skull is broad. The nostrils are on the sides and close to the tip of the snout. The lower jaws are still connected to the skulls in both specimens.

The bones are pure white and very soft, which made it difficult and slow for Will to free them from their rocky crust. The enamel of the teeth is a muted beige color. The teeth seemed to be cuspy rounded "molars" in the back of the jaws, preceded by smaller, cuspy "premolars," then some large "canines," and finally some tiny teeth in the front of the upper jaw. For someone like me who was at the time most familiar with mammals, this arrangement of teeth is very mammallike, sort of raccoony. But this animal was not a mammal.

Will and I took the specimens to the annual meeting of the Society of Vertebrate Paleontology, where we had great fun showing them around. It was obvious to several people attending that this animal was a crocodile, a strange one, but a crocodile nevertheless. They were correct. It is clear from the arrangement of bones and holes in the skull and lower jaw. But such a weird crocodile!

CROCODILES and their kin comprise one of the two living groups of Ruling Reptiles, the Archosauria. The other living group is the birds. That is right. Among living organisms, crocodiles are more closely related to birds than to anything else. Birds and crocodiles share a common ancestor somewhere back in the murky, distant past that no other living animals shared with them. But they do have some extinct relatives to which they are closely related. There are the dinosaurs (from which the birds, but not the crocodiles, descended), the flying pterosaurs, which are not birds at all even though they could fly, and a number of lesser-known groups. In their primitive states all of these groups resemble each other much more than any one of them resembles anything else. Much of the resemblance lies in the arrangement of the bones in the skull. They are also characterized by conical teeth set in holes along the jaw, but without having good roots to hold them in the sockets. (Living birds, of course, have evolutionarily lost all their teeth, but some fossil species had them, as did their archosaurian ancestors.)

Because of these shared features, and a few more, all of them—crocs, birds, pterosaurs, and dinosaurs—are considered to be archosaurs. No animals without those specific characteristics of anatomy can belong to the club. It is only the separate paths of evolution followed subsequently by crocs, dinosaurs, birds, and pterosaurs that makes each of them appear so different from each other in our eyes. All of those groups, in sum the archosaurs, are distantly related to the lizards and snakes, and more distantly related still to the turtles.

CROCODILIANS have an excellent fossil record going way back a couple of hundred million years, but there are only three groups still around. The first group is exemplified by the Nile crocodile, even now a common animal in many parts of Africa. There are also crocodiles in Australia and New Guinea, Asia, and America. Some inhabit salt water. There are dwarf crocodiles in West Africa. All of these are close relatives of the Nile crocodile. Then there are the alligators, now including the American alligator of the Gulf Coastal states, its cousin, the Chinese alligator, and the caimans of South America. They have blunt snouts compared with the Nile crocodile. The third group contains only the long-snouted gharial of the Indian region. All of the living species of all three groups are carnivorous and semiaquatic, meaning that they lead an amphibious life-style, hanging out in the water of swamps, estuaries, rivers, or lakes and then crawling up on land as urges and instincts take them to bask or reproduce. Among the twenty-two living species there is quite a variety of head shapes. Alligators have rather blunt snouts, while crocodile snouts are more narrow, and the gharial has the narrowest snout of all. The presence of long, thin, narrow snouts in aquatic animals indicates a preference for a fishy diet. The gharial has a menu more restricted to finny prey than do crocodiles or alligators.

All of the living crocodile clan share some important similarities in their anatomy that are different from some fossil crocs. For instance, in all the living species, the vertebrae join together in ball-and-socket joints. Each vertebra looks kind of like those in the tail of titanosaurid sauropods, but the resemblance is certainly separately evolved, and in the case of the crocs, ball-and-socket vertebrae are not limited to the tail. Living crocs also have a hard, bony secondary palate—a shelf of bone forming the roof of the mouth and separating the nasal passages from the mouth cavity. It is an important structure for crocs to have. The living species, with their nostrils on the top of their snouts, can hold their noses out of the water to breathe, yet their mouths can be open and full of water or food. Mammals, including us, have a similar bony palate, which serves the same function as that in crocs, walling off the air passages from the mouth. Crocs have certainly evolved in some interesting ways, as we can tell simply from looking at the living species.

But to the diversity of living species of crocs can be added their very rich fossil record and its 200-million-year history. Not all fossil crocodilians had complete bony palates or ball-and-socket vertebrae; in fact most of them did not. Some of them were not even amphibious. Some were strictly land-dwellers. Others were strictly marine, their tails evolving to look and function like those of sharks and their legs evolving into finlike paddles.

The structure of the secondary palate in various species is particularly important in deciphering the evolutionary history of crocs. In the most primitive group of crocodilian species, the secondary palate is not at all well developed, so the internal nares, the holes on the inside that are connected by the air passage to the nose holes on the outside of the skull, are way up at the front of the roof of the mouth. There is no secondary palate to speak of, and that is the primitive condition. The next grade of structure in the evolution of the crocodilian secondary palate is characterized by the internal nares lying quite far back and the air passage extending for a longer distance through the snout. In the most advanced evolutionary grade the internal nares are way back in the skull and the secondary palate is complete. Crocodilians with the more advanced grade of palate structure also have ball-and-socket vertebrae.

From Malaŵi we have skulls of the little croc (I will refer to it as the Malaŵi croc, for want of a better term), which shows it to be of the second, or intermediate, grade of crocodilian evolution with respect to the construction of the secondary palate. On top of that, rather than being a flattish skull, like Nile crocodiles and alligators, the Malaŵi croc skull is deeper. The nostrils are not placed on the top of the snout for snorkeling in water. Instead the nasal bones go forward to a point at the end of the snout and the nostrils lie below them.

But it was not the snout or even the secondary palate that caught my interest first. There was something else about the mouth of the Malaŵi croc that intrigued me more. This was not the musky, tusky orifice a crocodile should have. It was different. Having studied rats and other mammals for quite some time, one glance at that croc's teeth told me it was far out of the ordinary. This croc moved its lower jaw forward when it chewed. But how could that be? Modern crocs do not chew. They rip a hunk of flesh from a carcass and fling it down their throats, no fuss, no muss, no bother. But they do not chew.

The teeth of the living Nile crocodile are basically cones. Very sharp cones. Their jaw joints are hinges. They open and they close by rotating about a fixed point on the skull, snapping the jaws tight like a vicious pair of scissors. There is no motion at all at the joint, except the opening and closing of the jaw. Even we humans can slide our jaws around a bit at the joint, just try it. Crocodiles cannot do that. Their sharp teeth and fixed jaw joints are superbly adapted for grabbing and holding prey struggling in panic.

The diet of the Nile crocodile changes with the size, and consequently the age, of the animal. Younger and smaller individuals take a greater proportion of insects. Larger crocs eat fish, frogs, turtles, waterfowl, whatever they can catch. The big ones can grab a drinking antelope by the snout, haul it into the water, drown it, leave it to putrefy, let the meat soften and tenderize, then pull it apart and eat it. Crocs are mean. Even today they are a danger to people along many rivers and lakes in Africa. Every year several human beings die from croc attacks.

Of all the many, many different kinds of crocs, living and extinct, nearly all of them have teeth more or less like those of the Nile crocodile. A little more blunt, or a little more sharp, or a little more squished from side to side, but most all crocs have basically the same kind of conical teeth. And the jaw joint is the same in almost all of them too.

So the Malaŵi croc is strange for a crocodile. It has the head of a crocodile, but not so flat, and its teeth are strange, and its jaw joint is strange. The jaw joint has a long surface that allows the lower jaw to slide forward as the mouth is closed. Its upper ''molar'' teeth have a big central cusp whose point leans toward the back of the throat. A small but sharp ridge runs backward from the tip. Tiny cusps go along the edge of the base. Lower ''molars'' are almost exactly like the uppers, but with one big exception: The tip of the big cusp, and the ridge that comes off of it, point toward the front of the jaw rather than the back as in the uppers. It is as if a mirror were held to the back of an upper tooth, the mirror image being a lower tooth.

One glance at that and it is easy to conclude that those teeth had to work against each other. They did not grind enamel against enamel as mammals like you do while chewing, but the teeth did move toward each other as the beast chewed. The jaw moved not like a pair of scissors, but as the mouth closed, the jaw moved forward. This croc chewed from back to front, slicing and breaking food between its teeth. Rats chew from back to front. But self-respecting crocs should not.

The next step was to understand in even more detail the mechanism of how modern crocodiles chew in order to apply that knowledge to understanding the Malaŵi croc more thoroughly. It was also necessary to unravel which, if any, of the known species of crocs, living or extinct, our animal from Malaŵi was most closely related to. This was a formidable task because of the widespread fossil record of crocs. My friend Jim Clark was already an expert on crocodiles and their fossils. He had expressed an interest in the Malaŵi croc, so I invited him on board for the initial study. He would provide the perspective of his experience as a dedicated croc jock. The expertise he brought gave depth to the unfolding story of the unique animal we had.

Jim knew about the anatomy of modern crocodiles, particularly how the chewing muscles work, where they attach on the skull, and in which direction they pull when the jaw closes. It became clear to him that the anatomy of the Malaŵi croc jaw joint worked with the muscles that close the mouth to allow the lower jaw to slide forward when the mouth shuts. That agrees well with the interpretation made from the shape of the teeth.

The reason the jaws of other crocs do not slide is that there is a buttress of bone on the lower jaw that hooks around back of the joint surface of the skull. If that buttress were removed, the jaw could slide. The Malaŵi croc does not have it. The jaw could slide both ways, toward the front and toward the back, but we knew from the shape of the teeth that, even though the lower jaw moves back and forth, the power stroke was in the forward direction as the mouth closed. Food in the mouth would bank against the upper teeth and be crushed and slivered as the lower jaw slid toward the front end of the head.

Thus, the shape of the teeth, the anatomy of the jaw joint, and the function of muscles in living crocodiles all helped us to interpret the way this fossil species, 100 million years old, ate its food. The only living reptile whose lower jaw moves in this same way is the lizardlike tuatara that today inhabits small islands off New Zealand. It is not a crocodile. The muscles that move the tuatara's jaw forward are anatomically the same as those that move the Malaŵi croc's jaw. Rodents, whose jaws also move fore and aft, do it with different muscles. The similarity of chewing motions in the Malaŵi croc, the tuatara, and some rodents was evolved independently. This phenomenon, whereby an adaptive feature evolves separately in distinct evolutionary lineages, is called convergence. The evolution of a secondary palate in crocodilians and in mammals is another example of convergence. So is the ball-and-socket vertebrae of advanced crocodilians and in the tail of titanosaurid sauropods. The similarity among species caused by convergence is real but superficial, and it does not reflect a close relationship or common ancestry. Convergent evolution reflects a likeness in function and adaptation, not heritage. It is body form at work with life-style and ecology. The Malaŵi croc is a great example of it.

Jim also pointed out to us that, after all, the Malaŵi croc is not alone in the crocodile world in having an elongated surface on the jaw joint that would allow some movement. There is also a fossil species in South America that shares the same characteristic feature. It, too, is Cretaceous in age, but Late Cretaceous, a bit younger than the Malaŵi croc. It is called *Notosuchus*. There are other features besides the jaw joint in common between the two, for instance the way the snout is built. Our specimens from Malaŵi are not the same species, or even genus, but are in the same family, the Notosuchidae, as the South American form. The development of the chewing cusps on the teeth set the Malaŵi croc apart, uniquely, from every other croc in the world, even its closest South American fossil relatives.

This understanding of the relationships of the Malaŵi croc, and the distribution of its family members in time and space is really exciting. All along we had been interested in the Gondwana connection between Africa and South America. Now we had a family of crocodiles common to both providing further testimony of the influence of global geography on life in the Age of Reptiles. Moreover, *Notosuchus* from South America and the Malaŵi croc are different enough from each other to make the story even more interesting. Their common ancestor had to live prior to the Malaŵi croc, and it is not likely to have been exactly like either the African or South American form in its anatomy. It is still waiting to be discovered, somewhere in Gondwana.

The "mammalian" features of the Malaŵi croc, that is, its complicated, cuspy teeth and the complex way it moved its jaw in processing food, begs the question of its outcompeting mammals for a place in the African ecosystem during the Age of Reptiles. No mammals have yet been found in the Dinosaur Beds. But on the other hand, the sample of small animal fossils of any kind is sparse in Malaŵi. It is reasonable to expect mammals to turn up as more and more small fossils are found. It would be unfounded speculation at this time to suggest that mammals are absent from the Dinosaur Beds because the mammal niche was filled by the Malaŵi croc. Nevertheless the notion of competition between the two is not so farfetched as to be completely beyond consideration. After all, the Malaŵi croc did evolve convergently with mammals.

It is very likely that the Malaŵi croc processed its food more, and in a more sophisticated way, than other crocodiles. It chewed, but it did not chew exactly like mammals because the teeth do not seem to come in contact with each other, as happens in most mammals. But what did the Malaŵi croc chew? What was its diet?

All living species of crocodiles eat flesh of one sort or another. No crocodile species is known to be herbivorous. Small, young Nile crocodiles eat more insects and, as they grow larger, take progressively larger percentages of vertebrate prey, such as fish, frogs, birds, and mammals. I do not know at this point exactly what the Malaŵi croc ate, but it almost certainly was not a herbivore, based on the dietary habits of living crocs if nothing else. It is a small croc, probably not over a foot in total length, so it could not have taken large prey. Frankly I doubt whether it was overly particular about what it ate, pursuing more or less whatever it could catch. I suspect it may have eaten insects and spiders, maybe crayfish, crabs and other crustaceans, thin-shelled snails, and perhaps small frogs and the occasional fish caught along a riverbank. I suspect its foraging was more likely done on land than in water, perhaps occasionally in the shallows and backwaters of a stream or pond. It did not necessarily have the same hunting tactics as modern crocs. In fact it probably did not. The Malaŵi croc may have been a less stealthy, if more active, forager. Could this kind of animal have competed for the same food with early mammals?

Mammals are very rare in the Early Cretaceous. They are not particularly abundant anywhere in the world, certainly not as abundant as mammal fossils become after dinosaurs go extinct. Most are quite tiny, about the size of small mice. Those mammals that are known from the Early Cretaceous are either specialized herbivores or they have teeth suitable for eating a variety of small animal prey—they are carnivorous in the sense that they would eat whatever little molluscs, arthropods, or vertebrates they might catch. In general the carnivorous mammals known from the fossil record appear more diverse on a global scale than the herbivores during Cretaceous times. There seem to be more species of them. The diet of carnivorous early mammals, some of them anyway, might overlap a great deal with what is suggested for the Malaŵi croc.

In the fossil community represented in the Dinosaur Beds, I would expect to find both herbivorous and insectivorous mammals if the fossil record were complete. It would be unjustified to attribute the lack of all mammal fossils to competition with the Malaŵi croc, one reason being that there would be little competition, for food anyway, between the croc and plant-eating mammals. Nevertheless the Malaŵi croc might overlap to some extent in its habitat and ecological requirements with early carnivorous mammals, and therefore I do not completely rule out competition with them.

Of particular interest in this regard is the description of a new Early Cretaceous mammal from Brazil, *Candidodon itapecuruense*. This species is known only from a few small isolated teeth. What makes it so interesting is that the teeth appear to be quite similar to the Malaŵi croc's. Either *Candidodon* is a croc in disguise, which would not be overly surprising now that we know about Malaŵi, or it is a particularly striking example of evolutionary convergence. Either way, it provides an important direction for the study of Gondwana faunas.

There is still much we do not know about the Malaŵi croc. Our initial study investigated only the skull and teeth, and even those require more detailed study. In the 1987 field season graduate student John Congleton found a spot with half a dozen or so of the little crocs in it across the gully from CD-1. Another skull was found in the 1989 season. Now we have about a dozen really good specimens. There are six fine skulls, all with the lower jaws attached. We also have some skeletons with the bones still joined together more or less as they were in life. Some of these show the thin bony plates that armored the animal's back, similar to the condition in modern crocs.

All of the good specimens come from a small area of just a few square yards at CD-6 and across the gully. The skulls and skeletons occur in a coarse red sand with pebbles and nodules in it here and there. In fact, the croc occurs at several other localities, but just as a few bits and pieces, or single teeth. All of the really good ones are from that single spot. Some of the skeletons seem to be scrunched up, as if they were lying in a burrow and had gotten buried. Only detailed study will tell us for sure if the Malaŵi croc lived in burrows, but it is certain now that the occurrence of complete skeletons of the croc, all in the same area, with no other species of fossils to speak of found with them, is very different from the other fossil localities in the Dinosaur Beds. I think it owes its existence to the way the animal lived. Maybe its behavior in life controlled its preservation after death.

We shall learn more about how the Malaŵi croc lived when the anatomy of its skeleton is more thoroughly studied. Already some interesting features are coming to light. For instance, it looks as if this creature might have held its head up, as if you held your hand horizontally, palm down, forearm vertical, and your wrist bent at a ninety-degree angle. At least the parts of the neck vertebrae to which the appropriate muscles and ligaments would attach, and the position of the hole in the back of the skull where the spinal cord passes, suggest that the posture of the Malaŵi croc is not that of the Nile crocodile. And why should it be?

So the studies will continue. Should the reader be wondering what the Malaŵi croc is formally called, I must leave you hanging. There is one study, however, that definitely must be forthcoming. That is the one in which the Malaŵi croc is given a name.

I have some very happy feelings toward the Malaŵi croc. It was our first big strike in the Dinosaur Beds. It is clearly unique in the world. Its family is known from what is now Africa and from South America, possibly at the same time as the Malaŵi croc was living in the area that was to become the Dinosaur Beds, and certainly in geologically younger South American rocks. Its anatomy makes my imagination run wild. Just for fun, think of it holding its head up, searching for a bug (Figure 34). If it saw one hop, it dashed in for the kill, puncturing the tough morsel with its pointed canines, masticating the chitinous exoskeleton with cuspy teeth—teeth wielded by its piston jaw, forcefully punching forward, then rapidly pulling back. If it sensed danger, it dashed for its burrow. It wore a crocodilian coat of armor, but it behaved like a mongoose, a reptilian meerkat. It is almost like a small mammal in a crocodile costume, like a kid dressed up for a show. Its costume is as striking as any one might expect to see at Rio de Janeiro's Carnival in Brazil, where its closest relatives lived. The Malaŵi croc might have looked good among the fruit on Carmen Miranda's hat, going for insects that would be attracted to the bright colors—it is just 100 million years too old!

The Malaŵi croc would have been a good find by itself, but it is a part of a fauna, a community of animals. And it is not the only crocodilian member of the community preserved in the Dinosaur Beds. There are two other species of crocs as well, both known only from teeth. One, the more poorly

FIGURE 34: *The Malaŵi crocodile. This new species of small crocodile is shown in a gallery forest, with one croc rearing to capture a dragonfly lunch, another peering from its burrow. The frog looks jealous of the crocodile's success with the insect.*

represented of the two, has nondescript conical teeth. The other is represented by small, blunt teeth that are flattened from side to side but not really sharp. These teeth, like those of the Malaŵi croc, can also be traced to relatives in South America.

The little flattened teeth belong to a genus of crocodile called *Araripesuchus*. It has two species, the first one described from South America, and represented by two skulls and a skeleton. The other species was first discovered in Niger in West Africa. It is known from one skull. Isolated teeth of *Araripesuchus* also occur in Cameroon, West Africa, but they cannot be attributed to one or the other of the named species with any certainty. Both species are about the same age as the fossils from the Dinosaur Beds. With only isolated teeth from Malaŵi, little more can be done than to suggest that *Araripesuchus* is present, but that is an important statement to be able to make.

Araripesuchus, judging from the skulls that are known, is similar to the Malaŵi croc with respect to the development of the secondary palate. Both are about the middle grade of evolution, with the internal nares not so far back as in modern living crocodiles and alligators. The external nares in *Araripesuchus,* as in the Malaŵi croc, are not on the top of the snout but rather on the sides of the tip, and the nasal bones are long and pointed. The head is deep in both, not flat as in alligators. The teeth in the two are obviously different, so they did not eat the same way or possibly not even the same things. *Araripesuchus* does not have the long jaw articulation of the Malaŵi croc that allows it to chew from back to front. *Araripesuchus* is stuck with the scissorlike jaw closure of most other crocs. The vertebral centra are similar and primitive in the two, but the neural spines in the neck appear to be much longer in the Malaŵi croc, and the hole at the back of the skull for the spinal column is farther under in the Malaŵi croc, rather than more out the back of the skull as in *Araripesuchus*.

Araripesuchus, like the Malaŵi croc, was better adapted for a more fully terrestrial way of life than for a semiaquatic one such as the Nile crocodile has. That is clear from its hind limbs, which are longer than the forelimbs and less sprawling, more underneath the animal, than those in modern crocs. The shape of the head, deep with nostrils below the end, is not like that of semiaquatic crocs either.

The South American species, *Araripesuchus gomesii,* comes from one of the world's great fossil areas, from the Araripe Basin of Brazil. Thousands upon thousands upon thousands of fossils are known from there. Far and away most of the vertebrates known from the Basin are fish. That is because the rocks of the Araripe Basin are lithified sediments deposited in a great lake, one that persisted for several, if not tens of, millions of years. The lake apparently underwent at least one period when it dried out, and toward the end of its life the sea transgressed far enough inland to reach the lake. And along with the seawater came a few marine organisms.

At the time the Araripe lake came into existence, Africa and South America were still joined in the supercontinent of Gondwana. The separation had begun at the southern end of Africa, but the two continents were still connected through Brazil and several western African countries, most notably Cameroon. Lake Araripe does not appear to have been a deep rift-valley lake like Lake Malaŵi. Nevertheless it owed its existence to downwarping caused by the same structural features that would eventually lead to the formation of the South Atlantic, even if Lake Araripe was off to the side from the main rift. And it was deep enough at times to be stratified and to develop sterile bottom waters with no dissolved oxygen left in the water. Sometimes evaporation exceeded the inflow of fresh water, causing crystals of salt to grow in the sediments.

The rivers draining the interior of Gondwana, some of them at least, must have flowed into the widening gulf formed as southern Africa moved away from southern South America. It may have been reminiscent of the Colorado River flowing into the Gulf of California. The rift valley that would ultimately pry Africa and South America completely apart extended northward from the ancient gulf between the southern extremities of South America and Africa, then it branched. The climate in central Gondwana was arid. The place was close to being a desert. Yet there was enough water from rainfall to collect into lakes. Just as in the Great Basin of the American West today, for some of the central Gondwana lakes, notably Araripe, there were no outlets. Think of Great Salt Lake. Better yet, think of Lake Chad in Africa, quite solidly in the middle of a near-desert environment, yet permanently containing water, supporting an abundance of fish and other aquatic life, and fluctuating in size with the cycles of rainfall. Moreover, the location of Lake Chad, out in the exact middle of nowhere, in the middle of Africa, was dictated by geological structures that are genetically related to the opening of the South Atlantic, and therefore are cousins to the structures that formed Lake Araripe so long ago. The area of Araripe has undergone subsequent Earth movements and climatic change that have transformed the lake sediments into an eroding plateau and transformed Brazil into the lush green land that it is today. But it was not always like that. Lake Chad has not always been like it is now, either, but it has had a different geological history from Araripe.

Most of the really good fossils from Araripe are preserved in concretions—masses of limestone chemically precipitated from water around dead organisms. Had the organism not been there, the limestone may not have come out of solution and the concretion may not have formed. But because the concretions did form, they preserve animals in exquisite detail. The concretions can be plopped into a bath of acid and super skeletons will yawn into the light. They are truly magnificent fossils. The acid-preparation technique has only been used on them for a short time, but fossils in the Araripe concretions have been known for over a century and a half. Virtually every museum that is serious about fossils has some, and every rock shop has one or two for sale.

The concretions form as a reaction between the chemistry of the lake water and the organic matter of a dead organism. Thus they are only found in strata that reflect a suitable environmental chemistry. Given the varied history of Lake Araripe, only some of the strata contain concretions, but luckily many of the other strata also preserve fossils, even if they are not so spectacular.

The fish fauna from Lake Araripe is tremendous. There are at least twenty-one different genera. Virtually all of them are known from excellent complete skeletons. There is a kind of primitive shark. There is a ray. There is an abundance of bony fish. There are even two kinds of coelacanth, lobe-finned fishes that are distantly related to the first amphibians that came out of the water to conquer the land. Strangely enough, like Lake Malaŵi, Lake Araripe lacks lungfish, even though they are known to have inhabited Gondwana at the time, and as in Africa, there are lungfish living in South America today.

Besides fish there is a huge list of other species. There are vast numbers of insects—cockroaches, mayflies, dragonflies, termites, crickets, katydids, leafhoppers, grasshoppers, wasps, and more. There are spiders. There are shrimp and crabs. The diversity of animals is amazing. There are plants too. There are ferns and conifers and a variety of flowering-plant pollen. What Lake Araripe does not have is an abundance or diversity of land-dwelling vertebrates, and the reasons for that should be obvious: Unless a carcass ended up in the middle of the lake, it could not be preserved.

Araripe is an important site in paleontology because of its location, next to the place where Gondwana broke apart, and its age. In all probability it straddles the time interval when Africa and South America made their final separation. Therefore it provides us an absolute baseline of what to expect in both continents when they set out on their individual paths of history. There may have been geographic and ecological variation away from the center of the continents, but the area around Araripe was the same for both. It would be wonderful if there were more sites like Araripe, perhaps a few places directly comparable to it. But there are not, so we use what we have.

Some of the fish so beautifully represented in Brazil are known from less complete and less numerous specimens found in rocks of a similar age in Africa. The similarities with fossils in West Africa—Niger and Cameroon— are particularly strong, as you might expect in rocks of the same age that were so close together at the time they were formed. The similarities are not limited to fish. *Araripesuchus,* the crocodilian, is one of several animals known from both continents, but best known from Araripe. There is the turtle *Araripemys.* And there are frogs from both continents.

The flying vertebrates preserved at Araripe are exceedingly interesting, although none is preserved, or preserved so well, in Africa. There is a bird feather. There is also a mind-boggling diversity of pterosaurs, flying rep- tiles—archosaurs more precisely—related to dinosaurs and crocodiles. Their wing membranes, covered with little hairy projections, were supported by an immensely elongated forth digit, the ring finger. They were almost certainly fish-eaters. They congregated around Lake Araripe like terns and petrels over a bay, soaring, swooping, and dipping fish from the surface waters of the lake. There are no less than fourteen species found at Araripe. The really endearing thing about them is the unreal shape of their light-boned skulls. They have long snouts, but some of them have bizarre bony sails on their noses. These supposedly helped them cut through the water as they dove to catch a silvery, slithery fish.

There are a few dinosaur fragments from Araripe, but not many, and none of those that have been studied is particularly diagnostic. One has been called an ornithischian, and that would not be unreasonable considering that *Ouranosaurus* lived just across the rift in Niger and Cameroon. There is at least one theropod, again not surprising, and a couple of other specimens needing preparation or under study.

If we take things at face value, Lake Araripe was a large body of water in a flat, dry country. The land was open, the view unobstructed by dense vegetation (Figure 35). Low-growing ferns, horsetails, bushy shrubs, and occasional primitive flowering plants covered the ground. Herbaceous conifers grew on salty flats along the shore. All but the ferns and horsetails are only distantly related to living species. Trees such as monkey puzzles and other conifers that have no living descendants dotted the landscape and clumped like junipers on gentle slopes.

The waters of the lake teemed and its surface rippled with fish chasing mayfly larvae and shrimp. Crabs scavenged the shallows near the shoreland, but not the depths where there was no oxygen. A plethora of soaring pterosaurs chose the fish menu from their vantage in the air. They nested among the distant cliffs of hills and mountains associated with the rift valley and its structures, some of them visible on the horizon, and from which the pterosaurs launched themselves to fly and to glide with ease on thermal currents. Birds skittered in the scrubby trees nearby. Turtles and amphibious crocodiles sunned themselves. *Araripesuchus,* the small and agile terrestrial crocodile, pounced. Frogs hopped away, escaping among the ferns and horsetails, bouncing in the tubs that were dinosaur footprints, made when they trampled along the water's edge as they came to drink.

Compare that imaginary vision to the Dinosaur Beds of Malaŵi (see Figure 30 in Chapter 4), the same age, but way across the African portion of the Gondwana continent. The climate was seasonally arid, but not so hostile. The land was rough and broken, verdant in the rainy season, less so when it was dry. There were mountains nearby. Thick gallery forests of monkey puzzles and their coniferous relatives lined the permanent streams. The surrounding woodlands were open but grew more densely up hillside canyons. The open ground sported a cover of low shrubs, tiny flowers, and ferns. Cycads and similar-looking plants, distinctive with round, stumpy stalks topped with long, palmlike crowns of dark greenery, filled the intermediate heights between the herbage and the trees. In the rainy season water flowed briskly down from the mountain flanks in the channels of intermittent streams. Horsetails and ferns grew along the water's edge. Fish occasionally fought the currents. There was no lake, so there were fewer pterosaurs in the sky. But there were frogs and turtles along the banks, and they, too, like their cousins at Araripe, found comfort in the backwater ponds formed from dinosaur footprints.

FIGURE 35: A view of the Cretaceous lake at Araripe, Brazil. Lake Araripe was in the middle of a dry, flat country—the Gondwanan interior. It had no outlet. Its shores were dotted with horsetails, ferns, conifers, and occasionally a small flowering plant. Frogs, turtles, and crocodiles inhabited the shores. Dinosaurs visited to drink and left their footprints in the soft earth. The waters teemed with fish. Here a pterosaur is eating the coelacanth AXELRODICHTHYS.

Through the greenery, crashing this way and that, a family group of Malaŵi-saurus browsed, each stopping every few feet to pluck the foliage that grew in the easily accessible hemisphere around the front end of its body. Malaŵi-saurus used its long neck to take its head to the food. Stegosaurs munched, too, but their heads were carried lower to the ground and their necks were not so long. They ate the shorter plants. All of them, sauropod and stegosaur, were watched. When they walked too close to a colony of the mammallike Malaŵi crocs, the furtive little beasts took shelter in their burrows. When the dinosaurs passed by, when danger passed, out popped the crocs, searching anew for bugs (see Figure 34). The dinosaurs were being watched by something else as well. Imagine a young diplodocid on the other side of the river being stalked by a theropod.

Could that have been the way it was? Are those images of Araripe and the Dinosaur Beds realistic? That I do not know. We may never know. But they are reasonable pictures, given the information we have. That information is not extensive. There are some fossil leaves and pollen from Araripe. Additional leaves and pollen are known from nearby Cameroon. There are only a few tiny fruit or seedlike plant fossils from Malaŵi, and we have no idea what the plants that produced them looked like. Other inferences as to what the Cretaceous vegetation was like in Malaŵi or Araripe come from a general overview of the plant-fossil record. We have a pretty good idea of what was growing on the planet, and we have some idea of the distribution of species in different climates and in some ecological contexts. The reconstructed images of Araripe and the Dinosaur Beds are just best guesses, but they are consistent with the data, and they can be corrected when they need to be. For now, that is how I see them. To place them in perspective, these reconstructions should be viewed as hypothetical frames in a film of time. They are different from that presented for Tendaguru in Chapter 1. Tendaguru had different animals, apparently across the board, although some of them are grossly similar to those found in Malaŵi. The plants were different. At Tendaguru, 145 million years ago, there was probably a greater variety of coniferous plants. There were no flowering plants that we know of. In younger times, in the Late Cretaceous, flowering plants were on the rise. The pivotal time for them seems to be the Early Cretaceous, the time represented by Araripe and the Dinosaur Beds. Along with the abundance of flowering plants, the dinosaurs of the Late Cretaceous were different from earlier times.

No matter how correct or incorrect the vision of Malaŵi's Dinosaur Beds might be, no matter how precise and accurate the reconstruction, the time preserved in the Dinosaur Beds was only a temporary phase in the evolution of life. Every time interval becomes the next, and as time changes, things are no longer the same.

7

FOR
ONE
TOOTH

MY FIRST EXPEDITION to Malaŵi was completed. We had found no mammals, which is what we were primarily after on that trip. Luckily the mammallike crocodile more than made up for our shortfall in terms of excitement and scientific interest. The Malaŵi croc told us about a species, interesting in its own right, that was around at the time the very ancient ancestors of living mammals emerged. But early mammals in Africa were turning out to be frustrating and elusive. I did not get one in Kenya, where I first looked. That was strike one. I did not get one in Malaŵi, where I continued the search. That was strike two. Even worse, the prospects of ever getting tiny mammals from the sandy rocks of the Dinosaur Beds did not look promising. Nevertheless I still wanted to find them somewhere. I was more convinced than ever, stubborn in my opinion, that knowing about them was important for knowing about the mammals of the modern world, and that includes us. It was important to find them. If I was to avoid striking out altogether, my search for early mammals in Africa would have to go farther afield.

In January 1986 I had the opportunity to go to Cameroon in francophone West Africa (Figure 36). My French is abysmal, I am not proud to say, but what a great opportunity this was. A multinational project composed of

FIGURE 36: *Location map of Africa with Cameroon stippled. The Koum Basin is below the kink to the south of Lake Chad. The dinosaurs of the Koum Basin lived on the eastern side of the South America–Africa rift at the time (probably) that Lake Araripe existed on the western side of the rift.*

Cameroonians, French, and my old buddies from Pakistan and Kenya days, mainly British and American, was extending the search for more fossil evidence of human evolution. Virtually nothing of significance to that issue was known from all of West Africa. Nor were there any bona fide gorilla or chimpanzee fossils known from anywhere. The fossil record of the ape and human divergence needed work. Without doubt, West African fossils, if they could be found, would be very important for understanding the evolutionary history of the great apes and humans over the past twenty million years. This was too good a project for me to pass up, even though my major research interest had begun to shift to the much older rocks of the Cretaceous. Besides, Cameroon was the final point of contact between South America and Africa. If things got slow in the younger rocks, maybe I could get a peek at the ones that recorded the ancient rifting on the east side of the Atlantic, perhaps I might even find some fossils, maybe even early mammals. The other members of the expedition were agreeable to this; they could see the significance of the older rocks also. So off I went to Cameroon.

The name Cameroon has always sounded un-African to me in the same sort of way that Côte d'Ivoire, or Ivory Coast as we used to say, does not sound African. They do not because the words are not African. Cameroon is a European word. In the fifteenth century the Portuguese sailed into the estuary of the Wouri River and found it teeming with shrimp. The name of the country derives from the Portuguese word for "prawns."

The northern half of Cameroon, where most of the country's game resides, is also the best place to search for fossils. It is arid, but not so dry as northern Kenya. It, too, has a large lake in the north, just as Kenya has. Cameroon barely reaches to Lake Chad, a lake as we saw in Chapter 6, which has no outlet. The Bénoué River, full of hippos, flows across the countryside to the south of Lake Chad to its confluence with the Niger. The Bénoué provides a bounty of fresh fish, and it supplies water for small truck gardens, the products of which make their way to the bustling markets of northern Cameroon. The Niger debauches into the Ocean at the Gulf of Guinea, where its delta forms the eastern edge of the Bight of Benin.

Back in the north, the roads leading to the fossil grounds from our staging area at the École de Faune, the school of wildlife, in the dust-bowl town of Garoua are littered with army check posts. The soldiers are usually drunk on Beaufort or Trente-trois, the local beer, and they can be—like to be—rather frightening. They seem to enjoy it. Glaring through squinting, soggy eyes in the brilliant African sunlight, they fish for bribes, usually halfheartedly. Clutching their weapons, they scrutinize clearance papers from a discerning if illiterate perspective. They examine the gear in the back of the Toyota. Mostly they just cast glances from under heavy lids toward the rear window. Occasionally their clammy fingers, like the tentacles of an octopus, explore our goods as if searching for a valuable morsel. It is a chilling experience. But soon the soldiers' games are over and the check posts are in the rearview mirror.

Most of the people in this area of northern Cameroon are Fulbe. The men dress in flowing *kanzus* and cover their heads with embroidered *tarbooshes*. Their religion is Islam. They are farmers, growing cotton for export, millet, peanuts, tomatoes, and okra. And they are herders. Their cattle are long-horned zebu. Some of the men, especially the older ones, wear wide-brimmed straw hats with pinnacled crowns over their *tarbooshes*, tied under their chins. They greet each other enthusiastically, *"Jaam, jaam."* The more nomadic and traditional of the Fulbe, the Mbororo, may tattoo their faces, even today. Most men carry straight daggers. Leather is dyed purple, a remnant of the crafts of ancient Timbuktu, and worked into scabbards or into pouches to hold crystals of galena—lead ore—to be ground into black powder and used to accent the eyes of women. Strangely, in the far north, around Maroua, there is a tradition of horsemanship and swords. It, too, is a remnant of an ancient culture. It seems out of place, but in that part of tropical Africa horses can survive disease.

In the markets the people of northern Cameroon bargain with unsurpassed verve. Herbalists, experts in traditional native medicine, sell pharmacopoeial tree bark and strange animal parts, such as hyaena skin or hedgehog fur or bat wings or porcupine quills. Leather-covered amulets, each containing the jaw of a rat or the tooth of a mongoose, or perhaps a special seed, are sold to ward off evil. Traditional medicine and other practices are slow to be replaced, even when it would be to the benefit of the people. Livingstone, early in his career, gave up most of his medical work, except for severe cases, because he could not argue in nineteenth-century African logic against medicine men and the traditional belief in rainmaking. The natives insisted that there was no more connection between his medicine and the curing of disease than between their medicine and rain. He argued that rain falling after their ceremonies, as it occasionally did, was only coincidence and not due to their practices. They argued that he could show no better for his medicine. Sometimes rain did not come; sometimes patients died. There was no difference. Livingstone gave up the argument and concentrated on saving souls. Traditional medicine is still practiced.

Shops and kiosks in Cameroon are small and dingy. All of them carry stocks of tinned sardines, pilchards, and Maji, a soy sauce–like food additive. The larger and fancier shops are run by Lebanese traders. The Fali come down from the hills occasionally to visit the market and to buy at the shops. They are people of another, much more traditional look. Superficially they appear to my Western eye like the Masai of Kenya, only shorter in stature. They represent what is left of the tribes who lived here before the Fulbe migrated into the area and supplanted them.

THE CAMEROON Project started a year before I joined it. The French contingent was led by Michel Brunet from Poitiers, a suave continental with fieldwork experience in Iraq and Afghanistan. He is a specialist on mammals. With him was Abel Brillanceau, a registered wine taster and chain smoker of Gauloise cigarettes, an engineer and geologist. He managed vehicle logistics for the project and helped out with the geology. Jean Dejax was the tall, slim paleobotanist with a good sense of humor. Sevket Sen was a native Turk, but a naturalized French citizen. He had been with Michel in Afghanistan and was proficient in both fossils and paleomagnetism. He was there only in my first of three seasons. Other French colleagues came in the later seasons, or at times when I was not in the field. There were quite a number of them.

The American and British contingents were beginning to wind down their involvement after the initial expedition to Cameroon in search of fossil humans and gorillas. In the second expedition we continued to search for these things, but as the probability for finding them grew less and less as more and more area was searched unsuccessfully, we began to shift emphasis to the Cretaceous, specifically to the search for early mammals. The only person who provided continuity from the first trip to the next among the anglophones was Larry Flynn. He is a happy guy, originally from Cleveland, with whom I had been a graduate student at Arizona. He had spent time at Paris University, at the American Museum of Natural History, and he is now at Harvard. Larry is a competent field man, an excellent scientist, and a genuinely good human being. He is also fluent in French. I enjoyed getting back out into the field with him. There was also a graduate student from Wyoming, Kathy Flanagan, who had been an undergraduate at Arizona when Larry and I were graduate students there. This was her first trip to Cameroon.

The Cameroonian field component was led by Joseph Victor Hell, of their equivalent of a national geological survey. Joseph is a sedimentologist trained at Poitiers, where Michel, the leader of the French contingent, teaches. He had done his graduate work on the oil fields of the Gulf of Guinea, that part of the Atlantic that formed as the opening embayment between South America and Africa. He is a strong, energetic geologist, great fun in the field, and a former star soccer player. With him from the survey were Sodia, a technician, and also a cook. The first cook was sacked because he was drunk too often at breakfast. Sallee, the replacement, was much better, more reliable, and sincerely likable.

Once Sallee bought a goat from an Mbororo while we were in the field because it was cheaper than buying one in town. He needed the goat to pay for a bride, his only wife having died shortly before. The idea of a bargain was irresistible to Joseph, who was also contemplating marriage. He bartered for a big white zebu, closed the deal, and money changed hands. Arrangements were made for Joseph to return on a certain date to pick up the steer. When he did, the Mbororo was nowhere to be found. The zebu and the Mbororo herdsman were never seen again. Joseph had been cheated. He had to buy another cow in town for more money than he lost on his original bargain, but he is married now anyway. All is well that ends well.

Occasionally we had with us a generally unreliable driver named Samuel. I once caught him at 10:00 A.M. in the camp supply tent, in bed with a prostitute. For a number of reasons I thought this to be poor form. Samuel is a big boy and he can do what he wants—but not in camp. His activities certainly were not in the best interests of obtaining the expedition objectives. Besides, the presence of strangers, much less prostitutes, leads to pilferage. Joseph, as the ranking Cameroonian, called Samuel out and instructed him to dismiss his consort. Amorous Samuel was so drunk, he very nearly sloshed over flat on his face. He was not particularly contrite. Moreover, he was sulky for a day or two because his party had been put to an untimely end. Finally a rabbit was brought into our camp by a villager. Samuel purchased it and had it cooked. I cannot remember if he did it himself or if he had Sallee do it; probably the latter. He passed around portions of the delicious *lapin* as a peace offering. Samuel was happy again, and he behaved after that, but he was not given much rope.

FIELDWORK UNDER conditions of hardship can be trying, and strains can be exacerbated if results are slow to come. Cameroon was tough duty, mainly because fossils were hard to come by. The crew, being a mixture of different cultures, was called upon for special understanding, tolerance, and flexibility. It is important to have a positive force such as Larry Flynn involved in projects like that. It keeps things on an even keel to have a fair, unflustered mind to deal with petty, unnecessary, and even meaningless problems that might creep in with the aggravation and tedium of slow progress.

And progress was slow at first in Cameroon. The large crew divided into smaller groups to make exploratory missions. I took a group to the Mbéré River, which is in a spectacular valley with its steep southern wall rising sharply across the river from our camp. The valley floor was mostly covered with flaming-red laterite, an iron-rich tropical soil that destroys all fossils. It was dotted with abundant, orange-fruited palms and luscious avocado trees. Mushroom-shaped termite mounds emerged from the ground. Elephant grass grew in profusion. This was not the ideal place to look for fossils. Rock exposures were just plain miserable. We had to adapt a special strategy just to find them. We got local guides to take us around from place to place where they knew patches of good rock might brave the surface. We looked in all the water wells. No luck. We looked where women dug clay to make pots. No luck. We hiked the streambeds. Still no luck. But the valley was pleasant and the avocados were delicious.

The people of Cameroon are very enjoyable, but their eating habits can take a little getting used to. They have a catholic diet; they eat everything. There seemed to be nothing that moved about of which Joseph would not say, "It's a very good meat." Once when we were in town, Joseph ordered monitor lizard at the Ostrich Restaurant. It tasted like chicken. I saved the bones and brought them back to my lab in Dallas. Monitor lizard, to me, was odd enough, a culturally foreign dish, but another time while crossing the Mbéré River on a *pont des lianes,* a bridge of vines spanning the water, on a long walk in search of rock exposure, we met a man carrying a gunnysack. He and our guide, Daouda, the chief's brother, engaged in a lively conversation in the language of the Fulbe people. Inside the sack was a dead, dressed python of immense proportions. The snake's carcass was destined for the larder. In addition to the meat, there was a sticky wad of gooey yellowish python fat and some python eggs taken from inside the body. After continued palaver, Daouda stretched an oozy mass of fat onto a banana leaf. With this generous gift from his friend, we went on our way. I suppose Daouda enjoyed it.

After all the possibilities of rock exposures and all the leads on fossil localities within walking distance of the Mbéré River camp were exhausted, we were forced to expand the reconnaissance. We drove out from camp in the mornings, stopping at every little village to inquire about pottery clay. We were shown pits and scoured them for fossil fragments. No luck. Soon we were running out of days and traveling long hours to reach new villages. The process was becoming tedious. With four of us in the group, there were more people than necessary to do the job. It would have been efficient only with one or two people, and they would need the patience of Job.

I started to become concerned because there were no tangible, positive field results coming out of the Mbéré Basin. True, I was getting a handle on the regional geology, and I had gotten a first but rather uninspiring glimpse of the Cameroonian Cretaceous. But I wanted at least to get enough samples and raw data to derive some kind of scientific contribution from the sojourn at the Mbéré. At that time studies of molecular evolution were coming into vogue. DNA comparisons based on molecules taken from fresh liver or other organs could show how different, or similar, two species might be. I had already used fossils to try to figure out the relationships of rats in Pakistan and Kenya. It was grasping at straws, but if I could not get fossils, perhaps I could get some mouse livers for someone who would sample the DNA, and then the hypotheses based on fossils could be tested.

Rodents are always considered pests, disease vectors, and destroyers of grain. Humans wage a constant battle against them. They are never protected in the Developing World (and very few rodent species are endangered or protected in the Western world). By sampling their populations in the Mbéré Valley some contribution to understanding their biology and evolution could be made. Through that we would know more about biology and evolution in general. Because rodents are basically a plague, no one would ever care if they were caught, much less if their livers were donated to science. I was not concerned about catching anything from them; I had been inoculated for bubonic plague. The wild mice of the Mbéré Valley are not particularly insidious in their effect on humans, but had I known that the village of Lassa, for which the rodent-borne hemorrhagic disease Lassa fever was named, was just across the border to the west in Nigeria, I might not have been so anxious to gut the specimens and extract their organs.

It was the dry season, and the tall grass was being burned off, as it is over much of Africa every year, to make way for new growth more suitable for grazing cattle. I engaged a couple of village boys to catch rodents for me. They would set fire to a stand of elephant grass, then catch the mice scampering from hole to hole. It was effective, but there are certain hazards to this method when practiced barefooted. The boys alternated mouse catching with jumping up and down to cool the calloused soles of their feet.

My mouse collectors were successful in obtaining a small but diverse sample. They got perhaps half a dozen species. I decided to keep on collecting, so I bought a number of mousetraps at the market. One evening, near the town of N'Gaoundéré, named for a huge boulder perched atop a hill and shaped like an outy-style belly button, I chose what I thought to be a very likely spot to set the trap line. When I went to check the traps at dawn, I found some other people—Canadians, as I recall—also checking traps. They were after rodents for a different reason, and the spot had looked good to them too. Neither group had been aware of the other's activities. I had no idea anyone else in the nation of Cameroon was engaging in scientific rat trapping. I am certain they also did not. What an amazing coincidence that we should bump into each other, doing the same thing, at the same place, on the same night! Unfortunately for the trappers, the rats avoided both trap lines.

In order to preserve DNA, I was told by my molecular colleagues, the liver and other organs of the specimen were to be placed in ethanol. Well, I had no ethanol out in the field in the Mbéré Basin. So I used gin. Ultimately I turned the preserved specimens over to a molecular biologist with lots of African experience so that he could study them. Alas, technology is making my collecting method all but obsolete. Now there are cloning techniques to multiply minor amounts of DNA such as can be retrieved from stuffed museum specimens, and from that to make enough for comparative purposes. Mice can rest easier for it.

The Mbéré Valley did not produce fossils of any kind, much less ancient mammals. We headed back to headquarters in Garoua to regroup. It was decided that the Koum Basin, farther to the arid north, was worth a visit. A river, the Mayo Rey, cuts through the elongate basin from east to west. Along its valley there are exposures of rock. I saw purple shales of the Cretaceous. These were the best-looking sediments I had seen in all of Cameroon. Much of the ground was concealed by laterite and elephant grass. Still, the Koum Basin is drier than the Mbéré and it has much more rock exposure. The mere sight of those rocks after all the days of searching clay pits was enough to excite my spirit.

The Koum Basin is remote, lying as it does along the border with Chad. In certain seasons the evil, dust-laden winds of the harmattan blow south from the Sahara, choking and blinding people and animals and turning the sky yellow. At other times it is just hazy, a combination of dust and the ubiquitous smoke of African fires.

A road runs down the axis of the basin, along the north side, parallel to the Mayo Rey, from the town of Tchollire in the west to the village of Mayo Djarendi and beyond in the east. To the north of the road is the Boubanjida Game Reserve, teeming with wildlife. To the south is the river with exposures of rock. Animals are plentiful in the basin. While prospecting for fossils I once surprised a poacher rendering poison and fixing it to his arrows. In the dry season Western hunters pay fees to shoot the animals that stray off the reserve. Cameroon, even in this day and age, has a strong contingent of Europeans migrating south every year to hunt. In fact the government encourages it. It is big business. Africa has it as part of its long legacy. Most of the books written about Africa in the nineteenth century speak grandly of sport and game. But of course we have not been in the nineteenth century for a long, long time. Conservation and game management are beginning to mean something in developing Africa these days. When hunters in Cameroon go out into the bush, they often make their way directly to the Koum Basin, to the area bordering the game preserve. They stay at Rhinoceros Camp, a rondaval on the river terrace overlooking the Mayo Rey south of the village of Koum. They can hire a cook. They can find guides to take them out on the game trails and to dress their kills. As a consequence the area around the camp is littered with the bones of animals left over from hunters and scattered about by small animals and birds come to pick them clean. Rhinoceros Camp is centrally located for our work, and since it is close to the river, it is convenient for sieving. It is relatively safer than the more remote east end of the basin. We occasionally set up our tents and mosquito nets in the clearing there.

Elephants are too wise to stray far from the protection of the game reserve during the hunting season. In the rainy season, when fifty or so inches of rain falls, they come down past the villages along the road. Their dung and spoor are everywhere. Perhaps seeing modern elephant tracks is what turned our eyes to the telltale traces preserved in the rocks. On the very first trip to the Koum Basin, within the first day or two, Kathy Flanagan found dinosaur footprints near Rhinoceros Camp. With that we were finally getting somewhere in the Cameroonian Cretaceous.

We did not have long in the basin, only a few days. Bones failed to materialize around Rhinoceros Camp. We drove east to Mayo Djarendi and parked on the road near the river. We searched throughout the hot afternoon. Flanagan found a single scrap of bone. The next day we had to leave the basin because our flight from Garoua and out of Cameroon left in the evening. The field season was all but over. It was a five-hour drive from the Koum Basin to Garoua, three of them over grueling dirt roads. Still, Mayo Djarendi looked good. We decided to return to the area early in the morning to put in just a few hours' prospecting.

Walking and looking, walking and looking. Nothing turned up. We were to meet at the Land Cruiser at high noon—sharp. I looked at my watch; I had to make my way back right away. I sped along at a brisk walk, eyes glued to the ground moving under the pendula of my feet. All of a sudden my psyche was shaken. My left foot came down directly on top of a dinosaur bone.

There was no way to collect the bone in the time available. I could not even do a thorough survey of the area. We had to get back to town. Our Air Cameroon flight would not wait for us if we were late. I looked hurriedly around. There was a lot of bone weathering out. And there was small bone in the purple mudstone matrix entombing the dinosaur bits. This spot had to be worked. That was clear.

I took out my compass and read bearings to three distant hills. Then I built a cairn to mark the spot. The small stone I picked up last to crown my pile of rocks was a dinosaur tooth. Here was a good specimen that I could take back, identify, and use to make a case for future work. Then I took photographs. As a habit, I carry my camera in a plastic bag to keep it free from dust. After photographing the site, I filled the plastic bag with matrix to sample at least some small amount for microvertebrates because the sediment looked so promising. I labeled the bag KB-6, then placed it on my head, African style, and scampered back to the vehicle, and back home to the United States.

A year passed. During that time I planned return expeditions to both

Cameroon and Malaŵi. I would go to Cameroon in January, and then Malaŵi in July. I talked up KB-6. It was the only place of which I knew in Cameroon that had good bones, and I was the only paleontologist who had ever seen it, and then for only twenty minutes. I screened the sample I brought back. To my delight it produced bones. Nothing very good, but bones nevertheless. There was even a scrap of what I took to be a minute jaw, and that I took even further to be mammalian. On the strength of the discovery of KB-6, the dinosaur tooth I had brought back, and the meager but promising results from the initial sieving of a few pounds of sediment, Larry and I approached the National Science Foundation for funding. They responded positively. We had some money to do the work.

Now picture this. There we were back in the Koum Basin. I was surrounded by Larry, Will Downs, a graduate student, and my French colleagues. I could not find the site!

"Jacobs, are you sure you wrote down the bearings correctly?" Will asked, unable to hide his disgust but trying to be gentle.

"Louis, it was very hot when you were here before," began Michel's theory, spoken sympathetically, but with an edge I am sure I imagined. "Perhaps you did not walk so far from the road as you thought."

Four days we had been there, halfway around the world from our homes, searching for KB-6. It was humiliating. Since this was a multinational project, it was a multinational humiliation. What could have gone wrong? The French group, including one paleontologist who had risen in the ranks of the diplomatic corps, had to leave. That left the American contingent only, which was not quite so bad on my ego. Still, I had this subliminal, cloying apprehension that somehow honor was at stake. It felt like it does just before an anxiety attack.

Then John, my graduate student, found the site again. What a relief. It had been right there where we had been looking, where we had been standing while I felt so ridiculous. My bearings were even correct. What had gone wrong?

It was that damned burning of the elephant grass. It is done every year, but with no pattern to it. The previous year, when I found the site, the grass was unburned. This year it was. Once the grass around the site was burned, the ground was covered with black, obscuring ash. Soot covered the fossils, hiding clues. The area around KB-6 looked sufficiently different from the previous year that the bones lay hidden until they were stumbled over again. But now the site was relocated and the world looked better to me.

We spent the next month carefully quarrying. Our camp was on the sandy bank of the Mayo Rey at the far east end of the basin, well away from Rhinoceros Camp. To sleep, we stretched sisal twine from trees, on which we hung our mosquito nets. Tents were pitched for those who preferred sleeping away from the equatorial view of the night sky. There was a big supply tent and a cook tent. Guinea fowl and chickens were tethered to an acacia tree next to the cook tent. It was a pleasant camp, a twenty-minute walk from the site we were working. At night we could watch the distant—or sometimes not so distant—glow of burning elephant grass. We slept pleasantly, except toward morning on the occasions when a boisterous rooster chose to crow. The culprit became supper soon after that habit was developed. Once, before dawn had become a serious issue, a rooster took to crowing in the worst imaginable way. Larry jumped out of his sleeping bag, sacrificing himself to the chill air for the good of the camp, bound to quiet the bird. Barefooted and in his BVDs, Larry chased the bird around the acacia tree. It was not a fair match. The bird was tied. But Larry still caught it. He covered it with a bucket, which sent it gently back to sleep, insuring that it was fully rested for the stew pot.

A mosquito net was also erected over the quarry, not for bugs but for shade. It was something, a meager gesture, to cut the force of the sun's tropical rays and yet leave enough light for us to see what we were really after—mammals. There was plenty of small bone interspersed with dinosaur teeth and fragments of larger bones. There were lots of frog fossils.

The site had evidently begun as a stream deposit in the early stages of its formation. Then, as stream flow reduced, a pond had formed. It had teemed with frogs. The pond eventually silted up, entombing whatever bones and bodies had sunk to the bottom. Then a soil began to develop on the top of the muds that had filled in the pond and preserved the fossils. The ancient soil is interesting in its own right. It is impregnated with calcium carbonate, the caliche of semiarid environments. The streams and floodplains of ancient Cameroon were certainly not lowland forests and swamps. Within the ancient soil formed at the top of the pond sediments are clusters of elongate ovoid structures an inch or so long. These were clearly of biological origin. They are not fossil eggs, but what are they? They turn out to be the remains of insects, actually the homes of sweat bees or something like them.

The insect remains are really very interesting because it is not until about this time in Earth history, the Early Cretaceous, that flowering plants began their vast radiation and diversification. Looked at another way, it was not until then that the Earth gained the beauty of flowers with all their flamboyant colors and sweet scents. The colors and the scents attract insects, which in turn pollinate the flowers. If flowers were undergoing an evolutionary radiation 100 million years ago, the animals that pollinate them must have been coevolving right along with them. Otherwise, how could insect-pollinated plants reproduce, and what would the pollinating insects eat? Now, if the insects were diversifying along with the flowering plants, would it not make sense that the animals that eat insects would be coevolving right along with them? Here in Cameroon, at KB-6, we had the remains of social, flower-pollinating insects, at the same locality with dinosaurs, frogs, and who knew what else.

OBVIOUSLY WHAT I had hoped for was a mammal. All living mammals have hair and produce milk to nurture their young. They can be divided into three fundamental groups distinguished by their method of reproduction as well as other features (Figure 37). The first group of living mammals is the egg-laying monotremes. The second is the pouched marsupials, who give birth to poorly developed young, born at quite an immature stage. They are hairless and pink and blind, but their arms are strong for their size. They climb from the vagina, up the belly of the mother, pulling themselves along from hair to hair, until they reach the pouch. Once inside, the young marsupial swallows a nipple, and for most of the remainder of its life in the pouch, it is power fed milk by muscular contractions in the breast of the mother. It is a good life if that first journey can be made successfully. The third group of living mammals is the placentals, which retain a developing fetus in the uterus, nourishing it through a placenta.

The platypus and echidnas, or spiny anteaters, are monotremes. They alone among living mammals lay eggs. They are only known nowadays from Australia, Tasmania, and New Guinea. However, a fossil monotreme perhaps 60 million years old was recently reported from South America. The living opossums, kangaroos, wombats, and their relatives are marsupials. They are most characteristic today of the island continent of Australia, and to some extent, South America. The Virginia opossum is the only marsupial that now

FIGURE 37: *A sampling of modern mammals. Clockwise from upper left, a spiny anteater and a platypus, both egg-laying monotremes from Australia; an Asian sloth bear, a placental; and a pouched kangaroo, a marsupial, also from Australia. Mammalian distribution, even today, bears the stamp of events that occurred during the time of the dinosaurs.*

lives in the United States. There used to be many native North American marsupials, as shown by the fossil record, but the trash can 'possum is a recent immigrant from South America. Placentals are more numerous and more diverse than marsupials, and hugely more so than monotremes. Whales, dogs, cats, humans, fruit bats, elephants, in fact most familiar mammals, and their extinct relatives, are placentals. They inhabit most of the Earth.

One very important feature of mammals is that they are warm-blooded. There is a sophisticated physiological mechanism for internal temperature control of the body. That insures a reasonably constant, nonfluctuating temperature, maintained at an optimum for the biochemical processes that enable the organism to operate. The result, basically, is that mammals are more active animals more often than, say, lizards or most other reptiles. There are requirements that go along with being warm-blooded. Heat must be conserved. Hair, as opposed to scales, provides insulation and reduces heat loss from the surface of the body. Warm-blooded animals also require a more or less constant supply of food, fuel for the internal fires if you will, as opposed to reptiles. A snake may eat only once a week or so, but you eat every day and so do most other mammals. So do birds, which are warm-blooded, and so would have any other dinosaurs that might have been warm through similar processes of internal temperature control.

Because of the changes that have occurred with time in various evolutionary lineages, the casual observer might be hard pressed to recognize the tiny shrewlike creatures that were the earliest mammals and elephants, for example, as belonging to the same group of animals defined by the presence of hair and the production of milk. But they do. Unfortunately mammary glands, which produce milk, are not the sorts of things that are of much use in trying to understand fossil mammals because they are just not preserved as fossils. Neither is the structure of the uterus. Hair is occasionally preserved and fossilized, but not often enough to be of major significance in the fossil record. Some features of bone growth, apparently correlated with warm-bloodedness, can be observed in fossil bone under the microscope, but a broader understanding of both bone growth and warm-bloodedness is necessary to put the suggestions of microscopic bone structure to full use.

There needs to be a catalog of reliable characteristics of the skeleton with which to recognize fossil mammals. Such characteristics must be preserved in fossils, and to be of greater use, we should be able to observe them developing evolutionarily over time. Fortunately there are such defining skeletal characteristics in living mammals and that allows their roots to be traced well back into the fossil record.

The structural features of the skeleton have functional significance as well as genealogical importance. The demand for a constant food supply to maintain a constant warm-blooded body temperature and the energetics of such a life-style are intimately intertwined with the structural evolution of mammals. One of the most obvious features of most mammals is their posture. Unlike most crocodiles, lizards, or other such terrestrial reptiles, mammals are not sprawling, with their legs sticking out sideways from the body, then turning down at the elbows and knees. The front and hind legs of mammals are positioned directly under the body, transmitting the weight straight down the legs because of the more erect posture. Dinosaurs are a special case among the reptiles because their limbs, like those of mammals, are positioned more directly beneath the body.

The joints in the front and hind legs of mammals are generally more complicated, more sophisticated, than in reptiles, making for a tighter fit of adjacent bones at the joint. That is made possible by the way mammalian bones grow as compared with those of reptiles in general. The bone, an upper arm bone for example, is preformed in cartilage in a young and developing mammal. As it grows, bone salts, the stuff that makes bone hard, are deposited in the shaft of the bone and also at the ends where the joints are. Between the areas of bone-salt deposition, the cartilage keeps growing and the bone gets longer. After a while the deposition of bone salts outpaces the growth of cartilage, and the ends fuse with the shaft. When that happens, the bone essentially stops growing in size. That is why if you are twenty years old and five feet tall, you might as well give up ideas of playing professional basketball. You will not get any taller.

Reptiles, as opposed to mammals, generally but not always, have the ends of their limb bones encased in cartilage caps, where growth takes place while bone salts are deposited in the shaft. That growth can take place much longer, and therefore, maximum size of the individual is not fixed in many reptilian species in the same sense that it is in mammals. The result is that the joints in the limbs of reptiles, because their bones lack complex ends that fit together like intricate keys, have a looser, less efficient look to them than do the joints in the limbs of mammals. Couple this with the difference in posture, and the general impression is that mammals have evolved a much more efficient locomotor repertoire than most any other terrestrial vertebrates. It is not that reptiles are incompetent. They obviously do quite well with what they have. It is just that mammals are different. The utility of an efficient skeleton with respect to diet in a warm-blooded animal is in moving it to its food source, providing the tools—notably teeth and claws—with which to catch and procure a meal, or enabling it to flee to avoid becoming one.

Mammals bite and chew their food with their teeth and jaws, cutting meat as in carnivores and grinding herbage as in herbivores. Between those extremes are all the other adaptations for food processing—slicing, dicing, juicing, pulping—anything (almost) a Veg-O-Matic can do. Some mammal species have lost their teeth altogether and feed by lapping and sucking nectar or termites. Since mammals must feed at regular and closely spaced intervals to stoke the fires that maintain their body temperature, it is hardly surprising that the mammalian dentition provides a wealth of information on the dietary adaptations of fossil species. That is why it is so very fortunate for paleontologists that teeth are the most commonly preserved mammalian skeletal elements. They make good fossils because they are the hardest parts of the body, and therefore they resist destruction by geological and biological processes that retard fossilization.

A general feature of mammals is that the teeth are complicated. Mammals usually have a number of different-shaped teeth, and there is a division of labor between the incisors, canines, premolars, and molars. Many of the teeth have numerous bumps and cusps, as you can tell from running your tongue over those in the back of your mouth. The sophisticated cusp pattern of individual teeth enables the upper teeth to fit with the lower teeth in precise occlusion. This precise occlusion allows for precise function—the exact alignment of shearing crests and grinding mortars to produce the required result, masticated food. Mammals, as a rule, have one set of baby teeth and one set of permanent teeth. They do not continuously replace teeth the way dinosaurs did. The result is that precise occlusion is maintained throughout life.

Many structural features have important roles in the complicated and integrated process of mammalian chewing. The teeth are anchored securely in the jaws by multiple roots. Most reptiles, if they have roots, have only one for each tooth. Sockets into which the tooth roots sit are arranged along the edge of the jaws in one row. This is obvious to us, but many nonmammalian vertebrates have multiple rows of teeth, some on bones that never bear teeth in mammals. In modern mammals there is only one tooth-bearing bone in each half of the lower jaw, and the counterparts are connected at the chin. In some very early and extinct mammals, and in reptiles, there is more than one bone in each half of the lower jaw. That is the primitive condition. The additional bones are mostly toward the back of the jaw. That is very important because the jaw joint, where the lower jaw and the skull meet, is formed by different bones in modern mammals than in reptiles.

The jaw joint allows the mouth to open and close, so it is clear that its construction must bear some relationship to the way an animal chews. In mammals its construction is an adaptation that facilitates precise occlusion and the mammalian way of chewing.

The bones that form the mammalian jaw joint are called the squamosal in the skull and the dentary in the lower jaw. In reptiles the articulation is between the quadrate in the skull and the articular in the lower jaw. Through embryology, anatomy, and the fossil record, we can determine the homology of these bones between reptiles and mammals; that is to say, we can pinpoint exactly where in the mammalian skeleton the bones equivalent to the reptilian quadrate and articular are located. To do that we must examine the structure of the middle ear, a sensory organ located near the jaw joint.

Sound vibrations are transmitted from the eardrum to the oval window of the inner ear by bones in both reptiles and mammals. Reptiles have only one, but mammals have three bones in each ear. The possession of three middle-ear bones is a fundamental feature of all living mammals. In common parlance the three are called the hammer, anvil, and stirrup. Reptiles have only the equivalent of the stirrup. The equivalents of the quadrate and articular of the reptilian jaw joint have undergone an evolutionary transformation in the history of mammals to become the anvil and hammer of the mammalian middle ear. That is why reptiles have only one middle-ear bone, yet modern mammals have three. It is also why mammals have the jaw joint formed from different bones than reptiles, and why modern mammals have only one bone in each half of the lower jaw. All of those features are easily seen in the fossil record. And they are all related to the functioning of the teeth in precise occlusion, an adaptation for feeding that facilitates warm-bloodedness, because the jaw joint and the muscles that operate it must provide for precise occlusion to occur.

THE TEETH OF mammals deserve a closer look because they are the primary food processors for an animal. Everyone knows that various kinds of mammals have different diets and that their teeth look different. Meat-eaters such as lions look like they do when they roar because of their big, stabbing fangs. The teeth in the back of the jaws slice meat as cleanly as scissors cutting paper. Horses, on the other hand, are grazing animals that must grind large amounts of abrasive food, which is to say grass. Their cheek teeth are like millstones, not adapted for puncturing flesh at all. From these examples we can see two things: The shape of teeth is related to the ecology of mammal species and the range of shapes is quite vast. Natural selection surely plays a role in evolutionarily directing the shape of teeth with respect to diet. Species with very different evolutionary histories can evolve similarly shaped teeth simply as adaptations to similar diets.

Given the adaptational significance of tooth shape and the consequent likelihood of convergent evolution, it would be useful to determine a structural common plan from which all mammalian tooth shapes can be derived. That is not so simple, for one reason because living monotremes have no functional teeth. For marsupials and placentals it seems that the primitive pattern is like that of an opossum or a shrew. Ridges of the lower teeth shear across crests on the upper teeth. Then, as the jaw slams shut, the main cusps on the upper molars crush into basins on the lower teeth. This dual function, shearing and crushing, is what characterizes the teeth of the common ancestor of marsupial and placental mammals as judged both from theoretical considerations and from the fossil record.

As evolution proceeded, the crushing and grinding function became enhanced in disparate lineages of herbivorous mammals, such as kangaroos, which are marsupials, and horses, which are placentals. In those two species the teeth do not look so much alike, but the tapir, a close relative of the horse, has teeth quite similar to a kangaroo's. Pigs, humans, and even bears have teeth with low, rounded cusps that look very much alike because all three have diets that include a little bit of everything. In fact, fossil bear and javelina teeth have been misidentified as hominoid. In carnivores the primitive shearing function is perfected at the expense of structures relating to crushing and grinding. Thus, one primitive kind of tooth shape, one that could both shear and grind, gave rise to the incredible variety of tooth shapes seen in marsupials and placentals today.

What about monotremes? Their living members do not have functional teeth. The platypus has horny pads on its jaws, but luckily the vestiges of teeth can be seen as the animal develops. Some fossil species have teeth similar to the developmental stages of the platypus, thus providing important clues. It seems that monotremes comprise a branch that split off on its own course prior to the evolution of the kind of teeth that characterize marsupials and placentals. That makes all kinds of sense. Monotremes are also primitive because they lay eggs rather than give birth to live young as in the other two groups. The conclusion is that among the three groups of modern mammals living in the world today, marsupials and placentals have a more recent common ancestor than either does with monotremes, and therefore those two are more closely related to each other than either is to platypuses. What is really fortunate for paleontology is that this relationship can be seen with nothing more than isolated teeth.

Isn't it fascinating? Structural changes that function in hearing and in chewing have a common source in evolution that allows us to define mammals apart from the features of hair and milk and reproduction that do not preserve in the fossil record. The shape of teeth, which is ultimately enmeshed in the complex of jaw and ear changes, provides important evidence about the diet of extinct mammals and the evolutionary relationships among them.

A good bit of the early evolutionary history of mammals took place in the shadows, if not the footprints, of dinosaurs. Viewed in this way, we can imagine mammals as secretive, voracious, and tiny shrewlike creatures, scurrying from harm's way. These unobtrusive elements of the fauna emerged in their own right during the Age of Mammals, after the Great Dying, to become what they are now. But dinosaurs, except for birds, went extinct.

So when and where did the three groups of modern mammals—monotremes, marsupials, and placentals—representing every mammalian species alive today, first diverge from each other to evolve their separate ways? What were their earliest true members like? What were their ancestors like? Why did they diverge? Was it because Gondwana was fragmenting into the modern southern continents? These are basic questions about modern mammals, and I thought Africa might hold some answers. That is why I was in Cameroon looking for ancient fossils.

The attributes that anatomically define all living mammals as a single inclusive group appear to have evolved no later than about 100 million years ago, somewhere within the roughly 40 million years of time that is called the Early Cretaceous. The divergence of placentals and marsupials, it is thought, can be traced back to a common ancestor slightly later in time, later than the split between their common ancestor and the monotremes, but still in the Cretaceous.

But where did the monotreme-marsupial-placental common ancestor of the Early Cretaceous come from? We know from fossils that recognizable mammals evolved much earlier, around 220 million years ago in fact, at about the time dinosaurs originated. Even those species of over 200 million years ago have a long and unique history separate from reptiles. These very earliest mammals are quite different from the ones around today. They are even very different from the ones around in the Early Cretaceous. They were the inhabitants of Pangaea. They had the most fundamental skeletal features of mammals, but they had not yet evolved the features of the teeth, ears, and jaw to the extent seen in modern mammals. By 100 million years ago, after mammals had more than 100 million years of prior evolution under their belts, and after Pangaea had fragmented, some of the species reached the grade of modern mammals. It is within this Early Cretaceous complex that we must search for the origins of monotremes, marsupials, and placentals, because that is the time when the features that define these groups of mammals first evolve.

THE QUARRYING AT KB-6 continued. We wrapped many small specimens for preparation in the lab, but none of them was identified as mammalian. Matrix was collected—eight tons of it that year—and taken back to Rhinoceros Camp, where every bit of it was sieved. The small specimens and the sieved concentrate were shipped to my lab.

Months later, back in Dallas, I got a phone call. I was at home on a Sunday afternoon. It was my student, John Congleton, excited.

"I have a mammal!" he said.

Home run!

That was the first decent mammal specimen to come out of Cameroon— or from the entire African Cretaceous for that matter. The project continued to work KB-6 the next year and the next. In 1988 we went to set the camp in the usual spot on the banks of the Mayo Rey at the east end of the basin. At that time there was a lull in the shooting war between Libya and Chad. That left some armed Chadians with not much to shoot, but with plenty of time on their hands. They had taken to crossing the border into the Koum Basin. They became highwaymen, robbing people on the road. Thirteen vehicles returning from market at the border village of Mandingrin down the road from camp had been stopped all at once and robbed at gunpoint. To combat the threat, the authorities ordered all lorries to travel in even larger convoys. Soldiers in plainclothes, armed with machine guns, rode shotgun in each truck.

It looked like a situation that could turn sticky for a bunch of *wazungu* camped out in the middle of nowhere with so many fancy amenities, such as tents and sleeping bags, food and funds. I spread the word among the local villagers that we would be encamped for six weeks, just so that anyone interested would not think there was a need to rush into devilment. In five days we had stockpiled a supply of matrix for washing and completed the needed geological study around the site. I ordered camp struck without further notice. We moved to the relative safety of Rhinoceros Camp. Further work around KB-6 was done in day trips. We had no problems—luckily.

Since that first mammal tooth, a number of specimens have come to light, all important. None is particularly spectacular, but that does not matter. The first specimens from the African Cretaceous were the hardest to find. We broke the ground. Others will come more easily because now it is known where to look.

There are probably four species of mammals, at least, represented by fossils from the Koum Basin, but only one has yet been named. None of the Cameroonian mammal fossils are particularly like marsupials, or placentals, or monotremes, so far as I can tell. And none is particularly like the widespread mammals that inhabited the megacontinent of Pangaea, when all landmasses were joined and when mammals first evolved, 100 million years earlier than when the Cameroonian mammals lived. Their most similar relatives seem to be from rocks at least 40 million years older than they are, and found in England. That was a surprise.

As it stands now, it appears that mammals generally like those from Cameroon were widespread across the Northern and Southern Hemispheres at the beginning of the Cretaceous. They may not have been extremely abundant, but there were probably quite a few species of them. From this widespread stock, monotremes, the living egg-layers, evolved in the Southern Hemisphere. In that sense the Cameroonian fossil mammals are related to the duck-billed platypuses. Based on that logic, all other things being equal, they also laid eggs.

Some tens of millions of years after monotremes evolved, when Australia and South America were still connected through Antarctica, but after Africa had split off, the common ancestor of placentals and marsupials evolved. It evolved not in the Southern Hemisphere, but in the Northern. Geography continued to play a role. Descendants of the common ancestor gave rise to species that diversified into marsupials in North America, and placental mammals in Asia. Marsupials did not get to Africa until tens of millions of years later, and even then, coming from Europe as they did, they only inhabited North Africa. Their stay in Africa was only for just a brief period of time.

Toward the end of the Age of Reptiles, not long before dinosaurs became extinct, marsupials invaded South America from the north and spread across Antarctica to Australia. Then Antarctica split off from Australia and from South America. The geography of pouched mammals was following the arrangement of the continents (see Figure 9 in Chapter 1). That explains why the modern mammal fauna of Australia is so characteristic, with platypuses and koalas and kangaroos, but still resembles that of South America more fundamentally than anywhere else. Much, much later mice and dingos and humans hopped from island to island, finally to reach isolated Australia, as we shall see, long after placentals inhabited other continents.

Placental mammals have a complex geographical history, but their spread to southern continents comes after the major geographic reconfigurations of the Cretaceous. Placentals entered South America for the first time near the end of the Age of Reptiles, roughly seventy million years ago, probably about the same time marsupials were heading south. New discoveries indicate that, like marsupials, they carried on to Australia, but these early invaders never gained a strong foothold. Much later other placentals, such as mice, entered Australia perhaps as recently as eight or ten million years ago. Humans and dingos came even later. Why didn't the early placentals flourish in Australia like the marsupials did? That is a good question and no one knows the answer.

CAMEROON WAS BOTH good to us and bad. No matter how great the precautions, complicated situations can arise in the field. Tragedies do strike. In one way or another they can strike anywhere. We had a death.

In 1989 our colleague Abel Brillanceau, the chain-smoking wine taster, master of logistics, geologist, and good friend to us all, died of spinal malaria while in Cameroon. Either Abel was not taking malaria prophylaxis, as he should have, or he was and it did not work. The *Plasmodium* merozoite struck with a high fever. He was being airlifted to France when his heart stopped on the runway of the Garoua airport. He was gone.

We must assume that Abel was satisfied with his life, doing what he chose to do when the mosquito bit him. Still, he was a part of the effort. His fate could have visited any of us. We have no adequate way to honor our fallen colleague—but we try. Michel, Larry, and I, along with other friends on the project, named *Abelodon abeli* after him. It is the only fossil mammal ever named from Cameroon.

IT WAS with a great deal of effort that those first mammals were retrieved from the African Cretaceous. At the time I began planning the Malaŵi Project there were no fossil mammals of Early Cretaceous age, that is, between 144 and 97.5 million years old, known from any of the southern continents. Now, a decade later, they are known from South America, Australia, and Africa. They do not appear to be very common animals of the Early Cretaceous world, but they are there.

Was it luck that we found them in Cameroon, those pinhead-sized teeth? Maybe so, but we were looking for them. Is it luck when you fly halfway around the world, on two back-to-back overnight flights, to an African nation, then catch a two-hour domestic flight to the north end of the country, then drive five hours, three of them on jolting dirt roads, to get to the banks of a bilharzia-infested river, search the ground on foot for hour after hour until a likely spot is found, then collect eight tons of dirt, sieve it, transport the residue back, retracing your steps the same way you came, sort it under a microscope, and come up with a mammal tooth over 100 million years old?

Is it luck, skill, effort, or just plain crazy?

It is at least the first three. I am not sure about the last.

8

OTHER
NEIGHBORS

D INOSAURS, CROCODILES, AND mammals have shown themselves to be interesting in the Early Cretaceous of Africa. However, they did not live in a vacuum and they were not the only vertebrates for which this period is an important time of innovation. Many kinds of backboned animals in addition to birds and mammals were undergoing significant diversification during the interval prior to 100 million years ago. Some modern families of frogs and lizards probably had their origins then. A similar statement can be made for snakes. All of this evolution, leading to our modern world, was not independent of the rearrangements in the Earth's geography, nor was vertebrate evolution independent among its various subgroups or free from the influence of plants and insects, which were experiencing their own radiations. Food webs were undergoing some rather drastic modifications through all this coevolution. From that milieu emerged a world more recognizable, more closely similar to what we have now.

Subsequent to 100 million years ago the Earth's continents did not cease their adventure through time. The geography of continents and oceans continued to change. Mountains were uplifted and eroded. Climates changed. The Ice Ages waxed and waned. Extinctions occurred, most notably the Great Dying, but also many of lesser popularity. Evolutionary radiations occurred, replenishing the number of species inhabiting the Earth.

Evolutionary radiations can be defined as relatively short time intervals, geologically speaking, jammed full of lots and lots of evolution. The net result is usually the appearance of a large number of new species. If the time involved appears to be notably short, the radiation may be termed explosive. The flock of cichlid fish species living now in Lake Malaŵi is the product of an explosive radiation. It came about when a few species of the cichlid family got into the lake at some late date in its history. Some estimates, based on molecular differentiation of DNA in the cichlid species, suggest that the radiation began on the order of a scant couple of hundred thousand years ago. That is not much time at all from a geological perspective. Once there, the cichlids evolved rapidly to fill an astounding variety of fishy niches, utilizing much of the spectrum of the lake's habitats and its food resources. This was done, presumably, to the detriment and near exclusion of other noncichlid fish species.

The Age of Mammals, the Cenozoic Era in technical parlance, was initiated sixty-six million years ago by an adaptive radiation immediately following the demise of the dinosaurs. The timing is so precise that it is suggestive. Were the mammals, a group that had its evolutionary origins at about the same time as dinosaurs, in some way held back, prevented from achieving predominance, by an ecologically superior dinosaur clan? I do not know, but the possibility has suggested itself to many people. Throughout the sixty-six-million-year history of the Age of Mammals, after that initial radiation of species, the mammals did not simply rest on their land-conquering laurels. They continued to speciate and to radiate periodically throughout their history.

There seem to be at least two sorts of evolutionary radiations. One occurs when new connections are made between previously isolated landmasses through geographic changes associated with continental drift or other major physical processes. Often in such cases, the introduction of previously unrepresented species into a new area results in the production of new species, not uncommonly to the detriment of native species, similar to the case hypothesized for the cichlid fishes of Lake Malaŵi. In such a case it appears almost as if there are unfilled ecological niches waiting to be exploited. It is a matter of being in the right place at the right time and having the right equipment. Regardless of the specific details of Lake Malaŵi, but using it as an example, the current diversity of cichlids, plus hindsight, tells us that as a group the cichlids were evolutionarily able to exploit the situation in which they found themselves.

The other sort of radiation occurs when an adaptive threshold is crossed, a new way of making a living is devised, such as gnawing in rodents. Once a basic novelty is evolved, there are many, many variations on the theme to be exploited. That is a major factor, probably, in why there are so many species of bats and rats, these two being the most diverse groups of living mammals. The evolution of an innovative way to make a living, biologically speaking, is a recurrent pattern. It has happened over and over again in the history of life on Earth. The initial achievement of an adaptive feature, an accomplishment of ecological entrepreneurship, paves the way. Then descendant species fan out. Flight in vertebrates offers prime examples. Birds, which evolved as flying dinosaurs from a single ancestral species, exhibit an unequaled flamboyance, all tied, in one way or another, to the ecological door opened to them by the acquisition of their initial adaptation—flight. Pterosaurs, the other flying archosaurs, underwent a fine radiation, and it is regrettable for us that none have survived, because they would certainly be fun to watch. Bats are the third group of vertebrates to evolve true flight. There are more species of bats living today than any other order of mammals except for the rodents, who have undergone their own explosive and adaptive radiations, leaving them with an unequaled number of species in the terrestrial-vertebrate realm.

After the demise of the dinosaurs, the combined result of the basal Age of Mammals mammalian radiation, plus all the subsequent ones, is a vast number of species, a vast diversity of body forms, and a vast fossil record that reflects a lot of changes among the sum total of the species in various segments of the Age of Mammals. Thus the spectrum of mammals observable today shows immense differences in how various species live and what they look like. Compare a flying bat with a swimming whale. Compare a fruit bat, also called a flying fox, with its long snout and large Dracula wings, with a tiny leaf-nosed bat. They are very different. Compare a blue whale with a sperm whale, or a humpback, or a killer, or a blind river dolphin. All are whales, but they are very different. Compare any of them with their mammalian cousins that have also invaded the sea—seals, walruses, sea cows, sea otters. All of these different examples followed different evolutionary paths to end up at the same place, which is the world of today. We could use other examples and do the same exercise that we just did with whales. We could examine the diversity within the primates, or within all carnivores, or within all herbivores and we would reach the same conclusion: Mammalian diversity is astounding. And we have not even taken extinct species known only from the fossil record into account. The point is that there have been tremendous evolutionary changes in the mammals during the relatively short period of Earth history called the Age of Mammals—only sixty-six million years.

Other groups of vertebrates cannot boast such a track record. Some species living today appear so primitive, so unmodified from what the ancestor must have been like, that they stand out conspicuously from other living species. Many times the most primitive of living species in a given group of vertebrates resembles an ancient member of its evolutionary clade otherwise known only from the depths of the fossil record. Sometimes primitive living species have very poor fossil records. The lack of a good fossil record, or conversely the resemblance of the living species to a fossil species from early in its genealogy, suggests that the most primitive of living species are, in some sense, living fossils. Darwin recognized the concept in the *Origin of Species.* His examples include the platypus and the lungfish. He wrote of differential rates of evolution on the one hand, and of extinction on the other, both of which could result in living species appearing to be living fossils.

My favorite living fossil comes from the world of fishes, as does Darwin's lungfish example, but I think the hagfish is much more striking. At the earliest stages of their evolution, getting back beyond 500 million years ago, vertebrates had no jaws. The borders of their mouths were not supported by hinged, biting structures. Vertebrate ancestors fed by straining food particles through a basketlike organ in the throat. It is this basket that eventually evolved to become the gills and their bony supports, and, at the front end, the jaws. The evidence from anatomy and embryology is quite strong and unequivocal on the derivation of the jaws. The earliest vertebrate fossils belong to animals with soft fishlike bodies and hard, pointy "teeth"—not true teeth, but bony food-gathering organs nonetheless. These were conodonts. Vertebrates from a slightly younger time in the geologic record were covered with a bony shell formed in the skin. They had no jaws. Locomotion was probably through jerky flexing of their tails, moving the animals erratically from place to place, transporting the feeding basket to different spots on the ocean floor, where they snuffled in the bottom ooze to filter out digestible particles.

No such animals exist today—not exactly anyway. However, there are living animals with no jaws, and for that very big reason they are primitive among all living vertebrates. There are two groups of living jawless vertebrates. The more familiar of the two is the lampreys from the Great Lakes region. Lampreys are anadromous, meaning they live in the ocean most of their lives, but return to freshwater rivers and streams to breed. Besides having no jaws, lampreys have no bone in their skeletons, no scales, and no paired fins, unlike more familiar fish. They have only the fin that runs along the midline of the body and tail.

Lampreys not only lack jaws, they lack teeth as well. They obtain their food not as mud-grubbing filter feeders, but by sucking onto the side of a fish with their round, jawless mouths, then rasping a hole in the side of their victims with tough, horny structures inside their mouths. Tissue fluids from an abraded victim weep into the lamprey's gullet. Because lampreys attack commercially important species, they are well known to Great Lakes fishermen. They are vertebrate parasites, and like all parasites they tend to turn our stomachs. But let's have a look at the other group of living jawless fishes.

The lesser known of the living jawless fishes are the exclusively marine hagfish and slime hags. Quaint names, don't you think?

The hagfish and slime hags (Figure 38) are even more primitive than the lampreys because they have fewer semicircular canals in the inner ear, which

FIGURE 38: A hagfish beginning to feed on a fish carcass. It throws its body into a knot, which it then moves forward to push against the fish while it pulls with its head. A hole is ripped in the side of the fish, through which the hagfish— presumably happily—enters.

provide for balance and orientation, and they have only a single nostril. These were apparently the conditions in the most ancient of vertebrates, and the living hagfish have retained them as characteristic features. Hagfish are so primitive that some researchers do not even include them inside the vertebrates, placing them as their own special group that branched off the evolutionary tree even before lampreys. This is a rather moot point in our discussion since hagfish are clearly not related to anything but vertebrates.

Hagfish lack bone, teeth, and scales, like the lampreys, and therefore, they also have a dismal fossil record. Their place in evolution is decided more on the anatomy of living species than on fossils. The only known fossil hagfish, and the first one of the few known fossil lampreys that have been described, come from 300-million-year-old rocks in Illinois. The two living jawless fish groups were surely distinct well before then. Hagfish and lampreys are living fossils in the sense that they represent their fossil antecedents and have not evolved into completely different sorts of animals. Lampreys and hagfish may even have been separated on different branches of the evolutionary tree longer than any other pair of vertebrate species alive today—longer, for instance, than the human and lamprey branches have been separated. That is assuming hagfish and lampreys diverged before anything else—including the branch that we are on—split from the lineage that gave rise to modern lampreys. It is a matter of the geometry of the evolutionary tree. So hagfish might be more primitive than lampreys, but neither of them has jaws.

Hagfish have a different style of feeding from that of the lampreys. They are predators and they are strictly marine. Most of the dozen or so species of hagfish apparently burrow through bottom ooze in search of worms. Once they find one, it is hooked into the mouth by the alternate working of horny mouth parts.

Hagfish are also attracted to dead or nearly dead fish, which they enter and consume from the inside out. They have an interesting method of getting inside. The mouth design of hagfish is such that when the round, jawless orifice is appressed against the surface of a body, the tongue can be pulled back to create an increasingly strong grip, like a vicious Chinese finger puzzle. Usually the hagfish chooses a spot on the body of a dead fish where the flesh is rough, perhaps at an injury or at the anus or gills, anyplace where the hag can gain a better purchase. Then the hagfish loops its eellike body into a knot at the tail, which it slides forward on its body toward the head and finally against the carcass of the meal. It forces its knot against the body wall of the dead fish while pulling with its attached mouth until a hunk of flesh is ripped out, opening the door for entry. Once inside, dining is easier, if not more leisurely. When a morsel of food is swallowed, it becomes enveloped in a mass of mucus through which digestive juices pass and nutrients exit. Then the mucus-wrapped undigestible remains are expelled.

While their method of eating might strike the more anthropocentric of us as disgusting, that is not why these creatures have earned the names hagfish and slime hags. The real reason is that they secrete copious amounts of thick mucus from their long, slimy, pinkish purple bodies. In addition, coiled segments of protein are mixed with the mucus. These uncoil in seawater, serving to tangle the mess around the animal. They are not always in that state. Usually they are just average slimy. However, when danger threatens, the slime glands kick into high gear. It is a defense mechanism, and a good one. Not only humans find it disgusting, so do predators. They tend to pass, no doubt certain that the hagfish is not so good to eat, and they continue searching for a meal that is just a bit more appetizing. When the hagfish is out of danger, it again throws its body into a knot. As the knot moves forward from the tail to the head, the excess mucus is bulldozed before it down to the nose. Then the hagfish issues a big sneezelike convulsion, freeing itself from the slime, and swims off to continue its life.

Despite their life-style, hagfish deserve to be understood because they are of considerable commercial interest. On the negative side, they damage the catch in gill nets by feeding on trapped fish. But they also have a positive side, believe it or not. For one thing, they are eaten—by humans—in some parts of the world. And you probably did not know that hagfish provide eelskin for wallets. How ignoble to become a yuppie wallet after hundreds of millions of years of precious maintenance of the primitive status quo.

After all its long evolutionary history the hagfish may be the most primitive of living vertebrates, but paradoxically it is not necessarily very much like the earliest vertebrates from which it was derived. It is a living fossil because it has no jaws and because of a few other features. Its early jawless ancestors surely did not have the unique attributes seen today in living hagfish. The conodonts had hard "teeth" while hagfish do not. Being covered with armor plates, other early jawless vertebrates known from the fossil record could not tie themselves in knots, nor did they enjoy the defense of secreting enormous amounts of mucus and then sneezing it all away when danger passed. Perhaps hagfish evolved from cartilaginous ancestors that left no recognizable (or as yet decipherable) fossil record. Perhaps they evolved from conodonts. Even so, it would strain credulity to propose that hagfish, living fossils or not, are exactly like their ancestors of over 500 million years ago. Empirically, judging from all we can observe, evolution does not appear to work that way.

Organisms evolve as a well-integrated mosaic of features, some primitive like the ancestral condition and others advanced, or, in other words, derived from that of the ancestor. Hagfish are a mosaic. The lack of jaws is primitive, but the details of the horny biting parts in the round mouth are unquestionably derived relative to their ancestors. The mucus-flood defense is very likely a derived feature not present in the earliest vertebrates. The reason it is probably derived is because it is so specialized. If a structure is specialized, the options for the directions in which it can evolve further become limited. The lesson from all this is that although species living today have a long history of evolutionary transformations, some features of a species evolve faster than others. Even species that can legitimately be referred to as living fossils are unique and unlike their ancestors except in a very general sense and in a few very basic details.

Of course, not all groups of vertebrates evolve with the apparent excruciating slowness of slime hags on the one hand, or the apparent explosiveness of mammals on the other. There is no evolutionarily correct prescription. Each genealogy is different in detail. The history of organisms is complex, involving internal biological attributes of the individual and the species, external factors imposed by the physical environment and other interacting species, plus a big dose of statistical probabilities, or what we might commonly refer to as chance, maybe even luck. The various characteristics of a single species evolve as an integrated mosaic, some faster and some slower, so it makes sense that if we look at a community of animals, a collection of species all living in proximity, some will seem to be more evolved, while others appear less evolved. Some will be more like living fossils than others.

The different patterns of evolution of the individual species within a community will usually reflect, at least in some general way, the geography that has influenced their evolution, whether it be the dividing of supercontinents, the connection of an isthmus allowing animal migration, or the preservation of suitable protective refugia. We have already seen examples from the dinosaurs, crocodiles, and mammals of geographic rearrangements influencing the admixture of species present on a given continent at a given time. Frogs provide another example.

Frogs evolved just a bit before dinosaurs, crocs, and mammals. They are one of three living divisions in the vertebrate class Amphibia. The most ancient amphibians go way back in time to when vertebrates first left an obligatory aquatic life-style and began to invade terra firma. None of the living amphibians looks a great deal like their Paleozoic forerunners. Back then the amphibians looked like two-foot-long, and longer, spatulas having stubby legs and stout bodies. Their pancake-turner heads were fitted with jaws eager to snap shut on prey. None of the early amphibians was herbivorous. Even now, all are carnivorous, at least as adults. Frogs do not approach the size of the large early amphibians, and they are rather distantly related (within the Amphibia) to most of them, but while their skull bones are very different, living representatives of the class still show the broad, flat head and endearing Kermit the Frog smile of all amphibians.

Obtaining the land, as amphibians did, presents all kinds of problems. Since bodies do not float in air like they do in water, the most obvious problem involves supporting the animal's weight. Various structural modifications and experimentations occurred early in amphibian history. The backbone was reinforced, and the limbs strengthened. Drying out is a problem, more so than breathing.

Early amphibians had lungs like their fishy aquatic ancestors. Moreover, air-breathing through lungs could be supplemented by absorbing oxygen through moist skin. The downside of moist skin is that moisture is lost through it, dehydrating and killing the animal if the dehydration gets out of control. Living amphibians always have a tough time with that. They are most common around low, wet areas, ponds, or streams, and when they are found elsewhere, there are some sophisticated survival tricks brought into play.

Reproduction in modern amphibians follows a rather primitive pattern that in its basic form would be just as good for a fish. Usually the female sheds ova directly into the water and a male dumps sperm into the water to fertilize them outside of the female's body. Then, in most species, the developing amphibians undergo a free-living, fully aquatic tadpole stage. That is very unlike reproduction in reptiles and mammals, both of which have internal fertilization and fetal membranes, including an amnion, embracing the developing embryo.

Living amphibians comprise the caecilians, the salamanders, and the frogs (with their warty buddies, the toads). Caecilians have no legs. They live in the tropics, burrowing in the ground. A few species are fully aquatic, living the whole of their lives in fresh water. In Africa caecilians seem to be particularly fond of burrowing through the organic loam of banana plantations. They have a miserable fossil record, not very informative except for some tiny specimens from Arizona, dating from before Pangaea broke up. The Arizona specimens have legs. It should not be surprising that an ancient fossil caecilian has diminutive legs while living caecilians have none. Legless caecilians had to evolve from ancestors with legs. Nevertheless it is a truly wonderful thing to find them in the fossil record and to see them. It is a puzzle piece that fits perfectly into the hypothetical hole where it should.

Salamanders are often quite pretty with brilliant yellow or orange color patterns. They have long bodies and tails and broad, smiling faces. As they walk, they swing their bodies back and forth in an S-shaped curve, like the flexing of a fish tail. They are most diverse in the Appalachian region, but they are distributed all over much of the Northern Hemisphere. One salamander family entered South America, apparently relatively recently, and lives there today. Salamanders appear to have originated in the north after Gondwana separated in the breakup of Pangaea.

Frogs are currently worldwide in distribution, although like all other amphibians, they are limited by salt water. Their earliest record is from Madagascar. They evolved just a bit before the dinosaurs and mammals did. Throughout their 200-million-year-plus history frogs have been unmistakable as frogs. Once the structural and adaptive threshold of frogdom was passed, frogs were here to stay. It is a plan that works. There are many living species, and there is variety in what they do in nature, but basically a frog is a frog is a frog. They are not like mammals, many modern species of which bear little resemblance to the mammals of 100 million years ago. They are, in the sense of having a strong similarity to early fossil frogs, living fossils. Because they were around since the days of Pangaea, it is reasonable to expect that the separation of Northern and Southern Hemisphere landmasses had an effect on subsequent frog evolution, which it did, and that the later breakup of Gondwana also had an influence. Some of the modern distribution of frog families may well be related to the dissection of Pangaea, just as the distribution of salamanders is.

The genealogical relationships among living frogs have been studied from the perspective of their biochemistry, but not so much from their anatomy and early fossil record. That is in part because the anatomy of frogs, except in a few notable and important studies, is perceived as being monotonous.

Using the magnitude of immunological reactions among frogs, it was estimated that some of the modern families of frogs diverged from each other during the Cretaceous. One family of living frogs, the pipids, is now especially characteristic of Africa and South America. Often they are considered quite primitive among frogs. Pipids, the group that includes the midwife toads and the little mail order frogs for children, are nowadays entirely aquatic. Assuming that they have their origin in the time between the split of Pangaea and the breakup of Gondwana, the fossil frogs collected in Malaŵi and Cameroon ought to include pipids. That appears to be the case. Partial skulls from both Malaŵi and Cameroon are heavily constructed like modern pipids' skulls are. The best frog sample available to me is from the old Cretaceous pond in Cameroon. There are both adults and probably tadpoles there, but I have not been able to make more sense out of them than to recognize pipids. That seems to be the only family there, for now anyway.

Lizards and turtles, two groups of living reptiles, have a distribution pattern similar to amphibians and equally interesting. Thus we are beginning to see consistent patterns of biotic change emerge from the Age of Reptiles, initiated under the feet of dinosaurs and concluding with our own familiar modern world. Among the better-known lizards, the iguanas and their close relatives seem to have originated in Gondwana following the breakup of Pangaea. With further fragmentation of the southern landmass, chameleons emerged. Skinks, gekkos, racerunners, Gila monsters, and monitors may trace their geographic origins back to Northern Hemisphere landmasses after the breakup of Pangaea. Considerable mixing of Northern and Southern Hemisphere lizards has occurred since the end of the Cretaceous, just as it has for mammals, but the fossil record of lizards is less complete, or at least less intensively studied.

Turtles present a particularly interesting story because they are such an odd group of animals. In some ways, most notably in the structure of their skulls, they are the most primitive of reptiles. Amniotes, that is all those vertebrates having an amniotic membrane during fetal development, can be divided up into basically three different groups depending on the way their cheekbones arch. The architecture of cheekbones is important for how animals chew because some of the important muscles that work the lower jaw attach to them or contract next to them. To test this, feel your cheekbone to locate it in your face. Then slide your hand down toward the angle of your jaw and bite. You will feel the bulge of your masseter muscle. Then move your hand to your temple region and bite again. Now you will feel your temporal muscles. Both function when you chew. Your cheekbone provides a strut allowing the muscles to work efficiently.

Primitively the skull of vertebrates is constructed like a box with all the muscles for chewing confined within the box. The rearrangement of skull bones to form cheek arches opens up gaps, or windows, through which muscles can pass, allowing them to become longer and therefore stronger. The muscles often attach around the window opening, and when they contract, the bulge of the exerting muscle has a place to go, through the window, rather than being trapped in a boxlike skull. You, and other species in the mammal clade, have but one cheekbone arch on each side of the skull. Dinosaurs, birds, crocodiles, lizards, and snakes either have two or they have skulls that were modified from ancestors that had two. All living reptiles are of the two-arch skull variety, with one exception—the turtles. Turtles retain a boxlike skull, but modified in other ways. They do not have cheek arches at all and consequently their chewing muscles work differently from the basic plan of other reptiles. As a matter of fact, turtles do not even have teeth. Their jaws are covered by a horny beak.

Evolutionarily advanced turtles have sophisticated skulls and chewing muscles, which evolved in other directions from those taken by mammals. Nevertheless, because turtles lack cheek arches in the sense of mammals or as in other reptiles, and because geologically ancient and evolutionarily primitive amphibians lack cheek arches, turtles are considered primitive among the amniotes.

Their cheeks may leave a little something to be desired from an advanced amniote perspective, but turtles clearly have their own unique specializations. Just think about the shell. It is nature's own mobile home, the Winnebago of vertebrate evolution. To get an idea of just how remarkable the turtle shell is, reach behind your back and feel your shoulder blade. It juts out, right? Now feel your ribs below your shoulder blade. Your shoulder blade and your collarbone, the bones that make up your shoulder girdle, to which your arm attaches, all of it lies outside of your rib cage. Not so with turtles. The bony shell of turtles is made up mostly of ribs and the backbone. Obviously the shoulder blade—and arms, legs, tail, and neck, for that matter—are not attached outside of the rib cage. They could not be and still be seen extending out from inside the shell, or, more impressively in some species, the appendages could not be retracted completely into the protection of the shell. The skeletons of turtles, therefore, no matter how primitive the cheek arches might be, are very special structures.

There are two major groups of living turtles. The more common and abundant group comprises the hidden-necked turtles. The mechanism for drawing the head into the shell relies on a complicated suite of vertebral modifications allowing the neck to be essentially looped upon itself in an S-shaped curve and then rotated in a vertical plane back into the shell. The other major group is the side-necked turtles. They simply swing their heads to the side to fit it under the protection of the shell. The side-necked turtles are considered the more primitive of the two groups.

Turtles trace their origins back to the heyday of Pangaea, and there is good evidence that the two groups of turtles were distinct before the breakup of Pangaea began. However, as in the case of frogs and lizards, the isolation and disintegration of Gondwana had a major effect on the distribution of various turtle families as we find them today. The side-necked turtles are basically Southern Hemisphere in distribution, while S-necked turtles are much more widely distributed, including in the oceans of the world because some of them, such as leatherbacks and green sea turtles, have invaded the marine environment.

Fossil turtles were first found in the Dinosaur Beds of Malaŵi long ago. In fact one of them was named *Platycheloides nyasae* in 1928. *Platycheloides* is a side-necked turtle. The same kind of turtle is found in rocks of similar age in the West African nation of Niger along with other turtles most similar to those found at Araripe in Brazil. The fossil record of turtles is another case where ancient life reflects the large-scale geography of the Cretaceous. Until recently it was held among some researchers that green sea turtles, a living species, show a particularly informative life-style that harkens back to their ancestor's habits of 100 million years ago.

Green sea turtles are one of the S-necked species that have taken to the oceans (Figure 39). Females leave the sea only to scramble onto sandy beaches and lay eggs. There are several breeding centers for the species. Green sea turtles are herbivores. Some populations of them graze on sea grass off the coast of Brazil, but breed and lay their eggs over 2,300 kilometers distant, some 1,400 miles away. Each year a group of green sea turtles turns their beaks to the east and swims to the island of Ascension, an unprepossessing volcanic rock jutting above the surface of the ocean along the Mid-Atlantic Ridge. It is unclear exactly how the navigation is managed, perhaps by utilizing the sun or moon, perhaps ocean currents, perhaps the Earth's magnetic field, perhaps by a combination of several means. The most recent studies implicate the direction of waves and perhaps the local variation in the intensity of the Earth's magnetic field caused by the magnetic stripes in the sea floor as possible clues for turtle navigation (see Figure 8 in Chapter 1). Nevertheless the fact remains that a population of green sea turtles feeds off the coast of Brazil, then regularly the same group returns faithfully, it seems, to the same forsaken island in the middle of the Atlantic to reproduce. It was suggested at one time that the modern migration pattern of the green sea turtle was nothing more than an updated version of the ancient pattern of the ancestral breeding cycle established as Africa and South America split apart through continental drift. When those continents rifted apart, the South Atlantic Ocean formed. As they continued to drift apart, the Atlantic Ocean got wider and wider until the present geography was reached.

One fly in the ointment is the age of Ascension Island. It is nowhere near old enough to have been present in the early stages of the formation of the South Atlantic. It is quite young, not more than a few million years old. It is impossible that turtles were breeding on its beaches either late in the Age of Reptiles or early in the Age of Mammals because it simply was not there. The dilemma could be solved by realizing how geologically active mid-ocean

FIGURE *39: Green sea turtle. A population of these sea turtles nests on Ascension Island in the middle of the Atlantic Ocean.*

ridges are. There are always new volcanic islands being formed because molten rock is carried to the surface along mid-ocean ridges, new sea floor is created (see Figure 7 in Chapter 1), and sometimes in the heat of the geological moment lava is extruded through volcanoes to such an extent that a pile rises above the surface of the ocean water. Like Ascension, Iceland is an island on the Mid-Atlantic Ridge. In fact Iceland is the largest island on the ridge.

Once a volcanic island is formed along a mid-ocean ridge, two forces begin to act on it. First it begins an inexorable voyage away from the ridge due simply to the way plate tectonics works. New sea floor is created and older sea floor, including that on which volcanoes are stacked, moves laterally away. As sea floor moves away from the ridge, it cools and because it is cooler, it becomes denser. The cooler, denser sea floor away from the ridge settles deeper into the more plastic substance of the Earth's interior. The net result is that the islands that were once emergent above the ridge slowly submerge as they move away from the ridge.

The second force acting on the island is that of erosion. Waves immediately begin battering its surface as soon as it is formed. Such hostile actions by the ocean against the shores speed up the process of submergence. Eventually a flat top is pummeled onto the island and it sinks completely beneath the waves to become what is known as a seamount. The Hawaiian Islands, while erupted over a hot spot in the ocean crust rather than a spreading center, are a chain that illustrates the process. The youngest island is the big one, Hawaii. The islands are older in a line going to the northwest from Maui to Molokai to Oahu to Kauai. The oldest islands in the Hawaiian chain are no longer islands. They are the Emperor Seamounts. That is what is going to happen to Ascension Island. In time it will sink. When it does, turtles very certainly will breed there no longer.

So where will they go? The simple answer is just somewhere else. They will find a new place to lay eggs, or they will die out.

Now suppose that this turtle species with its exacting sense of navigation swims toward Ascension, but another island has sprouted nearby from beneath the waves along the mid-ocean ridge. Would they just lay their eggs on the new beaches? If the turtles were to find another island that way, it may not matter to the turtles that Ascension goes under. Is it possible that Ascension is one island in a long string of islands appearing and disappearing through time? It is easy to imagine such a thing if we look at the Hawaiian island chain on a map, strung along from a volcanic source, the younger islands fresh and high, the older islands lower and less rugged, phasing into seamounts. There are seamounts along the Mid-Atlantic Ridge, so the question becomes, have the green sea turtles leap-frogged from mid-ocean island to mid-ocean island as the South Atlantic widened for a period of 100 million years? What a neat story if they had.

The fossil record of sea turtles is less extensively studied than it ought to be in order to make sense of the history of the greens. Nevertheless turtles of a similar evolutionary grade had taken to the sea by Cretaceous times. They cannot have invaded the South Atlantic until it was open, obviously, so unless they were in the hypersaline waters off southwest Africa, which seems unlikely, green sea turtles probably did not exist around Africa, if they existed in the Cretaceous at all. Moreover, the life-style of green sea turtles in the Atlantic depends on the presence of large fields of sea grass, on which the species feeds, more than it depends on the beaches of Ascension Island, where only one population of the species lays eggs. There are no indications that turtle grass was widely distributed until the latter half of the Age of Mammals, perhaps around twenty million years ago or less.

Conclusive proof that the green sea turtles of Ascension Island are not the survivors of a long and majestic race of Mid-Atlantic seafaring turtles comes from a detailed comparison of their genetic material with that of other populations of green sea turtles. The molecules of inheritance clearly indicate that there has been mixing, at least to some degree, of the females from the various populations of the species. The Ascension Island population has not been separate all these years, and the colonization of the beaches in the middle of the Atlantic, while unquestionably an amazing feat of animal migration, is not necessarily the end result of a chain of longer and longer distance colonizations by a single contiguous population. It could be nothing more than happenstance that the beaches of Ascension are used as a nesting area, regardless of whether other islands along the Mid-Atlantic Ridge have, or have not, been utilized in times past.

The idea of island-hopping vertebrates is not limited to turtles, and it is not even limited to true islands, nor to animals that swim. It has been suggested that the rather constant supply of volcanic rocks to Iceland has maintained the island above the surface for tens of millions of years. That part of it lying over the Mid-Atlantic Ridge, the source of lava, remains emergent, but the lateral flanks of the island subside and disappear. It is similar to the notion of continually creating new islands along the ridge, except that with Iceland the island is always formed at the same spot. Thus, such terrestrial animals as may have been inhabiting Iceland twenty million years ago have never been without dry land, according to this theory, and the land surface where they lived acted as a sort of treadmill, with the inhabitants required to maintain their position over the ridge on younger and younger rock as time progressed. It is an interesting idea, but there is no direct evidence that volcanic islands have been particularly significant in this regard, at least so far as terrestrial vertebrates are concerned. But some evidence is suggestive.

One recent study introduces the possibility that the life of the Galápagos Islands, straddling the equator off the coast of Ecuador in the eastern Pacific Ocean, can be viewed from the perspective of islands through time, wearing to seamounts, subsiding and submerging while new islands form. This is an especially interesting suggestion because the Galápagos Islands played a central role in Darwin's formulation of evolution by natural selection. It is a unique set of islands with an interesting fauna and flora. The name Galápagos derives from the Spanish word for tortoise. Galápagos tortoises grow quite large, to over 100 pounds in fact. The islands were a regular stop for buccaneers and later for more legitimate sailing ships. The tortoises provided an easy source of fresh meat and they could be conveniently stored on their backs in a ship's hold for weeks without trouble.

Besides tortoises there are all kinds of noteworthy animals on the islands. Galápagos penguins survive at the equator because of the cold-water currents that come up from Antarctica along the west coast of South America. Marine iguanas are lizards that have taken to feeding in the sea off plants growing along the rocky shores of the islands.

Darwin was struck by the similarity of most of the fauna of the islands to that of mainland South America, yet each island held a different but related set of species. Darwin reasoned that each island in the archipelago provided a separate locus for natural selection and consequently for the differentiation of species, perhaps most famously the birds known as Darwin's finches.

If the Galápagos Islands are simply the last emergent rocks in a system that includes seamounts that were previously islands, the ancestors of the terrestrial inhabitants may have hopped from island to island through time. The implication is that their evolution has been more complex than that envisioned by Darwin. The evidence comes from the fact that there are seamounts associated with the present islands, and the limited biomolecular evidence suggests that the birds may not have had such a long separate history as the marine iguanas have had from their terrestrial cousins. It would not be particularly startling if they did not, because different species do not necessarily colonize islands at the same time. A more precise understanding is likely to follow detailed molecular studies and comparisons among islands and with the mainland of South America. Whether the history of Galápagos species is more or less complex, the result—obtained by the process envisaged by Darwin—is the same. Different but related species evolved on separate islands through natural selection.

ON THE OTHER side of the ocean's surface—the permanently wet side— the mid-ocean ridges and their islands have been of great biogeographic significance. The feet of volcanic islands form a substrate upon which coral and other organisms needing clean ocean water within the range of sunlight can flourish. Coral, because of the stony lime it secretes, actually builds rock. Clearly, then, marine organisms hop from the shores and lagoons of one island to the next, taking advantage of a fresh place to call home. As other invertebrates join the coral to build a complex community, so, too, do vertebrates join the party, particularly the vast array of coral-reef fishes. There is even a very likely case of a living fossil, called a coelacanth (its biology will be discussed at greater length in the next chapter), in which the animal, its kind supposedly extinct for eighty million years, now lives only along the steep sides of volcanic islands only five million years old or so. It is only known from the Comoro Islands between Madagascar and Africa, except for one specimen caught off the coast of South Africa.

Coelacanths are not deep-sea dwellers; rather they inhabit moderate depths. Their limited geographic distribution can only be explained by their hopping from island foot to island foot (or along volcanoes that never broke the surface of the sea) as those features were formed. Either that or we must admit that we simply do not know much about where animals live under the sea. The latter is true to some extent, and the former may be as well.

The colonization of the feet of islands by corals and other life demonstrates the importance of plate tectonics in creating new real estate and in adding to the diversity of environments available for life to invade and exploit. The coral-reef habitats are centered in the photic zone, the depth of water penetrated by light. Below the photic zone, on the seabed, the processes of plate tectonics provide other areas where life might thrive. Hot water escaping from inside the Earth through vents along ocean ridges provide for another kind of biological community, one that does not depend on sunlight for its primary energy but on chemical reactions. These hydrothermal vent communities are relatively new to us because exploration of the ocean floor is such a novelty. Nevertheless, there is a characteristic suite of organisms living in the dark depths, well away from any hope of sunlight. There are bacteria. There are molluscs and crustaceans. There are worms of many kinds, some growing to incredible lengths and having tentacles like flower petals. It is a whole different world, and one that in some respects may reflect life on Earth prior to photosynthesis and the abundant free oxygen that green plants produce. Organisms evolving in the warmth of a hydrothermal vent deep beneath the seas are sheltered from meteorites and climatic fluctuations that might drive species at the surface to extinction.

Chemosynthetic communities are not limited to hydrothermal vents along ocean-floor-spreading centers. There are other ways to establish an appropriate chemical environment for them. For example, and strangely enough, the carcass of a whale decomposing at the bottom of the sea provides the correct combination of factors for a small undersea island of chemosynthetic life to exist. It is a transient community, but still, it is a little enclave, just like an island, in an otherwise overwhelmingly phototrophic sea. Isn't that amazing? The conditions at a mid-ocean ridge and at a decaying whale carcass are sufficiently similar that the same general kind of community of organisms flourishes around each. What is so special about whale carcasses that they should do this?

The answer is that there is nothing really special about whales other than their size and perhaps their high oil content. If a whale carcass can support a chemosynthetic community under the sea, then so can any carcass of sufficiently large size to provide the right environment. So the bodies of vertebrate animals could have been acting as islands under the sea ever since large marine vertebrates evolved. Whales only go back 52 million years or so. However, large fish go back much earlier. The huge marine reptiles of the Mesozoic go back 200 million years, to the time of Pangaea. Plesiosaurs, ichthyosaurs, and mosasaurs, the three great reptilian lineages that ruled the sea during the Mesozoic, may have played a role in the evolution of hydrothermal-vent faunas way back then just as whales do now. Like the pattern seen on land, the whales—marine mammals—did not become the behemoths of the oceans—indeed they did not even evolve—until after the reptilian giants of the oceans became completely extinct at the Great Dying, the end of the Cretaceous.

SEA TURTLES evolved before whales, but never have they produced species comparable in size to the biggest marine mammals. Still, sea turtles achieve quite respectable dimensions. Moreover, they are reptiles and therefore they have a different metabolism from the warm-blooded mammals that maintain higher rates of bodily activities. Comparing the metabolic characteristics of a large reptile that undergoes taxing temperature changes (such as sea turtles) with those of a mammal might be very instructive and perhaps relevant to understanding dinosaurs.

Leatherback turtles, another species of the S-necked group, grow to between four and five hundred pounds in weight. They swim in latitudes ranging from the warm-water tropics to the frigid Arctic Circle. Thus, since they swim, they are forced to experience rather extreme conditions of temperature while remaining active. Their measured metabolic rates are below those expected in mammals of the same size, so the leatherbacks must be solving their problems of maintaining activity and body temperature in ways different from warm-blooded mammals. Not surprising.

In both large mammals and large reptiles, the sheer bulk of flesh between the inside and the outside of the body provides insulation against the loss of heat. However, leatherbacks must somehow dissipate their body heat while swimming in warmer waters, and conversely they must conserve their heat while swimming in colder North Atlantic waters. This is accomplished by regulating circulation, increasing the flow of blood to areas where heat can be more easily lost when the animal is in danger of overheating, and restricting the flow of blood when heat loss is detrimental. Central to the regulation of body temperature by leatherbacks, however, is large size and the insulation that bulk provides.

It makes a great deal of sense, then, that dinosaurs, at least the larger species, may have employed the same kind of gigantothermy in regulating their bodies as leatherback turtles do, simply because they were of large size. The conclusion, if that is so, is that gigantothermic dinosaurs could have been active through a wide range of temperatures. Other dinosaurs, particularly the smaller ones, may not have been able to control their body temperature in the same unconscious way. Some must have developed a true warm-bloodedness, even with small body size. We know that for certain because birds are warm-blooded.

Dinosaur geography provides evidence that these reptiles very probably were tolerant of a wide range of temperatures. The geographic distribution of dinosaurs is huge. It goes from the low equatorial tropics to the high polar latitudes. Early Cretaceous dinosaurs are known from Australia and Late Cretaceous dinosaurs are known from both Alaska and Antarctica. It is a tremendous geographic range, embracing extremes of temperature, but leatherback turtles have a similar range from the tropics to the Arctic, so it is not necessarily strange that dinosaurs do.

The average yearly temperature for Australia in the Early Cretaceous is estimated to be less than 5 degrees centigrade, which is only 41 degrees Fahrenheit. That is a yearly average of temperature based on the geochemistry of oxygen. Temperatures would have fluctuated with the seasons just as they do now. Austral winters were dark and very likely bitterly cold. Summers were warm. The Antarctic polar region was probably icebound.

Overwintering in harsh conditions—in the dark—with temperatures plummeting and food growing scarce, is difficult. Some dinosaurs, perhaps the smaller ones, may have been able to survive during the winter because they were active and warm-blooded. Other dinosaurs may have solved the problem by hibernating, sleeping through the tough times. Still others may have migrated to more pleasant climes on the northern side of Australia. That is all speculation. What is so interesting about the leatherback turtles with respect to dinosaurs is that they are reptiles, they suffer extremes of temperature, and they migrate. Most importantly we know something about how their body temperature is controlled and that it enables them to travel through the range of temperatures that they do. Perhaps some of the dinosaurs were similar.

TEMPERATURE, both inside and outside the body, is an important factor for all animals, but the outside temperature plays a peculiar role in some living reptiles. In most turtles, some lizards, and in crocodiles the temperature at which eggs are incubated at a critical time in their development determines the sex of the animal. Sea turtle eggs produce males if incubated below 28 degrees centigrade (82 degrees Fahrenheit), but they produce females if incubated above 29.5 degrees (85 degrees Fahrenheit) during the middle third of development. Therefore, since crocodiles, alligators, some lizards, and some other turtles develop in similar fashion, it is not unreasonable to assume that some or even most dinosaurs had a similar method of sex determination. It cannot be proven, but it has been suggested that changing climates toward the end of the Mesozoic may have affected the sex ratio of dinosaur species and thereby contributed to their extinction by disrupting the population balance.

THIS CHAPTER BEGAN by looking at differing rates and patterns of evolution resulting in adaptive radiations on the one hand and living fossils on the other. From the examples presented it should be clear that there is no set path that an evolutionary lineage must follow, but that the genetic potential of a species will limit its evolutionary options, as will the constraints imposed by its biological and physical environment. The physical processes of plate tectonics modify the Earth and create new environments for life to colonize. As the Earth's geography changes, so are life's strategies modified. Some generalities about the roots of the modern world begin to emerge.

Pangaea of 200 million years ago provided an interconnected canvas of continents across which was painted the rudiments of terrestrial vertebrate life for the modern world: primitive frogs, lizards, mammals, turtles, and perhaps birds. None had achieved the sophistication of their modern representatives. That came with the later stages of geographic rearrangement when Pangaea broke apart and Gondwana fragmented. The vicars left on drifting landmasses evolved their separate ways, often to reach different, but for each, more derived grades of evolution. The dinosaurs, too, evolved along the lines of geographical vicars, separated from each other by widening oceans and foundering land bridges. Only sporadically did landmasses conjoin to allow the mixing of their communities.

There is one additional case, in some ways the most intriguing, of the geographical distribution of animals through time that should be brought up here: the European fossil locality of Messel. Located in Germany near Frankfurt am Main, the site is roughly forty million years old. It is the remains of an ancient lake that existed around twenty-six million years after the Age of Reptiles, well into the Age of Mammals. Messel was originally excavated for oil shale. Such a large hole in the ground in crowded Europe will not go unnoticed by all sorts of people with jobs to accomplish. Messel was very nearly turned into a garbage dump until it was saved. Now it is a fossil reserve.

The fossils that are preserved at Messel are exquisite. Many species are represented by whole, articulated skeletons. Not only that, but some of the mammals have the image of their hair preserved as an organic film in the shale. Some even have the stomach contents of the last meal.

Being in the Age of Mammals, as it is, Messel has an interesting suite of mammalian fossils. The list includes insectivores, primates, rodents, bats— very nice bats—and other species. It even includes an anteating pangolin, a kind of mammal found today in Asia and Africa. They are covered in large, stiff scales, which make them look a lot like walking pinecones. However, the strangest of all mammals from Messel is another kind of anteater. It is an anteater that is the only European representative—fossil or living—of a group of specialized anteaters now living in South America (Figure 40). How could it have gotten to Messel without leaving a trace anywhere else?

The answer for some paleontologists is that this group of anteaters, and perhaps other groups of placental mammals, differentiated between 100 million years ago and the beginning of the Age of Mammals at 66 million years

Figure 40: South American giant anteater. A fossil related to this living species was found in Germany. Might similar fossils one day be found in Africa?

ago in what is now Africa. The timing would be later than the Dinosaur Beds of Malaŵi, or the Koum Basin in Cameroon, or Araripe in Brazil. It would also be younger than the separation of South America and Africa is usually considered to be unless the process of separation is actually more complicated than has been presented. There is no viable fossil record in Africa representing that interval, so the possibility cannot be excluded on the basis of what we currently know of African life. It is possible that the movement of Africa and South Africa away from each other during this interval was sufficiently complicated that island hopping, or perhaps contact, might just have occurred. If it did, the distribution of the South American anteater and its Messel relative might be explained. By Messel time the anteaters, primates, pangolins, early relatives of horses, and some other kinds of mammals had migrated into Europe, possibly from Africa.

I have no idea whether such a sequence of events actually occurred. The evidence is weak and inconclusive. However, it is an hypothesis that is plausible to the extent that it explains the Messel fauna, and it predicts that an undocumented episode of mammalian evolution occurred late in the Age of Reptiles in Africa. It also predicts which kinds of mammals should be involved in it. These predictions will be tested when fossils of the right age and in the right place are found. This could be another case of good fossils just waiting to be discovered.

Whatever the case, it is clear that toward the end of the Age of Reptiles the Earth was rich in biological diversity. In many ways it was recognizable as the parent of today's world. In one way, however, it was very different. Today's rulers, the mammals, did little but skulk furtively about in the Mesozoic world. They did not suffer from an identity crisis; they were clearly mammals and of the three major groups (placentals, marsupials, and monotremes) that we recognize today, plus some mammalian groups that have since become extinct. Yet it seems the mammals were almost intimidated by the dinosaurs. They simply and undeniably did not flourish during the Age of Reptiles. Only after the terminal Cretaceous extinctions, when dinosaurs and many other creatures went extinct, did the changing of the guard occur and a new period of faunal adjustment take place.

And now here we are.

9

A LIVING
DINOSAUR?

FOSSILS OF MANY KINDS representing the world of 100 million years ago can be found today, preserved in the ancient rocks of Africa. Many of them are strange. However, on one of my flights to Malaŵi I read in an airline magazine of something even more strange. It was a "serious scientific expedition" to Darkest Africa in search not of fossils, not even of living lions, hyaenas, or elephants, but of a *living* dinosaur. Not birds, but dinosaurs in the traditional sense. A sauropod. Something presumably resembling brontosaurus, or maybe a Malaŵi-saurus. The expedition I read about is not the first to propose the search. There have been at least four others. These are not scientific expeditions. They are science fiction—and not particularly good science fiction, either, judging from the 1985 motion picture *Baby: Secret of the Lost Legend,* which is based on such a search.

Africa, the Dark Continent, the land of the unknown, is a cliché, an allure even now. That mystique used to be justified. At least part of it goes back to the intense interest that the Victorian era took in the search for the headwaters of the Nile. In the latter half of the nineteenth century the geography of Africa really was much more poorly known than that of most other continents. Back then the Interior was a blank spot on the British map, even though in earlier centuries the Portuguese had a better reckoning of it. Now Africa is no longer so remote, so hidden, as it used to be. The big questions of old, such as the courses of its rivers and the traces of its mountains, are not obscure.

The River Nile originates from the lake region of East Africa and debauches into the Mediterranean Sea. The River Congo, through the Lualaba and the Ituri, has its headwaters near those of the Nile. It flows north then west from the lake region to drain the fetid swamps of Central Africa into the Atlantic. Only one great lake, Lake Malaŵi, drains south, out through the Shiré and then the Zambezi to the Indian Ocean. The rivers were highways when the continent opened up to Europeans. Explorers used them to travel through the land.

Daniel Defoe's fictional hero Captain Bob Singleton, the pirate, crossed the African continent through his author's pen, on paper and in the imagination, but much before his time. Defoe wrote Singleton's made up travel adventures more than a century before Livingstone actually did cross the continent in 1854. Livingstone followed a course along the Zambezi for most of the way. He made it to the Atlantic coast and then he made his way back. The truth of African exploration is stranger than fiction. Men like David Livingstone are not normal. He was caught up in the search for the headwaters of the Nile. Livingstone was a missionary, but he, like Richard Burton and John Speke, explored the Rift Valley where the great lakes of Africa hang like delicious wet grapes on a dry brown stalk. He searched for the headwaters of the Nile for years. He thought he had found them, but he had not. He was still searching when he died.

Henry Stanley searched for Livingstone and became infected with the fever of African exploration. *Bula Matari,* "the breaker of rocks," as Stanley became known to the natives, took on Livingstone's quest. He followed the course of the Lualaba, not to the Nile as he wanted but all the way to the Congo, even to the west coast of Africa.

It is all part of the tradition, this searching and exploration of Africa. The explorers, driven men, knew what they were looking for. They had their reasons, and the reasons were valid. The searches made sense to the nineteenth-century world. The Nile does have headwaters, and they were important to find. Livingstone was alive when Stanley searched, and he was important to find. The early explorers opened up the continent to Europe. There are no more blank spots on the map. The only way not to be aware of Africa nowadays is to ignore, for whatever reason, the common, hard-won knowledge of that continent.

Expeditions to Africa in search of living dinosaurs, like the one I read about in the airline magazine, are based on word-of-mouth reports of a legendary beast called *Mokele-Mbembe*. The phenomenon is no different from the reports of the Loch Ness Monster, Yeti, or Bigfoot. The only real difference is that in this case it is set in Africa. *Mokele-Mbembe*'s haunts are alleged to be the Likouala Swamp of the People's Republic of the Congo, right in the extreme depths of the continent. This is the northern part of the huge swampy region traversed by Stanley on his seven-month float down the Congo River. *Mokele-Mbembe* is thought to look like a brontosaurus—the word used by English-speaking searchers—based most strongly, in their opinion, on the identification of mug shots by natives. A man named Appolonaire encountered by one of the expeditions even sketched a crude effigy in the soil that was said to resemble a sauropod. He had seen the beast, he said, at the village of Pikunda, not far from the route Stanley took on his third African expedition. On that one Stanley left instructions with his rear guard to join him with extra supplies and ammunition. The rear guard never caught up with Stanley, partly because they heard he was dead. Supposedly he had been murdered in retaliation for the atrocities he allegedly bestowed on the natives. Rumors were rampant among the local populations that human arms and legs had been seen in Stanley's cooking pots. There was graphic evidence of a quality equal to that used in the search for *Mokele-Mbembe*. Stanley, who was assuredly not dead, wrote, "Sketches by an amateur artist are said to have been made of whole parties indulging in cannibal repasts."

Stanley, of course, had not been murdered, the English were not cannibals (any more than the natives were), and the sketches of Stanley's cooking pots had no bearing on reality. I do not know what the Congolese Appolonaire drew, or why, but the report that he sketched a sauropod does not substantiate their existence alive in the Congo.

Nevertheless an expedition to the Likouala Swamp could be scientifically very important if questions of more general significance were being asked: What is the diversity of life—plant and animal—in the Likouala Swamp? How many species are there? What is the ecological structure of the community? How does it compare with other tropical jungles, such as the Amazon? What is the contribution of the African tropics to the global ecological balance? What are the economically important species? Which species have medicinal properties? How has the swamp changed through geologic time? How is it being affected by human impact? Is it being destroyed? Are steps necessary for conservation? How can the people of the region best and most effectively utilize their resources?

If questions such as these were addressed, sauropods, if they existed, would turn up in due course. Whether they did or did not, we would have a much greater knowledge about this part of the world and it would be of much greater consequence.

But surely, one might insist, dinosaurs *could* be living somewhere in Africa, could they not? Sure, they could. And that would be fun. But how likely is it? The odds are so great against it that the probability of finding a living sauropod has, for all intents and purposes, reached zero. I regret that it is—sadly—a virtual certainty that none will be found alive. But it does make sense.

Not a single really new kind of large animal has been discovered in Africa since the okapi, a relative of the giraffe, was named in 1901, very nearly a century ago. And people have looked. The pygmy hippopotamus was discovered in 1912, but regular hippos were already familiar long before then. The giant forest hog was found in 1902, but people already knew that pigs were around. Almost certainly some less conspicuous small animals still remain to be discovered and described from many parts of the world. Things such as mice, insects, or fish are sure to have multitudes of unnamed species. Perhaps even some larger terrestrial species will be discovered. But while there may be species new to science, they are unlikely to be grossly different from what is already known.

The circumstances surrounding the European discovery of the giant forest hog, *Hylochoerus meinertzhageni,* are well documented, so they ought to be informative as to how new and large animals were discovered in the Victorian past. Richard Meinertzhagen, for whom the species was named, recorded the events in his diary. A soldier and an avid sportsman in the sense of early twentieth-century Africa, he spent much time afield. He lived in the bush, being stationed in several remote and mountainous posts in Kenya. He kept a scrupulous record of his daily life.

Meinertzhagen writes in his diary on 5 September 1902 while on a trip to the Aberdare Mountains,

> While wandering in the forest at dusk I saw two animals I have never seen before. Unfortunately I caught only a fleeting glimpse of them. . . . [One] was an enormous black pig, probably a forest variety of the warthog. Here again I only just saw the beast for a moment.

Then, in 1904, two years later, while on a punitive expedition against the Embu tribe of Mount Kenya:

> Just as we were emerging from the forest the leading man of my patrol fired a shot at something which I could not see, and on coming up I found he had killed a huge pig with long black hair, unlike anything I ever heard of. I put a piece of the skin into my haversack but left the carcass. I shall send to bring it in tomorrow. As we have several of the enemy in the vicinity I could not remain and examine her, for she was a sow, but I now wish I had brought home the skull, which was unlike that of any pig I know.

Then on 24 March 1904 he wrote,

> I may as well note down what I know of the huge forest pig which I found on 11 March in the Kenya forests. Up till now I have seen but one, a sow, and she after she had been killed. All I have of this beast is a small piece of skin. I asked all my Masai levies whether they knew the animal and they all said they did but that it lived in thick forest and was called *elguia* by them. They made their shields of its tough skin, and I actually purchased a shield which purports to be made from the forest pig. Its owner told me he bought the skin from a Dorobo hunter who had killed it on the Mau escarpment, which shows the animal has a wide range.
>
> Towards the end of the expedition my men found several large pieces of skin in villages. One piece in particular is enormous and could never have been taken off an animal much smaller than a donkey. The hair is long and black, measuring some 10 inches on the crest.
>
> On returning to Fort Hall I enquired from the Wakikuyu concerning the pig and found they all knew it well, calling it *numirra*. I have offered a cow to the first man who can get me a complete skin with the skull.
>
> I have sent all the skin I have, together with the above information, to Ray Lankester at the British Museum. I think there can be no doubt that the animal is new to science. It is exasperating not to have got a skull, but I live in hopes and shall hunt for him in forest when I get the chance.
>
> I am convinced that the pig I saw in the Aberdares . . . was this forest pig.

The elements of Meinertzhagen's ''discovery'' of the giant forest hog (see Figure 41) are personal observation, tangible remains, and verifiable general knowledge of the beast from local inhabitants. Science requires that there be something tangible, some repeatable, testable stream of logic, in order for an idea—or the claim of a new animal—to be accepted. African natives not only had names for the giant forest hog, they made shields from its hide. Meinertzhagen collected a piece of hide himself. In June 1904 Meinertzhagen even obtained a skull from one of the local inhabitants. That was particularly significant. Skulls are very important in mammalogy—the study of mammals—which is what the giant forest hog is, because almost every species can be distinguished by the structure of its skull bones and teeth.

Meinertzhagen wrote on 16 June,

FIGURE 41: *Giant forest hog. This species was unknown to the scientific community until early in the twentieth century. The circumstances surrounding its "discovery" were recorded and provide a model for how large "unknown" animals become known.*

But today I had even better luck. I had seen the tracks of pig in the forest and have often been out after them. It was only today when I was successful. I came on her in some thick stuff and killed her at about 40 yards. She is a young sow, and I was able to preserve the complete skull and skin, which I shall send to the British Museum. This is probably the first of her kind to be killed by a European.

So it was at the turn of the century. When Meinertzhagen moved to Nandi Fort in western Kenya in 1904, he found, "Forest hog are quite common here; I saw one today, and they frequently come into my vegetable garden at night." His infatuation with this animal continued. On 8 June 1905 he writes,

I received by today's mail the description and figure of the skull of my new forest pig. Though the beast occurs in the forest all round my house up here, my efforts to obtain specimens have so far proved fruitless; yet the natives know the beast well. I have offered a handsome reward for a specimen in the flesh, but I suppose they cannot conceive that anyone can be so mad as to want a pig and merely regard my whim as a form of insanity.

The hogs visited his garden:

I now have most English vegetables growing and they are now being raided by jackal, small antelope and forest pig. I sat up last night and saw a forest duiker and two forest pig, one an enormous boar, calmly rooting up my potatoes and tomatoes. . . . Some day I shall pepper those pig or put a bullet into one.

The discovery of the living okapi was not much different from the discovery of the giant forest hog. In 1900 the okapi was unknown to Western scientists, although now they can be seen in most zoos. The okapi is a short-necked giraffe that inhabits the deep jungles of the Congo Basin, where dinosaurs are suggested to be living now.

At the turn of the century pygmies told Sir Harry Johnston—the same Sir Harry who had earlier secured Nyasaland, now Malaŵi, as a British Protectorate—of a mulelike animal with zebralike stripes. He sent two pieces of the striped hide that had been given him back to Britain, and in 1901, on the basis of that evidence, it was named *Equus? johnstoni* after him. Later that same year, with better and more specimens, the beast was correctly determined to be a member of the giraffe family. Therefore, the name was changed to *Okapia johnstoni* because it is certainly not a zebra or deserving of the horse name *Equus*.

While the okapi is a distinct species of giraffe, some investigators early in this century thought that it bore some resemblance to extinct giraffes, also with short necks, which had been known from fossils for some time. Cryptozoologists, as such people who investigate claims of hidden species like to call themselves, picked up the okapi as an extinct animal found alive millions of years after it was supposed to have gone extinct, as *Mokele-Mbembe* is supposed to be. However, the okapi clearly is not one of the formerly known fossil species, notwithstanding the ancient record of the giraffe family or the primitive shortness of the okapi's neck.

The discoveries of the giant forest hog and the okapi are particularly enlightening when compared with the rumors of another animal, supposedly living in the same general area as the giant forest hog, but with no tangible proof of its existence. That one is called the Nandi bear. There are two theories as to what a Nandi bear may represent. One is that it is really a honey badger or ratel, a large member of the weasel family. The other is more appealing to long-lost-animal enthusiasts. It has been suggested that the Nandi bear is really an extinct mammal called a chalicothere. Chalicotheres have long, horsy heads, long front limbs, and claws on their fingers. They are gorilla-sized or larger. While chalicotheres have a long and seemingly good fossil record in many parts of the world including North America, Europe, Asia, and Africa, it is as hard to imagine their existence in western Kenya today as it is to imagine living sauropods in the Congo, monsters in Loch Ness, or Abominable Snowmen on the tops of mountains. If chalicotheres existed now, they would have been found out just like the giant forest hog was. If there is anything to the Nandi-bear story besides imagination, I suspect it may be the word-of-mouth description of gorillas passed across the continent from areas where they live to areas where they do not.

There are four genera of mammals—worldwide—known first as fossils, then discovered to have living representatives. One is a peccary, a pig relative from South America. One is a member of the dog family, also known from South America. One, not always put in this category, is a small, mouselike opossum known from Australia, the first live one, interestingly enough, being caught in a ski hut in the Australian Alps. The last example is a fruit bat from New Guinea. None of the fossils is highly distinguished from other, previously known relatives, and none is anywhere near the tens or even hundreds of millions of years of dinosaur antiquity. If sauropods, so very different from anything else alive today, were still extant in Africa, surely some remains of them, even a scrap of skin as in the case of the okapi or forest hog, would be available to verify the claim.

The showpiece of cryptozoological discoveries is the living fish *Latimeria* (Figure 42), the coelacanth discussed briefly in Chapter 8. It belongs to a group of bony fish that was thought to have been extinct for eighty million years. Then in 1938 Miss M. Courtenay-Latimer was intrigued by a strange fish caught in the Indian Ocean off South Africa near the mouth of the Chalumna River. A living coelacanth had been caught! This was truly a stellar discovery. While *Latimeria* itself, as a distinct species, has no fossil record, it *is* a member of the larger coelacanth group that had been unknown for the vast length of time between the Age of Reptiles and now. To this day, living coelacanths are known only from a small patch of the ocean. The first was caught by a South African fishing trawler. All the rest have been caught near the Comoro Islands between Madagascar and the African coast. The Comoros were the home of the porters who deserted Livingstone and reported him dead, leading to Stanley's search for Livingstone. Living coelacanths are known from nowhere else but those tiny spots, but mostly the Comoros, in all the vast, vast ocean.

Certainly this is an example of the fossil record somehow playing tricks on us. It does not adequately reflect the evolutionary history of coelacanths. Even until today there have been no fossil discoveries to fill the eighty-million-year gap in the fossil record. The reason most likely lies with the environmental preferences of fossil and living coelacanths. Fossil coelacanths are preserved in shallow-water environments, both fresh and marine, that are abundantly represented in the rock record. *Latimeria* lives in deeper water, 650 feet deep, 200 meters or so, in a marine environment, and in a very specific habitat as well. The rugged sea bottom along the steeply sloping feet of the Comoro Islands is formed from lava. *Latimeria* hangs out in and around caves in the lava rock, foraging and swimming about, for the most part casually. Such environments as those frequented by *Latimeria* are rarely preserved in the rock record, especially in such a state that fossils might be preserved with them.

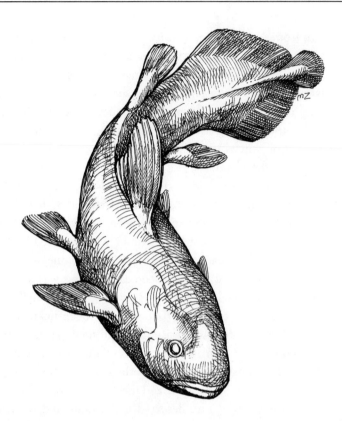

FIGURE 42: The coelacanth LATIMERIA CHALUMNAE. *The ultimate living fossil, coelacanths were thought to have been extinct for eighty million years until one turned up alive off the coast of South Africa.*

Moreover, they may not last all that long. The Comoros are volcanic islands, and as we have seen, oceanic volcanoes move away from their lava source by plate tectonics and become submerged to greater depths. *Latimeria*'s habitat in the Comoros cannot be older than the islands themselves, which is only a few million years. That creates an interesting paradox: Here is a living fossil, disjunct from its predecessors by eighty million years, yet living along the undersea slopes of an island perhaps only five million years old. Clearly *Latimeria* must either live undiscovered elsewhere besides the Comoros (and perhaps near the Chalumna River) or it is strictly limited in its distribution. Either way it has been doing some underwater island hopping along the feet of newly created volcanoes. I suspect it is severely limited in its geography and that it has been hopping volcanoes for a long, long time.

Latimeria is anatomically and behaviorally an extremely interesting animal. It is heavily built, and like some other fish that live at similar depths, its flesh is quite oily. The tail fin has three lobes, an extra one compared with other fish. The paired fins, representing the arms and legs of terrestrial animals, are fleshy with bony internal supports extending from the body into the fins, thus disclosing the coelacanth's cryptic evolutionary relationship to lungfish and tetrapods. It does not utilize its paired fins to walk along the bottom, but often its slow, deliberate movements are synchronized and alternating. Its movements appear as a fishy foreshadow of the locomotion in terrestrial vertebrates. It is a carnivore, feeding on fishes and squids, perhaps other things as well. Even though it is carnivorous, it is generally sluggish, leisurely maintaining its position in the water with casual flicks of this fin or that. Perhaps most intriguing of its behavioral traits is its habit of standing on its head. There are organs in the snout that are quite sensitive to electricity. The application of a small amount of electrical current to the water near a *Latimeria* will elicit a head-standing response. It has the same behavior naturally, without a researcher applying the current. That suggests that *Latimeria* uses electricity to sense its environment, possibly in locating other animals.

With *Latimeria* living now as it does, and with the ancient fossil record of coelacanths, which is reasonably good except for that eighty-million-year gap, showing a diversity of species and habitats for *Latimeria*'s cousins, the coelacanths must have a very complicated story to tell. Early on, coelacanths inhabited both salt and fresh water. The same kind of fossil coelacanth is known from the Cretaceous of West Africa and from Araripe in Brazil. (A pterosaur is eating a coelacanth in Figure 35). At eighty million years ago the more easily observed freshwater and shallow-marine species became extinct.

Descendant species such as *Latimeria* may never have been particularly abundant since the Cretaceous. They may have just bounced along from submerged island to submerged island, their range and abundance diminishing with the passage of geologic time. Because we know that *Latimeria* is different at the family level from other coelacanths, we know that evolution in the group did not stop, it just changed venue. *Latimeria* is a living fossil, to be sure, and the reason is because it still shows some primitive features, at least in its anatomy, that are little changed from older fossil species. In other regards *Latimeria* is undoubtedly derived with respect to the ancestral condition. It is a living fossil, but it is its own unique animal at the same time.

Even though the example of *Latimeria* is widely touted by the cryptozoology community, there is no meaningful analogy between the discovery of a new family of fish over fifty years ago, which in one sense is what the discovery of *Latimeria* amounted to, and the predictive ability to find living dinosaurs, also believed to be extinct since the Age of Reptiles. The difference should be obvious: We have the fish; we do not have the dinosaur. No matter how remote the Likouala Swamp is, it is not as remote as the ocean around the Comoro Islands, 650 feet down. It is much more likely that a living sauropod would be found, if they in fact existed, than that *Latimeria* would be found, much less observed and photographed in its natural habitat.

There is another big difference between the discovery of *Latimeria* and the search for living dinosaurs. The search for living dinosaurs is justified only on the basis of individual testimonies. There is no objective evidence for their existence in the present whatsoever. This approach had absolutely no role in the discovery of *Latimeria*. Miss M. Courtenay-Latimer was not out chasing rumors, nor searching for monsters under her bed or in her extended backyard. She was a museum specialist making collections of fish on a South African trawler. An odd fish was caught, and then, through the attentiveness of the captain, it was brought to her eye. She knew she would find fish on a fishing boat. Small wonder. The shock came when she recognized what the fish was. The scientific significance of her discovery cannot be challenged, but the existence of *Latimeria* came as no surprise to the natives of the Comoro Islands, who had caught them before. The scientific significance came from knowing what it meant. *Latimeria* is a living but distant relative of the fish ancestral to the first backboned animals to leave the water and take to the land permanently.

Even if sauropods were still alive, why should Darkest Africa be their home as opposed to, say, Long Island? The apparent reason is that Africa is unknown in the West, at least to those people mounting the expeditions to the Congo. Dinosaur survival in familiar, well-known, or populated corners of the United States would tax the credulity of even the most dyed-in-the-wool cryptozoologist, but it is acceptable, in some circles, to believe sauropods are in Africa. However, there is a more *ad hoc* reason that is usually offered.

The Congo Basin is considered by cryptozoologists—and, in fairness to them, by some scientists—to have been environmentally stable since the end of the Age of Reptiles sixty-six million years ago. The environment is not supposed to have changed in any significant way. At all. The end of the Age of Reptiles is the magic time because that is when dinosaurs vanished from the fossil record everywhere else in the world. If the swamps of Africa were never-changing, dinosaurs could have survived in the sanctuary of this slimy, murky, unknown refugium.

However, there is abundant and convincing evidence that environmental conditions in Africa have changed with time, that sauropods were not limited to swamps, and that the fossil record with its vast array of species contains not one sauropod specimen from any place on Earth, not one scrap of sauropod bone, since the Age of Reptiles ended. All that must be combined with the observation that there is not one shred of tangible evidence, not a piece of skin, not a toenail, no evidence at all that sauropods live today— anywhere.

It is extremely unlikely that the parameters defining the environments of the African continent have remained constant, have not wavered, for sixty-six million years. The Earth, as a sphere, shows variations in temperature as one goes from the tropical regions adjoining the equator to the temperate zones, and into the cold high-latitude boreal and arctic climates. In addition to variation in the sun's heating capacity relative to the curvature of the Earth, oceans and landmasses have different thermal properties, heating up and cooling down at different rates. Heat differential and the spinning of the Earth create atmospheric and oceanic currents, which distribute thermal energy about the globe in patterns specific to the shapes of the currents.

It should be obvious that physical changes in the geography of continents and oceans will change climate. If continents drift apart through plate tectonics, the climate will be different from what it is at times when landmasses are conjoined. Continents that change latitude through time experience an evolution of climate. The existence of shallow seas covering large portions of continents will affect climate. The formation of new oceans where none existed previously will modify ocean currents and influence climate. But on top of all that there are astronomical cycles that impose climatic fluctuations on the Earth. The amount of energy from the sun reaching the Earth varies in a recurrent fashion. There are several causes. The Earth wobbles on its axis of rotation in a predictable way, completing a cycle in about 26,000 years. The tilt of the Earth's axis also varies over a period of about 41,000 years. Moreover the Earth's orbit around the sun is not perfectly round, and there is variation in the time of year that the Earth is closest to or farthest away from the sun. This third variable has a cycle of about 100,000 years. All three of the cycles are perpetually influencing the amount of energy received from the sun—and its distribution on the globe—and therefore they influence climate through time.

The conclusion is quite clear: The climate and environment of any given place on Earth will change. It will change because of the effects brought about by the physical rearrangements of plate tectonics, and it will be changed by the imposition of astronomical cycles. Associated with all of that, there are any number of small- or large-scale influences on climate, some purely physical, others caused by biological activity. All of these various influences contribute to the overall pattern of climate through time, to the environments and ecosystems within which organisms evolve, and to the contexts in which species go extinct.

If climatic change is true from a theoretical perspective, then we should be able to see evidence of it in the rocks, and in fact we can. Evidence of glaciers and ice ages have long been seen in rocks. Ancient buried soils leave telltale clues as to the climatic condition under which they formed. Some of the most compelling evidence for past climate comes from fossils. The adaptations of plants and animals often indicate the restrictions under which they must live. Fossil pollen is frequently particularly informative when it can be recovered, which is surprisingly often. However, recent developments in geochemistry have provided some of the best new evidence of ancient climates.

The Earth's atmosphere is made up of a mixture of gases, mostly nitrogen, but also oxygen contributed by photosynthetic plants, carbon dioxide, water vapor, and other minor components. Atoms making up these gases come in various "flavors" at the subatomic level, and the alternative "flavors" are called isotopes. Any rock forming in chemical equilibrium with the atmosphere, or an organism—such as a clam, for instance—building its shell from elements in equilibrium with the atmosphere will reflect the isotopic composition found at that particular time in the air surrounding the Earth. Even though we are talking about elements and isotopes and atoms and molecules, sophisticated techniques allow the weights of different isotopes to be measured with great precision.

Oxygen atoms of concern here come in two isotopes. One isotope is heavier than the other. When dealing with such small particles as atoms and molecules, you would think that such a tremendously minute difference could not possibly have any consequence. But it does. Oxygen combines with hydrogen to form water molecules. Those with an atom of heavy oxygen will weigh more than a water molecule made with a light oxygen. Subtle differences in isotopic composition affect the physical properties of the water.

These slight differences influence the way the water molecules behave, particularly, how easily they go into the gaseous state by evaporation and, once there, how they condense and fall to the Earth as rain or snow.

The system is complicated, but the end result is that some variations in climatic parameters, such as temperature, have a correlation with oxygen-isotope composition, and that relationship can be measured. Since rocks or shells forming in equilibrium with the atmosphere will reflect the ratio of light-to-heavy oxygen at the time of their formation, a stratigraphic section, usually of marine rocks and fossils, will record the history of climate-related oxygen-isotope variations through time. That is how a long geochemical record of the Earth's climate is built up. Once the technology is at hand to make the measurements, and after good samples have been collected, it is basically quite simple to understand.

Isotopes of oxygen are useful paleoclimatic tools, but the temperature regime determined from them is usually an average for the Earth as a whole. That is enough to tell us that there have been episodes of significant global climate change. The evidence is clear on that. If the climate of the whole Earth has undergone changes, no place has been unaffected. Still, the climatic history of specific regions of the globe—the Likouala Swamp for instance—in contrast to the Earth's average climatic values measured through time, is often more difficult to decipher. A variety of methods is often used depending on what is available, including pollen samples extracted from sediments, environmentally sensitive ancient soils, fossil animals and plants, even the shape of the land—geomorphology, as it is called.

In order for swamps to exist, two basic requirements must be met: There must be adequate rainfall in the watersheds that empty into them, plus there must be a slow drain through which the accumulated water exits. That is what keeps swampy basins full. Water must pond and meander, stand and stagnate, rather than flow swiftly and cleanly out of the system. Modify either the amount of water or the efficiency of drainage and the conditions producing the swamp will be altered. The swamp will change. It will transform to reflect changing climate and rainfall patterns, and to reflect the development of mountains and other landforms that modify the drainage basins. Major Earth processes such as plate tectonics and continental drift create mountains and oceans, and as we know, they affect climate.

At 100 million years ago South America was just beginning to drift westward away from Africa. Since then the two have continued to drift apart.

A continuously widening Atlantic Ocean must affect oceanic and atmospheric circulation—and climate. After 100 million years ago, and well into the Age of Mammals, much of North and West Africa was inundated by fluctuating seas, some extending quite close to the Likouala region of the Congo. These seas had an effect on climate that would have been expressed in Central Africa.

The mightiest mountains of the African continent reflect geological history that occurred after the Age of Reptiles. Kilimanjaro, the highest peak in Africa; Kerinyaga or Mount Kenya, with the second-highest peak; and the Ruwenzories or Ptolemy's "Mountains of the Moon," on the eastern edge of the Congo Basin—these are all young constructions associated with the development of the East African Rift System. The Congo Basin drains the western side of the East African highlands. In West Africa, Mount Cameroon and the Adamoua Plateau, just to the northwest of Likouala, are much younger than the youngest-known dinosaurs. The geological construction of all these highlands must have affected not only climate but also drainage patterns. Those drainage patterns that make the Central African swamps were not there throughout much of the Age of Mammals. Sure, there were drainages, and some spots were lower and wetter than others, but based on geomorphology the landforms that make the swamps today simply did not exist until geologically more recent time.

The geological context of Africa clearly reflects the dynamics of the past and argues against an everlasting and abyssal Central African swamp. On top of all this add the fluctuations of global climate recorded in oxygen isotopes and the cyclic fluctuations known to have occurred due to astronomical influences on the Earth. Given these circumstances, there is virtually no geological reason to think that the Likouala Swamp would have remained unchanged since the days of the dinosaurs.

Moreover, environmental evidence from a number of sources indicates that no extensive lowland rain forests such as characterize the Congo Basin today existed in Africa at 100 million years ago. Clay minerals of that age, weathered from African rocks and blown out to settle gently on the ocean floor, are of the kind characteristically formed in seasonally arid environments, not in swamps. Ancient soils and fossils of plants with special adaptations for dry or salty habitats demonstrate seasonal aridity.

There is, unfortunately, no fossil record from the depths of the Likouala Swamp. The reason is straightforward enough. It being a swamp, sediments are being deposited, hidden under water and rank vegetation, rather than being exposed through erosion to disclose whatever fossils they might contain. Bones found in Niger, Cameroon, and Malaŵi show that African dinosaurs, including sauropods, inhabited a seasonally dry, hot land. The dinosaur fossils from Cameroon are located a short five hundred miles to the northwest of the Likouala. The geological changes that have resulted in uplift, erosion, and the discovery of fossils in Cameroon are related to the geological events that molded the northwestern margin of the Central African swamplands.

THERE IS ANOTHER related bit of science fiction—or rather pseudoscience—that is as equally untenable as living sauropods in Africa. It is the search for human fossils associated with dinosaur fossils. Glen Rose, Texas, a two-hour drive southwest of Dallas, is the world's headquarters for that search.

In this part of Texas the Paluxy River flows through 111-million-year-old rocks, roughly equivalent in age to those of Malaŵi, Cameroon, and Araripe in Brazil. The rocks at Glen Rose represent the remnants of old shorelines and mud flats from a time when the oceans covered much of what is now Texas. Dinosaur footprints—four-footed sauropods, strong-clawed three-toed theropods, and blunt "bird-foot" ornithopods—crisscross the ancient flats, preserving single moments of movement in the lives of these great beasts.

The existence of dinosaur trackways in the Paluxy River bottoms has been known since early in this century. The *Apatosaurus* at the American Museum of Natural History in New York, until recently, towered over Glen Rose footprints. Of course the bones of the *Apatosaurus* skeleton are about 145 million years old, and the footprints are considerably younger, a scant 111 million. The footprints bear the name *Brontopodus birdi,* named for Roland T. Bird who, with the help of WPA work crews, braved the floods of the Paluxy to collect fossils for the museum in New York. Footprints, as a special kind of trace fossil, not a part of an animal, but very certain evidence of its presence, and even its behavior, can be given their own scientific names.

During the Depression and after, a few of the local residents attempted to sell prints to bring in some scarce cash. Digging up dinosaur footprints is tough work. Apparently some ingenious entrepreneurs decided it would be easier to carve new footprints in stone rather than dig up old ones. The prints they chose to carve were in the shape of human feet.

Fundamentalists carried this a step further. (Excuse the pun; I could not resist it.) They identified some elongate erosional depressions—too large, but never mind—as human prints, making the claim that dinosaurs and humans walked together along the shore of the ancient Glen Rose sea. The claims are so outrageously false that the whole story would be comical were it not for the implications to public education of the fundamentalist agenda. Yet this nonsense is amazingly resilient. There is a museum outside of Glen Rose, the Creation Evidences Museum, that presents such absurdities as the petrified finger of a woman (really a burrow filling or concretion from the Glen Rose Limestone), abnormally large clothing to demonstrate that giants live, and a hyperbaric chamber. This last one is amusing. The logic goes something like this: In the days of Noah, with all that rain, the atmospheric pressure must have been much higher than it is now. Organisms, so the creationists say, grow to unnaturally large size under such atmospheric pressure. The hyperbaric chamber is a metal septic tank or some such container, presumably being converted to house kitty cats and other victims under pressure, allegedly to turn them into giants.

Believers in the association of dinosaur and human footprints reject virtually all intelligent explanation. And professional paleontologists, understandably, do not generally address the issue. If their time was spent continually dousing such frivolous backfires, legitimate research questions would go unaddressed. There is a tremendous body of knowledge testifying as to why the creationists are wrong on this issue. Libraries are full of it. Most all of what has been discussed in this book disproves it (and the rest is not relevant to the issue). Most creationists just simply choose to remain overzealous, unaware, uninformed, or purposely deceitful. There is no excuse for such shabby, innumerate logic when the problems the world faces require deliberate, considered, and reasoned solutions. Much to their credit, the latest falsifications of fundamentalist footprint dogma have been made not by professional paleontologists but by interested and curious, deeply wondering amateur paleontologists. Their attitudes are professional. Unfortunately whenever one allegation is disproved, another one, equally ludicrous, crops up.

There is a very simple reason why creationists cling to the Glen Rose footprints and insist on the co-occurrence of men and dinosaurs: Such an association would dispel the necessity of an Earth with vast antiquity. The entire history of creation, including the day of rest, could be accommodated in the seven biblical days of the Genesis myth. Evolution would be vanquished. For creationists, living dinosaurs would do the same thing. The fundamentalist creationist movement was involved in at least one of the Likouala Swamp expeditions.

In Africa I ran into a fundamentalist footprint phenomenon similar to what I was familiar with in Texas. In 1988 the Cameroon expedition discovered over two hundred dinosaur tracks along the Mayo Rey, a stream in the Koum Basin not all that far from where we found Mesozoic mammals. This is a strongly Muslim area of the country near the border with Chad. We were very excited with the discovery of lots and lots of tracks. Back at Rhinoceros Camp, where we were staying, I told our local laborers about our "discovery."

They had the perfect reply: "Why didn't you tell us that is what you wanted to find? We could have taken you there to begin with."

It was explained to us that the footprint locality was well known to the native populace. Of course they did not know about dinosaurs per se. Nevertheless, from their way of life, living in the bush as they do, they could certainly recognize spoor, not that that is hard to do with dinosaur footprints, even if they did not know what creatures had made the trails. Some of the more devout and imaginative of them claimed that they had seen, in amongst the tracks, the knee, elbow, and forehead prints of one of the genuflecting Islamic faithful praying to Mecca. In the depths of Africa religious fundamentalism was showing itself among dinosaur tracks, just as it does back home in Texas. My friends were unable to relocate the human prints, so they could not be shown to me. But my guides were sure they had seen them before.

Now, Muhammad was not born until the sixth century. I do not know when Muslim influence first began to be felt in northern Cameroon, but it could have been fairly late, maybe within the last couple of hundred years—maybe even later than that. How might creationists interpret this? Could they argue that dinosaurs are not an Old Testament legacy, drowned in the Noachan flood, that they lived well into later times—when we have, incidentally, abundant and elaborate written records—and also well into the time that the Earth's big animals were becoming generally familiar? It would mean nothing if such arguments were made—just so long as they stay outside the science classroom.

. . .

THE REAL IMPORTANCE of that site in Cameroon is in the footprints. Dinosaur tracks, as fossils, are interesting. Unlike body fossils such as bones or teeth, trackways preserve an instant in time. It is fossilized movement, and therefore it embodies the spirit of the behavior that movement entails. Dinosaur tracks are not so rare as you might think. Their preservation depends on dinosaurs moving across the right kind of ground, soft enough to leave an impression, yet firm enough and not so mushy as to fill in the shape or obscure definition. Some of the trackways in Cameroon show the track-maker progressing from firmer to sloppier substrate. The size and weight of dinosaurs can be estimated using mathematical equations based on footprint measurements. Estimates of speed and gait can be determined. Directions of travel can be seen, and the sizes or relative ages of individuals likely to be traveling in the same group can be contemplated.

At the main track site in Cameroon, called KB-17 because it was the seventeenth locality found in the Koum Basin, there are four superimposed stratigraphic levels, four bedding surfaces on the tops of four sequential sedimentary strata, that hold most of the trackways. The site itself is a stretch of the Mayo Rey in the middle of the basin. The south bank is formed of Cretaceous sandstone and siltstone, tilted down to the north at a ten-degree angle. The river in flood during the rainy season sweeps the sandstone clean and exposes the surfaces pocked with tracks. Tracks are not the only sedimentary structures present. There are traces of ancient plant roots in at least one spot. There are ripple marks in places, showing that water covered the mud. There are mud cracks, showing it dried out. There is even a dinosaur track made on a flat surface, without ripple marks, but inside the track are mud cracks. Water collected in the imprint of the dinosaur foot, making a little pool. As the water evaporated and soaked into the ground, the mud inside the print was left to dry. As it did, the mud shrank and cracked. All that told in one print.

We spent several days on the slab measuring toes, angles, paces, strides, everything necessary to reconstruct the site on paper in a detailed map. My graduate student, John Congleton, did a fine job on the study, as you can judge from the summary that follows. At KB-17 we measured forty-seven separate trackways with a total of nearly 250 individual prints. The identity of the tracks matched what we expected from the scrappy bones and teeth we had found in our quarries at the east end of the basin, so together the two sets of data complemented each other in what they could say about the dinosaurs that lived there. Both are important because no dinosaurs had ever been found in the Koum Basin before our expeditions went there.

Using body fossils, we could identify a couple of kinds of theropods based on meat-eating teeth. We also had a few sauropod teeth and one lousy tooth that could possibly have come out of a stegosaur's mouth. The sail-backed plant-eater *Ouranosaurus* (see Figure 3 in Chapter 1) was clearly present. The other members of the fauna, based on body parts, include crustaceans, lungfish and at least one other fish species, frogs, turtles, and crocodiles, most notably little *Araripesuchus*. And of course we got what we went there for— early mammals.

The footprints in the Koum Basin were all made by dinosaurs. Most abundant by far are theropod prints (like those of *Spinosaurus* in Figure 2). These show three narrow toes. More than one species is probably represented. Larger prints with three broad toes were made by *Ouranosaurus* in all probability. The smallest prints found are only about three inches or so in length. They also have three toes. They may represent a small species of dinosaur, or they could belong to young of one of the larger species. All three of the trackways made by the smallest feet were traveling to the northeast. We found no sauropod prints at KB-17, but just a short distance away there were unmistakable traces of sauropods walking in sticky mud. Their feet, adapted to bearing weight on the ends of pillarlike legs, sank deep into the ooze, leaving behind their traces, more holes than prints, as the feet were tugged from the mud that sucked to hold them in.

About half of the dinosaur trackways at KB-17 proceeded preferentially in a northeast-southwest direction. The other half were going the opposite direction. Perhaps the same individuals were going someplace in one direction and coming back from it in the other. Only one trackway is oriented east-west. Because the trackways are spread over more than four hundred yards' distance, they are on four different sedimentary bedding surfaces, and they represent several species of dinosaurs, the uniformity in the alignment of the trackways, whether coming or going, is striking. It suggests that some environmental obstruction, such as a river, controlled the avenue of movement. Perhaps the dinosaurs were moving parallel to a river channel, along its bank, or maybe they were constrained in the directions they could travel by some other physical barrier.

Most of the dinosaurs at KB-17 were walking when they left their prints; however, there are examples of other gaits as well. There are examples of trotting and sprinting, as determined from the length of stride, and even some cases of speeding up and slowing down. Smaller dinosaurs seem to have been more active and agile than larger ones. One trackmaker may have been injured, as its trackway indicates it was limping along its way. At first I thought we had the marks of a tail dragging in one of the trackways, but I was wrong. When we mapped it out, the trackway showed a theropod making a turn, its outside foot making a broad sweep on the substrate. The lack of tail drags everywhere is significant and tells us something about how dinosaurs held their tails: up off the ground.

The trackways I remember most pleasantly at KB-17 can be interpreted in a controversial manner, and I really have no way of supporting my contention, but here it goes. There are two trackways at the western end of the site, both three-toed theropods but one considerably larger than the other. The larger is strolling along, but curiously it is walking in a curving path. The smaller of the two is walking along beside it, in the same direction, paralleling the curve to a remarkable degree. Could this be an adult and its offspring traveling along together? If so, it reflects a sophisticated social structure. Why not? I imagine a mother with young. It would not be startling really, it is just that I cannot prove that the two were actually walking together at the same time purposely rather than their associated tracks being a spurious and fortuitous coincidence. Parental behavior in herbivorous dinosaurs has already been documented in nesting areas and with juvenile aggregates. They also formed herds and flocks, some of them anyway. Theropods may well have behaved in the same general way, caring for young and perhaps forming packs.

There are no living dinosaurs in Africa, at least in the sense of relict sauropods, but we have certainly been able to learn a great deal about the ones found there as fossils. We can appreciate them as living animals, as well we should, because we know that in a more appropriate sense dinosaurs *are* still living. As we have already seen, they are living in the form of birds, the descendants of theropods. Birds are dinosaurs that fly, that have colorful plumage, and delicate eggs, and parents that care for the young. They are not sauropods, tyrannosaurs, or any of the other popular Mesozoic denizens, but we can better imagine those beasts by having an appreciation for the living dinosaurs. Through birds we can watch the mating dances of cranes and speculate on the courtship behavior of *Ornithomimus*. Birds, as dinosaurs, provide a fascinating new dimension to dinosaur biology—and a window through which to view it.

Ever since their origin from theropods, birds have undergone a marvelous radiation beautifully exemplified in tropical Africa. Is it not more grand, more inspiring, to see birds as living dinosaurs evolving through time with the ecology of a changing Earth, to learn about the past as it was and for what it means to the future, than to hold fast with no good reason to the notion that sauropods still live or that humans walked with giant dinosaurs? The Age of Reptiles is simply an expired world that no longer exists except through its legacy—its foundation for our modern world.

10

THE GOOD OF
DINOSAURS

T HE FIELD SEASON is over for me. It was successful. We got fossils. Now I am in the airplane and the people of Mwakasyunguti are on the ground. I got the fossils and now I am leaving. From here in the airplane, flying over, the valley of the Dinosaur Beds looks insignificant. It is like a large-scale version of driving past pedestrians. The perspective is so different. Can Mwakasyunguti matter, this speck lying in the valley so far below me? Can Malaŵi? It is so out-of-the-way and such a small place. Its telephone directory is a puny half-inch thick—including the yellow pages—for the whole country.

It is easy to be cynical about Africa. Long ago the geologist J. W. Gregory wrote that Livingstone's death in 1873 "closed the work of the dreamers . . . henceforward they [would be] unimportant." That can never have been less true than now in present-day Africa. Without dreams there is no vision. Without vision, how can problems be solved? Without Africans of vision, how can Africa solve its problems?

I suppose that if Mwakasyunguti does not matter in the great scheme of things, Malaŵi does not. If Malaŵi does not, Africa does not. And if Africa does not matter, neither does the world at large. All of them matter, or none of them does. In the final analysis, we all have to live on this Earth.

So Mwakasyunguti does matter. It is not insignificant. Still, the problems of such a tiny country as Malaŵi, stuck way off in Africa, appear insuperable. And a hunt for dinosaurs in such a place appears ludicrous, sometimes even to me. But it is not.

There is so much about working in a different culture that is incongruous. So much of Africa is incongruous. Much of what I do not understand is pleasant, such as the sign on the business establishment bellowing out, WELD- ING AND DISCOTHEQUE. What can that mean? On the other hand, some of what I do not understand is not pleasant at all.

One of the biggest problems Malaŵi faces can be blatantly observed on the main highway. The road south from Lilongwe to Blantyre, where our fossils are prepared in the laboratory for study, runs for part of its length along the country's western border with Mozambique. On the right side, in Mozam- bique, homes and shops stand dilapidated and vacant—bombed out. Such doors as remain slap ineffectually in the breeze on the remnants of rusty hinges. Tumbleweeds. It is deserted. Across the road, in Malaŵi, life teems among crowded shacks. Here are the refugees of Mozambique's decade-and- a-half not-so-civil war, which has lasted since the Portuguese pulled out of their ill-prepared colony. The majority of the refugees in Malaŵi are women and children. Mozambiquan men are mostly dead, conscripted, or elsewhere. Malaŵi, a country of some eight million inhabitants, has over 850,000 refugees living in its borders. In one district, refugees outnumber Malaŵians nearly two to one.

The political boundaries of Africa are European impositions. With nepo- tism royal, Queen Victoria transferred sovereignty of Kilimanjaro to her first grandson, Kaiser Wilhelm II of Germany. In 1890, just before Nyasaland became a protectorate, Britain and Germany were negotiating between them- selves to define their respective spheres of influence on the Dark Continent. The Livingstone Mountains went to the Germans. That is why the Living- stones today are in Tanzania and Malaŵi territory stops west of them. The British sphere of influence, up until World War I, ended at the Songwe River, now the border between Malaŵi and Tanzania. This northern area of what is now Malaŵi fell to the British only because, during the sphere-of-influence negotiations, Britain relinquished claim to the North Sea island of Helgoland, turning it over to Germany in exchange for the territory south of the Songwe.

But the political boundaries of Africa are traditionally meaningless from a fundamental cultural perspective, just as those of East and West Germany were, or North and South Korea are. The refugees from Mozambique are the same people—Yao, Ngoni, Sena, and other tribes—as live in the areas across the Malaŵi border where they settle in refugee camps. The culture is the same, the language is the same. Often this is not enough to induce a humanitarian response to the tragedies of war in adjacent countries. Malaŵi, the Warm Heart of Africa, does have a humanitarian philosophy, accepting refugees from their war-ravaged neighbor and caring for them. But it is not easy. The number of refugees has swelled tenfold since 1986.

The refugees are almost all illiterate peasants, subsistence farmers resigned to simple lives. They do not want to be in Malaŵi. They want to be home. Farming the land. There is relatively little migration of refugees from the camps in rural border areas to urban centers; consequently crime has not yet skyrocketed the way one might have predicted with such a massive influx of impoverished, downtrodden people.

Refugees receive humanitarian assistance, the basics for survival: food and clothing. The daily food ration is just over two thousand calories, barely at the acceptable medical limits. Food rations are made up of maize meal, pulses (meaning peas and beans), sugar, salt, edible oil, some dried fish, and dried skim milk. Pellagra, a nutritional disease caused by lack of niacin found in fresh vegetables, is becoming common. Supplementary food is provided to malnourished children and to pregnant or lactating women in the form of *likuni phala,* a marginally higher-protein mixture of 80 percent maize, 10 percent peanuts, and 10 percent pulses.

Each family is allotted one cooking set, once, and two water containers, again only once. Other nonfood items include soap—a bit over one pound per family per month, one blanket every two years for each person, and clothing. Infants receive a yard and a half of cloth, boys and men get a pair of shorts and a shirt, girls get a dress, women get a two-yard length of cloth and one blouse or T-shirt.

The total value of life placed by the world on the 850,000 refugees was $24 million last year. Less than thirty dollars a head. And the refugees did not cause the war. Neither did Malaŵi.

All parties involved agree that life is more than thirty dollars' worth of beans and blankets. The attempt to solve the problem surely deserves more support. But it is not forthcoming. The help that is available comes from the international community, in particular from the United Nations High Commission for Refugees, and from private aid groups.

To Malaŵi the greatest costs are hidden, yet they are severe. Health, sanitation, education, and social services are strained beyond capacity. The roads and physical infrastructure are being worn out. The land is being deforested for firewood. Malaŵi is a small country with hardly enough land for its own agricultural uses. Its own population is burgeoning. Jobs are scarce even for Malaŵians. How can they sacrifice more? Still, the Malaŵians remain humanitarian, hospitable, and open.

There is no resolution to the refugee problem except repatriation. That has two basic requirements: The refugees must feel it is safe to return home, and they must be able to eke out a living once they are there. The latter is not a big requirement. Subsistence farming in the mud-and-thatch villages of rural Africa is hand-to-mouth in the best of times. But even if the people are willing to go home just in the reasonable aspiration of surviving in their own homeland, they cannot do so until the war quits. Perhaps that will be sooner than later. If there ever was a fathomable reason for the hostilities, this war has gone on so long, so viciously, and so ruinously that reasons probably cannot be remembered, much less matter at this stage. Many of the combatants, like the mercenary *ruga-ruga* of the slavers of old, now simply kill for food and plunder.

Voluntary repatriation is understandably not going well. There is a very effective grapevine for war information among the refugees; they will know when it is safe to return. At this time in most of Mozambique it is not. Nowadays about five thousand refugees per year return to "safe" areas. Most of the repatriates are the heads of households. Their families remain at the refugee camps, and with unfortunate frequency, the repatriate, not expecting to survive in his homeland, flees again for the sanctuary of the camp. In the camps there is little to do, no land to farm. There is no official jobs program, it being difficult enough to find work for Malaŵians, but vocational training is part of the repatriation plan—health workers, teachers, metal workers, carpenters. A few private aid organizations have meager self-help and food-for-work schemes.

There is little else that can be done with tight money. Even if money were easy, only peace will really solve the problem. Friendly, peaceful Malaŵi will do what it can for its beleaguered neighbor. Malaŵi's roads, its forests, its farmers deprived of land now used for refugee camps, and its health, educational and social systems must cope. African resignation comes into play, once again allowing people to live with the problem. At least, in the effort to provide adequate water, Malaŵians get some benefit from newly drilled wells. But the problem must still be solved.

The refugee problem is acute, but Malaŵi must also face the chronic problems of development common to all countries of the impoverished world. The process of development is interminable. It seems to progress at the same unnoticeable pace at which erosion wears away granite. While the impoverished world develops, the Developed World moves ahead with R&D, producing faster computers, lasers, CAT scans, and all the other accouterments of the next century. It is really easy to be cynical about the prospects for the Developing World. How can it ever catch up? How can it solve the problems that hinder it from making progress? On the other hand, how are mountains ever eroded to the sea?

Malaẁi has been independent for twenty-nine years, about the same length of time as most African, indeed most all developing countries. The maturing process for a nation does not take place overnight. It takes time. It took time for all the developed nations too. And for Malaẁi the process must take place in the distinctly African context that exists now.

Africans have an African perspective, not Western by any means, but one that is instilled by their traditions. This perspective derives at least in part from the social dynamics of extended families. They are close-knit, and often there are large numbers of children. Extended families provide a sort of traditional insurance against the tribulations of old age and other hardships that can be eased and alleviated by familial compassion. Commercial insurance and pension funds, our usual methods, are not generally affordable to most Africans. Although the government provides the medical and other social services its means allow, these are limited. In Africa large families are the safety nets that help people cope with what they cannot control—drought, disease, death, hunger. But large families cause overpopulation. With development and progress a new safety net must be found.

Religion, always a big cultural factor, traditionally included the spirits of animals and ancestors, but those beliefs are now often mantled with the cloak of Western missionary indoctrination. This combination gives some of the introduced Christian religions a distinctly African flavor. Some aspects of missionary faith are readily accepted. Alfreda Ibui in Nairobi once told me she liked Christianity. "Otherwise twins are bad luck, and my sons would have been killed."

African traditional religion has not been destroyed, it has evolved to fit modern Africa. Traditions change, but slowly. At each step something of social value, derived from past tradition but suited for the present, must always remain. Social systems must retain integrity. It is part of the maturing process.

Freedom and independence for Malaŵi was won, so it is said, through Unity, Loyalty, Obedience, and Discipline. Early on, President Banda identified the three great enemies of the people as poverty, disease, and ignorance. The four traditional qualities of the people that led to independence are still trained on these enemies as the path to economic development. The country is racially fully integrated, but citizens of Asian descent, who are often successful merchants, are allowed to open their shops only in greater Blantyre, Lilongwe, Mzuzu, and Zomba. This is supposed to be a kind of affirmative action whereby more black shopkeepers are introduced throughout the country. The policies of the government, if not the traditions of the people, insure access to opportunities for women.

The economic strength of Malaŵi is its agricultural system. It is the lifeblood of the country. Malaŵi is usually self-sufficient in food, even exporting to neighboring countries. It produces cash crops such as tobacco, sugar, cotton, tea, and macadamia nuts. It is primarily through agricultural development with concomitant growth in support industries that the battle against poverty is being waged. Moreover, today Malaŵi is setting an example in sub-Saharan Africa by producing charcoal from the lumbering wastewood of commercial plantations, thereby providing fuel for urban populations and easing somewhat the pressure for firewood on natural vegetation.

Despite the burdens placed on them, health care and services are steadily improving. Access to hospitals and medical workers is increasing. There are widespread programs for inoculation, nutrition, hygiene and sanitation, and safe drinking water. There is an active effort to face the AIDS threat. They had better make an active effort: The problems caused by refugees pale in comparison to the reality of AIDS in Africa. Since the disease strikes those in their prime of life, active people full of vigor, and it imposes ten years or so of impressed service as an unwitting carrier of the virus, the tragedy must only get worse before it gets better. Death from AIDS is becoming more and more commonplace, removing some of the most talented and energetic from the labor force and from the ranks of middle management. Who will see to the everyday running of the country as the next century begins? Who will care for the thousands upon thousands of orphaned youngsters, their parents gone and their aunts and uncles dying, as their parents will have done, from AIDS, and their grandparents passing on through attrition? What happens to extended-family safety nets when there is no one left in the family to extend a hand?

It is easy to be despairing and decide there is no hope. But there must be.

Life must adjust, even to this latest atrocity. It is easy to be complacent from across the sea, but AIDS is here, too, and the magnitude of the problem in this country has not seen its limit. In Malaŵi the efforts to combat the AIDS virus are being increased through enlightenment programs. Poignant educational slogans, such as Death by AIDS is the death of Malaŵi, catch the minds of the people. Education simply must work if the ravages of the disease are to be mitigated. Luckily education has had a long and accepted tradition in Malaŵi. Ignorance is combatted through a system of local village schools such as the one in which our friend Lightwell teaches, boarding schools for secondary education, vocational and trade schools, teachers' colleges, and the University of Malaŵi. The university is staffed with foreign and domestically trained Malaŵians and some expatriates. Many Malaŵian professionals are educated abroad, quite a few in America, where Banda received his training.

The road to development is potholed and arduous. There is a long way to go. But Malaŵi has made progress by keeping focused on its real enemies: poverty, disease, and ignorance. Will Malaŵi ever be homogenized into the Western world? Why should it? Will it overcome the hardships imposed by the refugee problem? It has to. Will it survive the AIDS epidemic? It must. What are the alternatives?

Malaŵi is an optimistic country that has followed its own path since independence. Those are appealing qualities, imparting self-respect, allowing it to be happy. There may not be an Apple computer in every hut, but there may come to be, with hard work and vision, full-bellied, healthy, wise people in them. It is wisdom, within a realistic context, that charts the course of destiny. Malaŵi will set its own course. Quiet, peaceful, little Malaŵi. No one hears of it in the West. Ever since independence, all the way till now, it has been too stable.

BECAUSE OF ITS stability, the friendliness and hospitality of the people, and the relatively efficient bureaucracy, Malaŵi is a good place to run an expedition. The scientific agenda of my Malaŵi Project has changed over the last decade. That is the way it should be. Hypotheses evolve as more is learned; new strategies must be devised to answer new questions. But one objective has not changed since its inception: The project should contribute to Malaŵi, not parasitize it. This objective is independent of the scientific results of the project to the extent that it can be, recognizing that the continued existence of the project rests primarily on the adequacy of the science. I would not argue that this project has been a major force in the battle against poverty, disease, and ignorance. The only ammunition the project has supplied against disease is the dispensing of a few aspirins and some quinine tablets. I do hope, on the other hand, that there may be some positive manifestations, however minuscule, with regard to the mitigation of poverty and alleviation of ignorance.

Over the years the cost of fieldwork in Malaŵi has amounted to nearly $200,000, much of it coming from the National Geographic Society. Considering I have run five field seasons and done some laboratory work there, this sum is, by some measures, not much money. By others, it is. Excluding international travel expenses, most of the money was spent in Malaŵi, and much of it in economically underdeveloped portions of the north. In Mwakasyunguti, where the equivalent of one U.S. dollar pays a man for a day's labor, and I am the only employer, the impact of the Dinosaur Project, in those relative terms, is considerable indeed.

Each field season the project has specific goals and objectives. The Mwakasyunguti labor force helps those goals be realized. The villagers are one of the components that make for a successful season. Good results position the project for continued funding, which means more employment. As the project blossoms, new avenues must be traveled.

Early on I realized that dinosaurs in Africa present formidable logistical problems. This was not much of a bother in the first two expeditions because collecting dinosaurs was not a primary goal, finding mammals was. I got a mammallike crocodile instead, but that animal is not large enough to cause problems. Then in the 1989 season the emphasis began to shift, and from 1990 dinosaurs have been the main thrust. Once the bones were out of the ground, how would I ever get them prepared out of their jackets? Clearly the cost of shipping plaster and bone biscuits to my labs in Dallas, then shipping finished bones back, was prohibitive. I had to find another way.

The solution was to train a person in the technical skills required in fossil preparation. Sending someone to the States for a few months had distinct advantages. For one thing it is much more cost-effective than sending bones. For another it is a much more long-range solution, supplying to Malaŵi in-country technical expertise to handle their own paleontological resources on a continuing basis. This obviously appealed to the Antiquities Department, who assigned Fidelis, who had been with me in the field every time, the responsibility of learning to be a fossil preparator. I obtained some private funding, enabling Fidelis to come to Dallas for three months in 1989. There he worked intensively with Kent, learning all the techniques we could teach him and gaining practical experience on the fossils. I provided him with much of the equipment necessary to have a functioning, efficient preparation laboratory. Now there is one in Malaŵi where there was not one before.

Technical expertise is only half the battle. What happens to the bones once they are prepared? There is no professional paleontological expertise in Malaŵi, so the pleasures and responsibilities of the scientific investigation have been left to the American contingent. While we are happy to study the fossils, the arrangement is not ideal. For one thing, there is more to do than Dale and Will and I can handle. For another, I find the whole concept of entering into a cooperative expedition in a foreign country, obtaining the professional advantages, then abandoning the country at the close of the project to be latter-day intellectual exploitation and viscerally displeasurable.

I would have to train a Malaŵian student. It is not always so easy to find an appropriate candidate. Why, for instance, should little Malaŵi want to have a professional paleontologist? What good does it do the country? Would not all the really good students be interested in medicine, law, economics? Of course, most are interested in pursuing those subjects. But individual interests vary, and there are people intensely interested in the Earth and the life on it. They can be found in Malaŵi just as they can be found in every other country. Moreover, Malaŵi has a first-class Department of Antiquities in the Ministry of Education and Culture. It runs the National Museum, protects the nation's monuments, surveys the country's cultural and archaeological resources, and conducts scholarly research. The professionals of the department teach courses at the University of Malaŵi.

A vertebrate paleontologist is not such an absurd thing for an educational organization, whether a museum or university, in a developing country to have. The research of paleontology can be as high-tech, or as low-tech, as facilities allow. That translates to the fact that some legitimate and important lines of investigation can be pursued at relatively low cost. Paleontology is a bargain. Moreover, a paleontologist must be familiar with a great number of disciplines. To take examples from this book, effective paleontology requires knowledge of geology, ecology, anatomy, animal behavior, and any number of other subjects. When staffing positions are limited, a vertebrate paleontologist can go a long way toward rounding out a department. The country of Malaŵi will be needing talented young people, broadly proficient in a number of professional skills. A paleontologist could do other things as well as fossils. A paleontologist could be seconded into service with the country's geological survey or water department. Natural hazards such as landslides and floods need evaluation, and cities need to be planned accordingly. The medical school might need instructors in human anatomy. The university might require instructors in science. Museums need talent. All of these organizations need what is too often lacking in every country: competent, well-informed, knowledgeable leaders. A developing country such as Malaŵi could do much worse than recruit a rigorously and broadly trained paleontologist. So could many universities in this country.

The authorities at the Department of Antiquities, in response to the exciting results we were obtaining, created a new position for a professional paleontologist. Now, if I trained a Malaŵian for a Ph.D., there would be a job waiting on the return. The student could, as a research topic, devote the necessary long hours to the intense study of the collection of bones from Malaŵi that is even now being prepared by Fidelis. It will take at least as long to prepare the bones as to study them for a dissertation. Preparation has a head start, so the science will not be delayed.

The future departmental paleontologist must have the necessary training for the appropriate management and administration of paleontological re-sources, the interest and ability for original research, and the inclination to teach through the Malaŵi higher education system to bring the relevant concepts of Earth and life sciences to a broader, better-educated audience. If everything goes according to plan, Malaŵi can manage its own paleontological resources, and my value to their country, such as it is, will diminish. That would be the measure of success.

It is very difficult, for me anyway, to predict the odds for a student's success. So much depends on the fortitude of the individual. This is true under the best of conditions, when there is a large applicant pool, and when universities can selectively pick and choose who will be admitted. It is often more difficult with foreign students, steeped in unfamiliar cultures. In cases like that of Malaŵi, one person will be a paleontologist and assume all the responsibility that the position will obtain. One person is selected from the country, from among people who are eager but not knowledgeable about the subject or perhaps not even predisposed to a consuming dedication to it. Who knows, perhaps the person might turn out to dislike fossils. Then you are stuck. All the eggs are in the basket of the single person selected for training.

I enlisted the help of my Malaŵian colleagues in the search for an appropriate candidate. Requirements were a strong math and science background and an excellent performance at the University of Malaŵi. The Department of Antiquities interviewed the most promising candidate. That was Elizabeth Gomani. She has a strong background in math, computers, statistics, chemistry, and Earth science—a very appropriate background. In 1989 and again in 1990 Elizabeth joined the expedition in the field to get some practical paleontological experience. This also allowed me the opportunity to evaluate her as a potential student, for her to decide if she really wanted to pursue this option, and for us both to get a chance to know each other. My opinion: Elizabeth has what it takes.

Elizabeth arrived to start graduate school two years ago last January. She started in the winter semester. Her flight over brought her through Chicago, where she saw snow for the first time. That evening she saw television for the first time. The next day she ate pizza and a red apple for the first time. I took her on a tour around campus. I showed her the brass floor plate under the dome of the main hall. Afterward, walking down the street, she examined each manhole cover very carefully. She is doing well. Malaŵi now has technical expertise and it will soon have professional expertise to handle its fossils—all of them, dinosaurs included of course. And for the purposes of the project, when Elizabeth has completed her training, like a dinosaur in the traditional view, I will go extinct.

Dinosaurs have great popular appeal in Malaŵi, just as they do everywhere else. With all the fieldwork we were doing, it was inevitable that the word about our activities would suffuse into the public sphere and that this would eventually swell into national excitement. It was very important to generate excitement at the right time, not too soon, before the scientific significance of the project could be guaranteed, and not too late, when the enthusiasm would be of no help for insuring continued success.

The 1990 season was the right time. Bones we had, and now we needed to keep the project rolling. Fidelis had received his training, and the wheels were turning to get Elizabeth into graduate school. Benefits to the country were becoming apparent. Moreover, Caltex Oil in Malaŵi had decided to make a donation to the project (and they have continued to support us subsequently). They wanted publicity for their part, so they informed the press. A reporter and a photographer were present when Mr. Allen, the Caltex representative, presented the check at our arrival in early July. The result was a front-page story, short but informative, in the *Malaŵi Times* and a report on

Radio Malaŵi. It was heard at Mwakasyunguti before we got to the field. Then, in August at the end of my time in the field, reporters and photographers came to the site. A feature article appeared shortly after in *Quest,* Malaŵi's foremost magazine.

All this fans the flames of excitement in the general public—adults and children. No one ever thought that dinosaurs, those strange, bizarre, faraway creatures, would actually be found in tiny, peaceful, nothing-ever-happens Malaŵi. Yet they were, and some people had known it for years. Now it is everybody's turn. Trivial as it may seem in some regards, the dinosaurs are a source of national pride, of *esprit.* That is good.

With increased interest will come some complications. People will want to see the dinosaurs. Others will want to own them. Visitors to the northern reaches of Malaŵi might want to see the site, or perhaps take home a souvenir. As all too often happens, that generates a commercial demand for fossils. That would be bad. The paleontological resources of the country belong to all its citizens, not to just a select few. The scientific value belongs to the world. The fossils of Malaŵi are fragile. They are a nonrenewable resource. Those who would have a memento on their mantel do more harm than they know; the careless removal of fossils from the surface of the ground destroys the clues that give fossils meaning and that provide a means to finding still-buried specimens. In Malaŵi such behavior carries a risk: The fossil resources of the country are protected by law, and the Department of Antiquities is serious in the extreme about living up to its caretaker responsibilities. They intend to nip any problem in the bud. An appropriate strategy for protection is being devised. It involves educating locals, and perhaps establishing a site museum along the lines of Dinosaur National Monument in Utah. It almost certainly will require a small but permanent staff at Mwakasyunguti. A few jobs will be created. That will be good.

Still, the public demand for dinosaurs must be met for three reasons: It is fun, it is profitable, it is educational. The fun of extinct animals is undeniable. It is obvious. So is the profitability. Walk through most any store in the United States that sells goods for children and you will see the dinosaur motif. Breakfast cereal, spaghetti, Halloween costumes, T-shirts, postcards, backpacks, rockers, TV shows, coloring books, cassettes, posters, windup toys, board games, video games. You name it. The phenomenon of dinosaurmania is worldwide. If anyone knows the economic value of this persistent and never-ending craze, I have not been able to find out. Yet it must be tremendous. In some form or other this commercial phenomenon will develop in Malaŵi. And that will be good.

The kicker about dinosaurs is that they are just as good at selling science as they are at selling toys or breakfast cereal or canned spaghetti. They might even be the best single thing around for attracting people to science at all levels, kindergarten through graduate school. Not everyone who likes fossils will become a paleontologist, but that is not the point. Paleontology *itself* does not need a recruiting drive. A lot of people like the subject matter of paleontology just for what it is. They will like what paleontologists do, even if they are not paleontologists themselves.

The educational aspects of my work in Malaŵi I find most intriguing. In effect the dinosaurs are a tool, the bait, if you will, to stimulate healthy curiosity and the good habit of enjoying it. Education is an iterative process, constantly being redone and embellished in individuals and constantly re-peated for each age group of children. Many of the demands and requirements are the same for any classroom, whether it be in rural Malaŵi or in an affluent private school in the United States. Therefore these African dinosaurs ought to have educational value for everyone everywhere. They teach about the history of life and of the Earth, as dinosaurs from anywhere do. They teach specifically about Malaŵi. Malaŵian schoolkids know where the United States is; how many Americans of any age know where Malaŵi is?

How can the educational potential of these dinosaurs best be realized? In Malaŵi the Antiquities Department will place them on display in the National Museum in Blantyre. There may also, in time, be a site museum at Mwaka-syunguti, and perhaps a small traveling exhibit. Supplementary booklets for various grade levels are planned. Outside of Malaŵi news of this work will eventually filter down to children's books. But to me it would be much more electrifying to resurrect these dinosaurs in lifelike creativity and let them tell their own story by touring the world for all to see. Then there would be some interest generated—in Africa, in Malaŵi, and in science. It only takes money.

OF COURSE ALL this presupposes that the Malaŵi dinosaurs have a worth-while story to tell. I think they do. Just look at what we have seen. At least thirteen kinds of backboned animals have been found in the Dinosaur Beds, plus a few seedlike plant remains, and two kinds of freshwater invertebrates. Bones are abundant and well preserved, allowing us to determine a great deal about the animals of ancient Africa. The age of the fossil remains is Early Cretaceous, falling somewhere between 144 and 97.5 million years ago. This interval is generally the most poorly known of any in the Age of Reptiles, but it is important because it is in this time interval that the animals and plants of the modern world emerge. Malaŵi provides a major source of information about the terrestrial animals, particularly large animals, on the Earth during that time. It may be the best in Africa for its age. But it is not an isolated occurrence. It exists in a global context, its very presence governed by the grand principles of geology and biology. What it contributes to our knowledge of the world as a whole, and Africa's place in its evolution, is greater by far than any little details about any specific animal. It is important to know this big picture because if the world of the Early Cretaceous was not as it was, the world of today would not be as it is. Do we not want to understand what we can do to the world of tomorrow, to plan rationally for the future?

The Dinosaur Beds are a unique window into the past for at least two reasons. They preserve a fauna, a suite of animals, the likes of which is found nowhere else in the world. It has relatives elsewhere, and that helps us to understand its place, but no other locality preserves exactly the same amalgam of species. Moreover the Malaŵi fossils represent the community of animals living just at the time Africa was becoming isolated from South America. On top of that, the bones are preserved in sediments reflecting environments that are in some ways different from the usual environments where dinosaurs are found. That tells us something about their ecology.

Five species of dinosaurs, at least, occur in northern Malaŵi. The carnivorous ones are the most poorly represented. That makes sense. Carnivores are high on the food chain, and in a balanced community they should not outnumber their prey. The herbivores are a spiky-plated stegosaur that feeds on low plants close to the ground and at least two kinds of sauropods that eat taller plants. One of the sauropods is a new and different species of diplodocid, represented at first by a small jaw, probably from a baby. Last field season we recovered more of it. The other sauropod is the titanosaurid Malaŵi-saurus. That species is the best represented of all the dinosaurs in Malaŵi. Parts of the skeleton are known from sets of bones articulated as in life. Other bones are scattered. Very interestingly, parts of the skull, the lower jaw, and some teeth have been found. In comparison with the Malaŵi-saurus sample, of the more than 150 species of sauropods that have been named worldwide, perhaps only two dozen are reasonably well represented by fossils. Of these, skulls are known in less than half. The fossils of Malaŵi-saurus include the only sauropod-skull material known in all of Africa from between the time of Tendaguru and the end of the Age of Reptiles—an interval of nearly eighty million years. With such nice material of this sauropod, its relationships can be worked out. It is not like *Diplodocus* or *Apatosaurus*. It does not have the long skull, pencillike teeth, or scalesome, flailsome tail of those two. Its arms are shorter than *Brachiosaurus,* and its teeth and snout are different from both *Brachiosaurus* and *Camarasaurus*. It is hardly surprising, then, that regal Malaŵi-saurus allows for the revision of ideas about the family tree of sauropods, especially with regard to the place of titanosaurids. Titanosaurids, while having some derived features unique to their own family, and while being much more characteristic of the Cretaceous than the Late Jurassic heyday of the sauropods, are basically primitive in their anatomy.

One of the interesting features of Malaŵi-saurus is its size. At thirty feet long and perhaps a dozen tons in weight, it is small for a sauropod. As I said earlier, of all the bones collected in Malaŵi from all the many different spots in the Dinosaur Beds, none approaches the size of a truly large sauropod. This includes everything collected by colonial expatriates in the 1920s, Migeod in 1930, and all the bones my crews have collected. Malaŵi-saurus is only one third the size of *Diplodocus*. Why should that be? While in the field I thought of two possible explanations. Perhaps the bones come from young individuals. Even the dinosaur giants must grow from hatchlings, but none of the places where bone is found appears to be a nesting area or other social aggregation brought about by the behavior of baby dinosaurs. If not babies, maybe the bones from Malaŵi are those of dinosaur teenagers, as it were. On the other hand, maybe Malaŵi-saurus really was a small sauropod species. Cretaceous sauropods are poorly known all over the world, and most real giants appear to have lived millions of years earlier, but I have to admit there is something amusing, even appealing, about a thirty-foot-long sauropod dinosaur, a pygmy if you like, living in Africa over 100 million years ago where today, after all that time, pygmy humans live. There is, of course, no connection between dinosaur and human pygmies. Malaŵi-saurus is a distinct species of animal; human pygmies are just a population of the one global human species with a smaller average height. But still, the thought of pygmy sauropods is entertaining.

Sauropods have often in the past been depicted as creatures of the low-lands—swamps, seashores, sluggish riverbanks, and bayous. Indeed, their footprints are most often found in rocks representing these environments. The rocks of Malaŵi's Dinosaur Beds were deposited by fast-flowing streams that drained the hilly country at the feet of mountains. The terrain was probably fairly rugged and the vegetation not particularly dense, except perhaps for the galleries along watercourses. The vegetation was certainly not as dense as that in a rain forest. The weather was hot and seasonal, oscillating between wet and dry seasons. The sampling of this kind of environment, as provided by the Dinosaur Beds, may be relevant to why the sauropods were small. Was the countryside too rough for fifty-ton behemoths? Did the young of giants live in the hills, away from the lowlands?

Allow me to speculate a little further. The really giant sauropods are very specialized animals. They had to evolve from species smaller and more primitive than themselves, but those ancestral species are currently unknown to paleontologists. They must have lived where the really big ones did not, otherwise we should have found them at Tendaguru or Dinosaur National Monument or some other famous dinosaur hot spot. Malaŵi-saurus is both small for a sauropod and it has some primitive features in the vertebrae and the skull. This has some very important implications for dinosaurs.

Titanosaurids, as a family, are the last of the sauropods. They are most common in rocks younger than the Dinosaur Beds, not in Africa, but in India and South America. They also appear in the Late Cretaceous of Europe and in North America (the beast called *Alamosaurus*), where they went extinct at the Great Dying that marks the end of the Age of Reptiles. Malaŵi-saurus provides a kind of missing link between older Cretaceous titanosaurids and those of the Late Cretaceous so common in the rest of the world. The titanosaurids may have evolved in Africa and then skipped over to South America just prior to the opening of the South Atlantic Ocean. Some forty million years after they left Africa, they were in North America.

The bizarre mammallike crocodile from Malaŵi tells us to expect the unexpected. We cannot always predict accurately what we will find in the unknown past, even though we can construct hypotheses that make reasonable predictions. The Malaŵi croc was unexpected, but it does not violate the body of knowledge upon which paleontology is based. It is just an interesting discovery, appealing in its way just as the dinosaur discoveries from Malaŵi are. Does the presence of the mammallike croc have any relevance to the apparent absence of true mammals from the Dinosaur Beds? Maybe so, but even if it does not, it demonstrates that viable, long-lived, functioning ecological communities can be made up of species vastly different from those around today, each with its special role in the web of life. As exemplified by the Dinosaur Beds, the ecosystems of the past are not simply junior-league models of those that exist today. They were different, and they had to be modified for the world to become what it is.

All of the studies done thus far are preliminary. More work needs to be done on everything. The frogs are unstudied, the mammallike croc is not yet named, nor are Malaŵi-saurus or our new species of diplodocid formally named. The stegosaur and theropods need detailed examination. What will they tell us? The questions go on and on. It will be years before the final reports are completed. It will be years before Elizabeth has turned in her finished dissertation and returned to her country to undertake new investigations in Malaŵi's fossil beds. Even after that has happened, scholars will forever employ the specimens collected in our Malaŵi expeditions, and those from Cameroon, just as they use books in a library, for their own research purposes. Ideas will constantly be revised, eternally updated, never static. What we think now about Malaŵi-saurus and the other fossils from Africa is sure to change in the future. In one sense that means that what is being said today is sure to be wrong, or at best, not completely right; in a more important sense it means that what is being said now will help us be closer to the truth next time.

THIS IS HOW it was when I left Ngara camp:

August 3, Friday.

Lightwell was in camp this morning because Kent and I are leaving today. He came quietly up to me.

"Excuse me, sir," he said, "may I speak to you?"

I was heading for my tent. "Sure," I answered. "Can you talk while I pack my gear?"

Lightwell followed me over to the subdued light beneath the green canvas of my Malaŵi home.

"Sir, I have prepared a sort of report, which I would like to read because you are leaving."

"Okay, go ahead."

Lightwell started to read. I stopped him.

"I think this is for the whole group. Let's go back and gather everyone," I suggested.

Around the table, under the shade of the tamarind tree, Lightwell began.

"First, before I read my report, please let me say that if anything was done that offended you, please forgive us, for you are visitors here and we never do anything to offend you. But if we did something that offended you without our knowledge, I am sorry. I have heard that Yasaki misbehaved and had to be sacked for being rude. I am sorry. He embarrassed us."

We echoed warm sentiments, and I assured him of our deep feelings for all the people of Mwakasyunguti, including Yasaki. Good-byes in Malaŵi are always glorpy.

Lightwell read his handwritten note with trembling lip:

Farewell Report

It is my great appreciation and sincere gratitude for you once more coming here to visit my country, in particular my village Thawilo.

I again thank you for the best time I spent with you here on Saturday, 28th July. I extend my sincere gratitude to you also for the good and fruitful ideas you shared with me on that day. May I take an opportunity for thanking you once again for the point of developing my home area. Because of this some of my home brothers are able to get a sort of employment whereby they can obtain money for their living. In addition to this development, my village bears its importance and great fame in the country. It is my absolute belief that people always tend to neglect places found in remote areas or away from the main road. But with the case of Thawilo, in particular Mwakasyunguti village, no one can neglect it as it is now. So for you to discover such an expensive thing in my home area, it is because of the great wisdom poured in you. Therefore, may you and your family be healthy and strong all the way to Dallas in the United States of America as you will be going back home. May you have such an excellent wisdom so that all the best quality businesses planned and prepared for you may be fulfilled.

It is of no wonder that you have left people of Thawilo with great excitement and healthy pockets for such an unforgettable development you have introduced in the area. To say for sure, people in Mwakasyunguti village never forget you though you leave them because you have brought a sort of development in Thawilo. They always feel happy with you when you live among them. Although time has come now for you to leave them, spiritually you will always be among them. Please, may your families remember us here.

I once more say thanks are due to you, Dr. Louis Jacobs, Dr. Dale Winkler, Kent D. Newman, and William Downs. I wish you all a good journey.

YOU ALL DESERVE BEST WISHES AND THANKS!

L.S.E. MKWALA

LIGHTWELL SADALA ENDSON MKWALA

My own emotions about Malaŵi, its people, and its future jostled within me as we rattled off down the tarmac to Karonga, through the territory Mlozi and his slavers had savaged a century before. We drove past the sign for the Synod of Livingstonia, past the World War I graves, past Karonga Teachers' College, past the bright, new regional hospital, to the airport.

"Will it fly today?" I asked the Air Malaŵi ticket agent.

Through a broad grin he replied, "I hope so."

EXPEDITION MEMBERS

1984 Malaŵi Expedition

R. Jerry Britt (Southern Methodist University)
William Chilinda (Department of Antiquities)
William R. Downs (Southern Methodist University and Northern Arizona University)
Louis L. Jacobs (Southern Methodist University)
Zefe M. Kaufulu (Department of Antiquities)
Biswick Khomba (Department of Antiquities)
Petros Mfiri (Karonga)
Fidelis Morocco (Department of Antiquities)
Greavens Mwanza (Karonga)
Lloyd Nyalwa (Karonga)
Nicola Stern (Harvard University)

(Our son, Matthew, was born in September after the 1984 Malaŵi Expedition. In May 1985, Bonnie and I took Matthew with us to Kenya while we did our work on younger fossils. That year I dug dinosaurs and other bones in Texas and Arizona.)

1986 Cameroon Expedition

Sodia Adamou (Yaounde)
Abel Brillanceau (Université de Poitiers, France)
Michel Brunet (Université de Poitiers)
Jean Dejax (Museum national d'Histoire naturelle, Paris)
Kathryn M. Flanagan (University of Wyoming)
Lawrence J. Flynn (Harvard University)

Emile Heintz (Museum national d'Histoire naturelle)
Joseph Victor Hell (Institute de Recherche Geologique et Minière,
Garoua)
Louis L. Jacobs
Jean (last name not known, Garoua)
Jean-Pierre (last name not known, Garoua)
Sevket Sen (Université de Paris VI)

1987 CAMEROON EXPEDITION

Sodia Adamou
Abel Brillanceau
Michel Brunet
John D. Congleton (Southern Methodist University)
Jean Dejax
William R. Downs
Vera Eisenmann (Museum national d'Histoire naturelle)
Kathryn M. Flanagan
Lawrence J. Flynn
Emile Heintz
Joseph Victor Hell
Louis L. Jacobs
Yves Jehenne (Université de Poitiers)
Guy Mouchelin (Université de Poitiers)
David Pilbeam (Harvard University)
Sallee (last name not known, Garoua)
Samuel (last name not known, Garoua)

1987 MALAŴI EXPEDITION

John D. Congleton
William R. Downs
Louis L. Jacobs
Alfred Kapira (Mwakasyunguti)
Zefe Kaufulu
James Khomu (Department of Antiquities)
Brighton Missiska (Mwakasyunguti)

Mjuda Missiska (Mwakasyunguti)
Wellington Missiska (Mwakasyunguti)
Lightwell Mkwala (Mwakasyunguti)
Fidelis Morocco
Kent D. Newman (Southern Methodist University)
Alisa J. Winkler (Southern Methodist University)
Dale A. Winkler (Southern Methodist University)

1988 CAMEROON EXPEDITION

Sodia Adamou
Abel Brillanceau
Michel Brunet
John D. Congleton
Jean Dejax
Joseph Victor Hell
Louis L. Jacobs
Guy Mouchelin
Sallee

1989 MALAŴI EXPEDITION

William R. Downs
Elizabeth Gomani (University of Malaŵi)
Louis L. Jacobs
Joseph Kapira
Zefe Kaufulu
James Khomu
Laura MacLatchy (Harvard University)
Augustine Maxwell (Ngara)
Patson Maxwell (Ngara)
Yasaki Mhango (Mwakasyunguti)
Mjuda Missiska
Wellington Missiska
Lightwell Mkwala
Fidelis Morocco
Ronald Mwagomba (Karonga)

Kent D. Newman
Gresham Ngwira (Ngara)
Dale A. Winkler

1990 Malaŵi Expedition

William R. Downs
Elizabeth Gomani (Department of Antiquities)
Louis L. Jacobs
Alfred Kapira
Joseph Kapira
James Khomu
Augustine Maxwell
Patson Maxwell
Yasaki Mhango
Dyson Mkwala (Mwakasyunguti)
Mjuda Missiska
Wellington Missiska
Fidelis Morocco
Ronald Mwagomba
Kent D. Newman
Gresham Ngwira
Alisa J. Winkler
Dale A. Winkler

(There was no African field season in 1991, but Dale Winkler and I went to the Department of Antiquities to prepare fossils in their laboratory with Fidelis Morocco.)

1992 Malaŵi Expedition

John Chilachila (Department of Antiquities)
Elizabeth Gomani (Department of Antiquities and Southern Methodist University)
Louis L. Jacobs
Alfred Kapira
Joseph Kapira

James Khomu

Saulos Makale (Mwakasyunguti)

Banana Joe Missiska (Mwakasyunguti. I cannot resist giving the derivation of Banana Joe's name. His given name in Tumbuka sounded very much like the Chicheŵa word for eggs. He apparently did not like that. On a trip to Lilongwe he was visited by spirits in his sleep, so he says, and they instructed him to change his name to Banana Joe, which he did.)

Keni Missiska (Mwakasyunguti)

Mjuda Missiska

Wellington Missiska

Dyson Mkwala

Fidelis Morocco

Ronald Mwagomba

Kent D. Newman (Southern Methodist University and Plano Independent School District, Wilson Middle School)

Gresham Ngwira

Locala Nyilongo (Mwakasyunguti)

Louis H. Taylor (Western Interior Paleontological Society, Denver)

Thomas Thwindwa (Ngara)

Dale A. Winkler

SUGGESTIONS FOR FURTHER READING

(This is not an exhaustive bibliography, only an introduction to the literature, but it should lead the interested reader to the wealth of published sources available about the topics of this book. Some references are relevant to more than one chapter, but each is listed only once, in the most appropriate place.)

CHAPTER 1. THE FORGOTTEN DINOSAURS OF AFRICA

Albritton, C. C. 1986. *The Abyss of Time.* Freeman, Cooper and Company, New York.

Blaikie, W. Garden. 1910. *The Personal Life of David Livingstone.* John Murray, London.

Campbell, R. J. 1930. *Livingstone.* Dodd, Mead & Company, New York.

Crichton, Michael. 1990. *Jurassic Park.* Alfred A. Knopf, New York.

Colbert, Edwin H. 1973. *Wandering Lands and Animals.* E. P. Dutton & Company, Inc., New York.

Darwin, C. 1859. *The Origin of Species.* John Murray, London. (A variorum text edited by Morse Peckham [1959, University of Pennsylvania Press] indicates that the passage mentioning Livingstone was changed in the fifth edition to, "Livingstone states that good domestic breeds are valued by the negroes in the interior of Africa who have not associated with Europeans.")

DeSalle, Rob; Gatesy, John; Wheeler, Ward; and Grimaldi, David. 1992. "DNA Sequences from a Fossil Termite in Oligo-Miocene Amber and their Phylogenetic Implications." 257:1933–36.

Drummond, Henry. 1884. "Geology of Central Africa." *Nature* 29:551.

————. 1888. *Tropical Africa.* Hodder and Stoughton, London.

Gould, Stephen Jay. 1980. *The Panda's Thumb.* W. W. Norton & Company, New York.

————. 1983. *Hen's Teeth and Horses Toes.* W. W. Norton & Company, New York.

————. 1985. *The Flamingo's Smile.* W. W. Norton & Company, New York.

Hallam, A. 1973. *A Revolution in the Earth Sciences.* Clarendon, Oxford.

Hillis, David M., and Moritz, Craig. 1990. *Molecular Systematics.* Sinauer Associates Inc., Sunderland, Mass.

Jacobs, Louis L.; Winkler, Dale A.; and Downs, William R. 1992. "Malaŵi's Paleontological Heritage." *Occasional Papers of the Malaŵi Department of Antiquities* 1:5–23.

Kenyatta, Jomo. 1938. *Facing Mount Kenya: The Tribal Life of the Gikuyu.* Secker and Warburg, London.

Kipling, Rudyard. 1978. *Just So Stories for Little Children.* Weathervane Books, New York. (There are, of course, many editions of this delightful work. The advice of the kolokolo bird is from "The Elephant's Child." A few other descriptive terms from other stories have also been used.)

Maier, Gerhard. 1989. *Tendaguru Through Time: The Information Trail of a Scientific Expedition.* The University of Alberta, Unpublished Research Project submitted to the Faculty of Library and Information Studies.

Migeod, F.W.H. 1930. "Report on the British Museum East Africa Expedition. Season 1929." *Natural History Magazine* 2(1930): 185–98.

————. 1931A. "British Museum East Africa Expedition. Account of the Work Done in 1930." *Natural History Magazine* 9:87–103.

————. 1931B. "Digging for Dinosaurs." *Discovery* 12:142–45.

Morell, Virginia. 1992. "Thirty-Million-Year-Old DNA Boosts an Emerging Field." *Science* 257:1860–62.

Parkinson, J. 1930. *The Dinosaur in East Africa: An Account of the Giant Reptile Beds of Tendaguru, Tanganyika Territory.* H. F. & G. Witherby, London.

Paul, G. S. 1988. "The Brachiosaur Giants of the Morrison and Tendaguru with a Description of a New Subgenus, *Giraffatitan,* and a comparison of the World's Largest Dinosaurs." *Hunteria* 2:1–14.

Scotese, Christopher (chairman). 1990. *Atlas of Phanerozoic Plate Tectonic Reconstructions.* Technical Report 90, Paleomap Project Technical Report No. 10-90-1, University of Texas, Arlington.

Simpson, George Gaylord. 1963. *This View of Life: The World of an Evolutionist.* Harcourt, Brace & World, Inc., New York.

————. 1983. *Fossils and the History of Life.* Scientific American Books, New York.

William, G. 1982. *The Road to Jaramillo.* Stanford University Press, Stanford, Calif.

Wilson, J. Tuzo; and others. 1972. *Continents Adrift.* W. H. Freeman and Company, San Francisco.

Chapter 2. Tahiti Without Salt

Anderson-Morshead, A.E.M.; and Garland, Vera. 1991. *Lady of the Lake: The Story of Lake Malaŵi's M. V.* Chauncy Maples. Central Africana, Blantyre, Malaŵi.

Avise, John C. 1990. "Flocks of African Fishes." *Nature* 347:512–13.

Bemis, William E.; Burggren, Warren W.; and Kemp, Norman E. (editors). 1987. *The Biology and Evolution of Lungfishes.* Alan R. Liss, Inc., New York.

Carter, Judy. 1987. *Malaŵi: Wildlife, Parks and Reserves.* MacMillan Publishers Ltd., London.

Clark, J. Desmond; Haynes, C. Vance; Mawby, John E.; and Gautier, A. 1970. "Interim Report on Palaeo-Anthropological Investigations in the Lake Malaŵi Rift." *Quaternaria* 13:305–54.

Cole-King, P. A. 1987. *Lake Malaŵi Steamers.* Department of Antiquities, Lilongwe, Malaŵi.

Colin, J.-P.; and Jacobs, L. L. 1990. "On the Age of the Malaŵi Dinosaur Beds." *Comptes Rendus de Academie des Sciences, Paris* 311:1025–29.

Dixey, F. 1927. "The Mlanje Mountains of Nyasaland." *The Geographical Review* 17(4):611–26.

———. 1928. "The Dinosaur Beds of Lake Nyasa." *Transactions of the Royal Society of South Africa* 16:55–66.

Fryer, G.; and Iles, T. D. 1972. *The Cichlid Fishes of the Great Lakes of Africa.* T.F.H. Publications, Neptune City, N.J.

Gibbons, Ann. 1991. "Jawboning Prehistory." *Science* 253:846.

Johnston, Harry H.. 1897. *British Central Africa.* Methuen, London.

Konings, Ad. 1990. *Konings's Book of Cichlids and All the Other Fish of Lake Malaŵi.* T.F.H. Publications, Neptune City, N.J.

Lewis, Digby; Reinthal, Peter; and Trendall, Jasper. 1986. *A Guide to the Fishes of Lake Malaŵi National Park.* World Wildlife Fund, Gland, Switz.

Mateer, Niall J.; and others. 1992. "Correlation of Nonmarine Cretaceous Strata of Africa and the Middle East." *Cretaceous Research* 13:273–318.

Meyer, Axel; Kocher, Thomas D.; Basasibwaki, P.; and Wilson, A. C. 1990. "Monophyletic Origin of Lake Victoria Cichlid Fishes Suggested by Mitochondrial DNA Sequences." *Nature* 347:550–53. (See also the comments on this paper in *Nature* 350:467–68.)

Meyer, Axel; and Wilson, Allan C. 1990. "Origin of Tetrapods Inferred from

Their Mitochondrial DNA Affiliation to Lungfish.'' *Journal of Molecular Evolution* 31:359–64.

Moir, Fred. 1923. *After Livingstone.* Hodder and Stoughton, London.

Moir, Jane F. 1891. *A Lady's Letters from Central Africa. A Journey from Mandala, Shiré Highlands to Ujiji, Lake Tanganyika, and Back in 1890.* James Maclehose & Sons, Glasgow. (Reissued with a new introduction in 1991 by Central Africana Limited, Blantyre.)

Nyamweru, Celia. 1980. *Rifts and Volcanoes: A Study of the East African Rift System.* Thomas Nelson and Sons Ltd., Nairobi.

Reinthal, P. 1990. ''The Living Jewels of Lake Malaŵi.'' *National Geographic* 177(5):42–51.

Sturmbauer, Christian; and Meyer, Axel. 1992. ''Genetic Divergence, Speciation and Morphological Stasis in a Lineage of African Cichlid Fishes.'' *Nature* 358:578–81.

Young, E. D. 1877. *Nyassa: A Journal of Adventures.* John Murray, London.

CHAPTER 3. JOURNALS FROM THE GROUND

Benson, C. W.; and Benson, F. M. 1986. *The Birds of Malaŵi.* Montfort Press, Limbe, Malaŵi.

Bernstein, J. 1990. ''The Dark Continent of Henry Stanley.'' *The New Yorker,* 31 December 1990: 93–107.

Clough, Juliet. 1989. *Malaŵi: The Warm Heart of Africa.* Hanns Reich Verlag, Munich.

Davidson, Basil. 1978. *Let Freedom Come: Africa in Modern History.* Little, Brown and Company, Boston.

———. 1980. *The African Slave Trade.* Little, Brown and Company, Boston.

———. 1991. *African Civilization Revisited: From Antiquity to Modern Times.* Africa World Press, Inc., Trenton N.J.

Fotheringham, L. Monteith. 1891. *Adventures in Nyassaland; A Two Years' Struggle with Arab Slave-Dealers in Central Africa.* Sampson Low, Marston, Searle, & Rivington, London.

Howson, P. J. 1972. *A Short History of Karonga.* Department of Antiquities Publication II, Government Press, Zomba.

Johnston, Harry H. 1930. *A History of the Colonization of Africa by Alien Races.* New revised edition. Cambridge University Press, Cambridge.

Kandoole, B. F.; and Phiri, K. M. 1989. *Malaŵi 25: Twenty-five Years of Independence in Malaŵi, 1964–1989.* Silver Jubilee Commemorative Book. Dzuka Publishing Company Limited, Blantyre, Malaŵi.

Kayira, Legson. 1965. *I Will Try*. Doubleday & Company, Inc., Garden City, N.Y.

Lamport-Stokes, Barbara. 1989. *Blantyre: Glimpses of the Early Days*. The Society of Malaŵi, Historical and Scientific. Blantyre, Malaŵi.

Livingstone, David; and Livingstone, Charles. 1865. *Narrative of an Expedition to the Zambesi and Its Tributaries; and the Discovery of Lakes Shirwa and Nyassa 1858–1864*. John Murray, London.

Livingstone, W. P. 1921. *Laws of Livingstonia: A Narrative of Missionary Adventure and Achievement*. Hodder and Stoughton Limited, London. (Written by David Livingstone's son.)

Mukasa, Ham. 1975. *Sir Apolo Kagwa Discovers Britain*. Edited by Taban Io Liyong. H. E. B., Heinemann, London.

Nelson, H. D.; Dobert, M.; McDonald, G. C.; McLaughlin, J.; Marvin, B.; and Whitaker, D. P. 1975. *Area Handbook for Malaŵi*. U. S. Government Printing Office, Washington, D.C.

O'Toole, Thomas. 1989. *Malaŵi . . . in Pictures*. Lerner Publications Company, Minneapolis. (This is a good middle-school geography text.)

Pachai, B. (editor). 1972. *The Early History of Malaŵi*. Longman Group Limited, London.

Ransford, Oliver. 1966. *Livingstone's Lake: The History of Malaŵi*. John Murray, London.

Rotberg, Robert I. (editor). 1970. *Africa and Its Explorers: Motives, Methods, and Impact*. Harvard University Press, Cambridge, Mass.

Schoffeleers, J. M.; and Roscoe, A. A. 1985. *Land of Fire: Oral Literature from Malaŵi*. Popular Publications, Limbe, Malaŵi.

Shaxson, A.; Dickson, P.; and Walker, J. 1985. *The Malaŵi Cookbook*. Blantyre Printing and Publishing Co. Ltd. for the Government Printer, Zomba.

Sheriff, A. 1987. *Slaves, Spices & Ivory in Zanzibar: Integration of an East African Commercial Empire into the World Economy, 1770–1873*. Ohio University Press, Athens, Ohio.

Stanley, H. M. 1872. *How I Found Livingstone*. Sampson Low, London.

———. 1909. *Autobiography of Sir Henry M. Stanley*. Dorothy Stanley (editor). Sampson, Low, Marston and Company, Ltd., London.

Wassermann, J. 1933. *Bula Matari, Stanley, Conqueror of a Continent*. Translated from the German by Eden and Cedar Paul. Liveright, Inc., Publishers, New York.

Wills, A. J. 1985. *An Introduction to the History of Central Africa: Zambia, Malaŵi, Zimbabwe*. Oxford University Press, Oxford.

Young, E. D. 1868. *The Search After Livingstone*. Letts, Son, and Company, London.

CHAPTER 4. THE ROAMING TITAN LIZARDS

Alexander, R. McNeill. 1989. *Dynamics of Dinosaurs and Other Extinct Giants.* Columbia University Press, New York.

Benton, M. J. 1989. "Evolution of Large Size." In Briggs, D.E.G.; and Crowther, P. R. (editors), *Palaeobiology: A Synthesis.* Blackwells, Oxford, pp. 147–52.

Berman, D. S.; and McIntosh, J. S. 1978. "Skull and Relationships of the Upper Jurassic Sauropod *Apatosaurus* (Reptilia: Saurischia)." *Bulletin of the Carnegie Museum of Natural History* 8:1–35.

Bonaparte, José F.; and Powell, Jaime E. 1980. "A Continental Assemblage of Tetrapods from the Upper Cretaceous Beds of El Brete, Northwestern Argentina (Sauropoda - Coelurosauria - Carnosauria - Aves)." *Mémoires de la Société Géologique de France, Nouvelle Serie* 139:19–28.

Calvo, Jorge O. and Bonaparte, José F. 1991. *Andesaurus delgadoi gen et s.p. nov.* (Savrischia-Souropoda), Dinosauria Ttanosauridae de la Formacion Rio Limay (Albiano-Cenomaniano), Neuqven, Argentina. Ameghiniana, Vol. 28 (3–4):303–10.

Carpenter, K.; and Currie, P. J. (editors). 1990. *Dinosaur Systematics: Approaches and Perspectives.* Cambridge University Press, Cambridge. (This is a fine book about dinosaurs and it contains a very important paper on sauropods by the dean of sauropodologists, John S. McIntosh. The reference edited by Weishampel, Dodson, and Osmólska listed under the next chapter also contains an excellent contribution by McIntosh.)

Carroll, Robert L. 1988. *Vertebrate Paleontology and Evolution.* W. H. Freeman and Company, New York. (This is the standard text for vertebrate paleontology.)

Colbert, Edwin H. 1983. *Dinosaurs: An Illustrated History.* Hammond Incorporated, Maplewood, N.J.

Coombs, Walter P., Jr. 1975. "Sauropod Habits and Habitats." *Palaeogeography, Palaeclimatology, Palaeoecology* 17:1–33.

Depéret, Charles. 1896. "Note sur les Dinosauriens Sauropodes & Théropodes du Crétacé Supérieur de Madagascar." *Bulletin de la Société Géologique de France* 24:176–96.

Dong Zhiming. 1990. "On Remains of the Sauropods from Kelamaili Region, Junggar Basin, Xinjiang, China." *Vertebrata PalAsiatica* 28:43–58.

Dong Zhiming, Peng Guangzhao, and Huang Daxi. 1989. "The Discovery of the Bony Tail Club of Sauropods." *Vertebrata PalAsiatica,* 7:219–24.

Gillette, David D. 1991. *"Seismosaurus halli,* gen. et sp. nov., a New Sauropod Dinosaur from the Morrison Formation (Upper Jurassic/Lower Cretaceous) of New Mexico, USA." *Journal of Vertebrate Paleontology* 11(4):417–33.

Haughton, S. H. 1928. "On Some Reptilian Remains from the Dinosaur Beds of Nyasaland." *Transactions of the Royal Society of South Africa* 16:69–83.

Huene, F. von. 1929. "Los Saurisquios y Ornithisquios de Cretacéo Argentino." *Anales del Museo de La Plata* (series 2) 3:1–196.

Huene, F. von; and Matley, C. A. 1933. "The Cretaceous Saurischia and Ornithischia of the Central Provinecs [sic] of India." *Memoirs of the Geological Survey of India, Palaeontologia Indica* 26:1–74.

Rothschild, Bruce M.; and Berman, D. S. 1991. "Fusion of Caudal Vertebrae in Late Jurassic Sauropods." *Journal of Vertebrate Paleontology* 11:29–36.

Wild, R. 1991. *"Janenschia* n. g. *robusta* (E. Fraas 1908) *pro Tornieria robusta* (E. Fraas 1908) (Reptilia, Saurischia, Sauropodomorpha)." *Stuttgarter Beiträge zur Naturkunde, serie B (Geologie und Paläontologie)* 173:1–4.

CHAPTER 5. AFRICAN DINOSAURS, BEFORE AND AFTER

Barinaga, Marcia. 1992. "Evolutionists Wing It with a New Fossil Bird." *Science* 255:796.

Chatterjee, Sankar. 1991. "Cranial Anatomy and Relationships of a New Triassic Bird from Texas." *Philosophical Transactions of the Royal Society of London, Series B* 332:277–346.

Chiappe, Luis M. 1991. "Cretaceous Avian Remains from Patagonia Shed New Light on the Early Radiation of Birds." *Alcheringa* 15:333–38.

Chure, Daniel J.; and McIntosh, J. S. 1989. "A Bibliography of the Dinosauria (Exclusive of the Aves) 1677–1986." *Museum of Western Colorado Paleontology Series* 1.

Dong Zhiming. 1988. *Dinosaurs from China.* China Ocean Press, Beijing.

Ehrlich, P. R.; and others. 1983. "Long-term Biological Consequences of Nuclear War." *Science* 222:1293–1300.

Elliot, David K. (editor). 1986. *Dynamics of Extinction.* John Wiley & Sons, New York.

Gratz, A. J.; Nellis, W. J.; and Hinsey, N. A. 1992. "Laboratory Simulation of Explosive Volcanic Loading and Implications for the Cause of the K/T Boundary." *Geophysical Research Letters* 19(13):1391–94.

Hecht, Max K.; Ostrom, John H.; Viohl, Günter; and Wellnhofer, Peter (editors). 1985. *The Beginnings of Birds.* Freunde des Jura-Museums Eichstatt, Willibaldsburg, Ger.

Hildebrand, Alan R.; and others. 1991. "Chicxulub Crater: A Possible Cretaceous/Tertiary Boundary Impact Crater on the Yucatán Peninsula, Mexico." *Geology* 19:867–71.

McIntosh, John S.; Coombs, Walter P., Jr.; and Russell, Dale A. 1992. "A New Diplodocid Sauropod (Dinosauria) from Wyoming, U.S.A." *Journal of Vertebrate Paleontology* 12:158–67.

Norman, David B. 1985. *The Illustrated Encyclopedia of Dinosaurs.* Crescent Books, New York.

Padian, Kevin (editor). 1986. *The Origin of Birds and the Evolution of Flight.* California Academy of Sciences, San Francisco.

Sereno, Paul C. 1991. "Basal Archosaurs: Phylogenetic Relationships and Functional Implications." *Journal of Vertebrate Paleontology* 11, Supplement to 4, 1–53.

Sereno, Paul C.; and Rao Chenggang. "Early Evolution of Avian Flight and Perching: New Evidence from the Lower Cretaceous of China." *Science* 255:845–48.

Turco, R. P.; and others. 1990. "Climate and Smoke: An Appraisal of Nuclear Winter." *Science* 247: 166–76.

Weishampel, D. B.; Dodson, P.; and Osmólska, H. (editors). 1990. *The Dinosauria.* University of California Press, Berkeley. (This is the best book on dinosaurs I know of. The chapter by McIntosh on sauropods is the best summary of the group that exists.)

Wellnhofer, Peter. 1991. *The Illustrated Encyclopedia of Pterosaurs.* Crescent Books, New York.

Wolfe, Jack A. "Palaeobotanical Evidence for a June 'Impact Winter' at the Cretaceous/Tertiary Boundary." *Nature* 352:420–23.

CHAPTER 6. THE CROCODILE OF CARNIVAL

Bonaparte, José F. 1991. "Los Vertebrados Fosiles de la Formacion Rio Colorado, de la Ciudad de Neuquen y Cercanias, Cretacico Superior, Argenyina." *Revista del Museo Argentino de Ciencias Naturales "Bernardino Rivadavia" e Instituto Nacional de Investigation de las Ciencias Naturales, Paleontoloía* 4(3):15–123.

Buffetaut, E. 1979. "The Evolution of the Crocodilians." *Scientific American* 241(4): 130–44.

Carvalho, Ismar de Souza; and Campos, Diogenes de Almeida. 1988. "Um

Mamífero Triconodonte do Cretáceo Inferior do Maranhão, Brasil.'' *Anais da Academia Brasileira de Ciências* 60(4):437–46.

Clark, J. M.; Jacobs, L. L.; and Downs, W. R. 1989. ''Mammal-like Dentition and Mandibular Movement in a Mesozoic Crocodylian.'' *Science* 244: 1064–66.

Cott, Hugh B. 1961. ''Scientific Results of an Inquiry into the Ecology and Economic Status of the Nile Crocodile (*Crocodilus niloticus*) in Uganda and Northern Rhodesia.'' *Transactions of the Zoological Society of London* 29:211–357.

Graham, Alistair; and Beard, Peter. 1973. *Eyelids of Morning: The Mingled Destinies of Crocodiles and Men.* New York Graphic Society, Ltd., Greenwich, C.T.

Jacobs, B. F. 1990. ''Lower Cretaceous Diaspores from Malaŵi.'' *National Geographic Research* 6: 516–18.

Jacobs, L. L.; Winkler, D. A.; Kaufulu, Z.; and Downs, W. R. 1990. ''The Dinosaur Beds of Northern Malaŵi, Africa.'' *National Geographic Research* 6: 196–204.

Maisey, John G. (editor). 1991. *Santana Fossils: An Illustrated Atlas.* T.F.H. Publications, Neptune City, N.J.

Ross, Charles A. (consulting editor). 1989. *Crocodiles and Alligators.* Facts on File, New York.

CHAPTER 7. FOR ONE TOOTH

Bonaparte, José. 1990. ''New Late Cretaceous Mammals from the Los Alamitos Formation, Northern Patagonia.'' *National Geographic Research* 6(1): 63–93.

Brunet, M.; and others. 1990. ''New Fossil Mammals from the Early Cretaceous of Cameroon, West Africa.'' *Comptes Rendus de l'Academie des Sciences, Paris* 310, II, 1139–46. (We named *Abelodon abeli* in this paper.)

Denis, Alain. 1984. *Beyond Sight: Cameroon.* Editions du Damalisque, Paris.

Godthelp, H.; and others. 1992. ''Earliest Known Australian Tertiary Mammal Fauna.'' *Nature* 356:514–16.

Hargreaves, J. D. 1963. *Prelude to the Partition of West Africa.* MacMillan Press Ltd., London.

Hiiemae, Karen M.; and Crompton, Alfred W. 1985. ''Mastication, Food Transport, and Swallowing.'' In Hildebrand, M.; Bramble, D. M.; Liem, K. F.; and Wake, D. B. (editors), *Functional Vertebrate Morphology.* The Belknap Press of Harvard University Press, Cambridge, pp. 262–90.

Jacobs, L. L.; and others. 1988. "Mammal Teeth from the Cretaceous of Africa." *Nature* 336: 158–60.

Pascual, Rosendo; and others. 1992. "First Discovery of Monotremes in South America." *Nature* 356:704–706.

Rich, P. V.; van Tets, G. F.; and Knight, F. 1985. *Kadimakara: Extinct Vertebrates of Australia.* Pioneer Design Studio, Victoria, Aus.

Savage, R.J.G.; and Long, M. R. 1986. *Mammal Evolution: An Illustrated Guide.* Facts on File Publications, New York.

Vickers-Rich, P.; Monaghan, J. M.; Baird, R. F.; and Rich, T. H. 1991. *Vertebrate Paleontology of Australasia.* Pioneer Design Studio Pty., Ltd., and Monash University Publications Committee, Melbourne.

CHAPTER 8. OTHER NEIGHBORS

Bardack, D. 1991. "First Fossil Hagfish (Myxinoidea): A Record from the Pennsylvanian of Illinois." *Science* 254:701–703.

Bonaparte, José F. 1986. "History of the Terrestrial Cretaceous Vertebrates of Gondwana." *IV Congess Argentina Paleontologia y Bioestratigraphia* 2:63–95.

Bowen, B. W.; Meylan, A. B.; and Avise, J. C. 1989. "An Odyssey of the Green Sea Turtle: Ascension Island Revisited." *Proceedings of the National Academy of Sciences, U.S.A.* 86:573–76.

Brasier, M. D. 1974. "Turtle Drift." *Nature* 250:351.

Briggs, D.E.G. 1992. "Conodonts: A Major Extinct Group Added to the Vertebrates." *Science* 256:1285–86.

Carr, Archie. 1967. *So Excellent a Fishe: A Natural History of Sea Turtles.* The Natural History Press, Garden City, N.Y. (This is a classic of natural history. It has been reissued as *The Sea Turtle* by the University of Texas Press.)

Carr, Archie; and Coleman, P. J. 1974. "Seafloor Spreading Theory and the Odyssey of the Green Turtle." *Nature* 249:128–30.

Carson, Hampton, L. 1992. "The Galápagos That Were." *Nature* 355:202–203.

Christie, D. M.; and others. 1992. "Drowned Islands Downstream from the Galápagos Hotspot Imply Extended Speciation Times." *Nature* 355:246–48.

Ciochon, Russell L.; and Chiarelli, A. Brunetto (editors). 1980. *Evolutionary Biology of New World Monkeys and Continental Drift.* Plenum Press, New York.

Duellman, William E.; and Trueb, Linda. 1986. *Biology of Amphibians.* McGraw-Hill Book Company, New York.

Estes, Richard, D. 1983. "The Fossil Record and Early Distribution of Lizards." In Rhidin, Anders G. L. (editor), *Advances in Herpetology and Evolutionary*

Biology: Essays in Honor of Ernest E. Williams, pp. 365–98. Museum of Comparative Zoology, Harvard University, Cambridge, Mass.

Estes, Richard D.; and Pregill, G. (editors). 1988. *Phyletic Relationships of the Lizard Families.* Stanford University Press, Stanford, Calif.

Gaffney, E. S.; Hutchinson, J. H.; Jenkins, F. R.; and Meeker, L. J. 1987. "Modern Turtle Origins: The Oldest Known Cryptodire." *Science* 237: 289–91.

Gingerich, P. D. 1990. "African Dawn for Primates." *Nature* 346:411.

Gregory, R. T.; Douthitt, C. B.; Duddy, I. R.; Rich, P. V.; and Rich, T. H. 1989. "Oxygen Isotopic Composition of Carbonate Concretions from the Lower Cretaceous of Victoria, Australia: Implications for the Evolution of Meteoric Waters on the Australian Continent in a Paleopolar Environment." *Earth and Planetary Science Letters* 92:27–42.

Jensen, David. 1966. "The Hagfish." *Scientific American* 214(2):82–90.

Lack, David. 1947. *Darwin's Finches: An Essay on the General Biological Theory of Evolution.* Cambridge University Press, Cambridge, Eng.

Lewin, Roger. 1989. "New Look at Turtle Migration Mystery." *Science* 243: 1009.

Lohmann, Kenneth J. 1992. "How Sea Turtles Navigate." *Scientific American,* January:100–106.

Martill, D. M.; Cruickshank, A.R.I.; and Taylor, M. A. 1991. "Dispersal via Whale Bones." *Nature* 351:193.

McKenna, M. C. 1983. "Holarctic Landmass Rearrangement, Cosmic Events, and Cenozoic Terrestrial Organisms." *Annals of the Missouri Botanical Gardens* 70:459–89.

Paladino, F. V.; Dodson, P.; Hammond, J. K.; and Spotila, J. R. 1989. "Temperature-Dependent Sex Determination in Dinosaurs? Implications for Population Dynamics and Extinction." *Geological Society of America Special Paper* 238:63–70.

Paladino, F. V.; O'Connor, M. P.; and Spotila, J. R. 1990. "Metabolism of Leatherback Turtles, Gigantothermy, and Thermoregulation of Dinosaurs." *Nature* 344:858–60.

Reisz, Robert R.; and Laurin, Michel. 1991. *"Owenetta* and the Origin of Turtles." *Nature* 349:324–26.

Rich, T.H.V.; and Rich, P. V. 1989. "Polar Dinosaurs and Biotas of the Early Cretaceous of Southeastern Australia." *National Geographic Research* 5: 15–53.

Rich, P. V.; Rich, T. H.; Wagstaff, B. E.; Mason, J. McEwen; Douthitt, C. B.;

Gregory, R. T.; and Felton, E. A. 1988. "Evidence for Low Temperatures and Biologic Diversity in Cretaceous High Latitudes of Australia." *Science* 242:1403–1406.

Sansom, I. J.; Smith, M. P.; Armstrong, H. A.; and Smith, M. M. 1992. "Presence of the Earliest Vertebrate Hard Tissues in Conodonts." *Science* 256:1308–11.

Smith, C. R.; Kukert, H.; Wheatcroft, R. A.; Jumars, P. A.; and Deming, J. W. 1989. "Vent Fauna on Whale Remains." *Nature* 341:27–28.

Squires, R. L.; Goedert, J. L.; and Barnes, L. G. 1991. "Whale Carcasses." *Nature* 349:574.

Steadman, David W.; and Zousmer, Steven. 1988. *Galápagos: Discovery on Darwin's Islands.* Smithsonian, Washington, D.C.

Stock, David W. and Whitt, Gregory S. 1992. "Evidence from 18S Ribosomal RNA Sequences That Lampreys and Magfishes form a Natural Group." *Science* 257:787–89.

Storch, Gerhard. 1992. "The Mammals of Island Europe." *Scientific American,* February:64–69.

Tunnicliffe, Verena. 1992. "The Nature and Origin of the Modern Hydrothermal Vent Fauna." *Palaios* 7:338–50.

Chapter 9. A Living Dinosaur?

Arens, William. 1979. *The Man-eating Myth: Anthropology and Anthropophagy.* Oxford University Press, Oxford, Eng.

Bird, Roland T. 1985. *Bones for Barnum Brown: Adventures of a Dinosaur Hunter.* TCU Press, Fort Worth.

Darwin, Charles. 1962. *The Voyage of the Beagle.* Leonard Engel (editor). Doubleday & Company, Inc., New York. (This is edited from the 1845 version.)

Defoe, Daniel. 1990. *The Life, Adventures, and Pyraces of the Famous Captain Singleton.* Oxford University Press, Oxford, Eng. (First published in 1720.)

Eve, Raymond A.; and Harrold, Francis B. 1991. *The Creationist Movement in Modern America.* Twayne Publishers, Boston.

Forey, Peter. 1990. "The Coelacanth Fish: Progress and Prospects." *Science Progress* 74:53–67.

Forey, Peter. 1991. "Blood Lines of the Coelacanth." *Nature* 351:347–48.

Fricke, H. 1988. "Coelacanths: The Fish That Time Forgot." *National Geographic* 173(6): 824–38.

Fricke, H.; and Hissman, K. 1990. "Natural Habitat of Coelacanths." *Nature* 346:323–24.

Fricke, H.; Reinicke, O.; Hofer, H.; and Nachtigall, W. 1987. "Locomotion of the Coelacanth *Latimeria chalumnae* in its Natural Environment." *Nature* 329: 331–33.

Fricke, H.; Schauer, J.; Hissman, K.; Kasang, L.; and Plante, R. 1991. "Coelacanth *Latimeria chalumnae* Aggregates in Caves: First Observations on their Resting Habitat and Social Behavior." *Environmental Biology of Fishes* 30:281–85.

Gillette, D. D.; and Lockley, M. G. (editors). 1989. *Dinosaur Tracks and Traces.* Cambridge University Press, Cambridge, Eng. (We published the first notice of dinosaur footprints from Cameroon in this book. Since then my former student, John Congleton, completed a thorough study of them for his master's thesis.)

Gorr, T.; Kleinschmidt, T.; and Fricke, H. 1991. "Close Tetrapod Relationships of the Coelacanth *Latimeria* Indicated by Haemoglobin Sequences." *Nature* 351:394–97. (See also the comments on this paper in *Nature* 353:217–19, 1991.)

Huxley, Elspeth. 1959. *The Flame Trees of Thika: Memories of an African Childhood.* Chatto and Windus, London. (This very pleasant book is mentioned here in part to balance Meinertzhagen's cold-blooded account, listed below.)

Lockley, Martin. 1991. *Tracking Dinosaurs, A New Look at an Ancient World.* Cambridge University Press, Cambridge, Eng.

Mackal, Roy P. 1987. *A Living Dinosaur? In Search of Mokele-Mbembe.* E. J. Brill, Leiden, Netherlands.

Martin, C.G.C. 1980. *Maps and Surveys of Malaŵi.* A. A. Balkema, Cape Town, S.A.

Meinertzhagen, Richard. 1983. *Kenya Diary (1902–1906).* Eland Books, London. (First published in 1957.)

Nelkin, D. 1982. *The Creation Controversy: Science or Scripture in the Schools.* Beacon Press, Boston.

Simpson, G. G. 1984. "Mammals and Cryptozoology." *Proceedings of the American Philosophical Society* 128(1): 1–19.

Smith, J.L.B. 1956. *Old Fourlegs: The Story of the Coelacanth.* Longmans, Green and Co., London.

Strahler, A. N. 1987. *Science and Earth History: The Evolution/Creation Controversy.* Prometheus Books, Buffalo, N.Y.

Thomson, Keith S. 1991. *Living Fossil: The Story of the Coelacanth.* W. W. Norton & Company, New York.

Thulborn, Tony. 1990. *Dinosaur Tracks.* Chapman and Hall, London.

Chapter 10. The Good of Dinosaurs

Alexander, Caroline. 1991. "Personal History: An Ideal State." *The New Yorker,* 16 December 1991:53–88.

Gregory, J. W. 1913. *Livingstone as an Explorer: An Appreciation.* James MacLehose and Sons, Glasgow.

Howgate, Mike. 1989. "A Pteranodon in Every Bite." *New Scientist,* June 1989:67–68.

Teplitz-Sembitzky, W. 1991. "Wastewood as a Source of Woodfuel: The Case of Malaŵi and Its Relevance to Sub-Saharan Africa." *Natural Resources Forum,* February 1991: 59–65.

INDEX

Louis Jacobs received his Ph.D. from the University of Arizona in 1977. His doctoral research was based on fossils he collected in Pakistan. After a short time in northern Arizona he moved to Kenya to become Head of the Division of Palaeontology at the National Museum, working for Richard Leakey. He has conducted extensive field work in the United States, Pakistan, Mexico, Kenya, Cameroon, Malaŵi, and Yemen. He recently discovered the first dinosaur known from the Arabian Peninsula. He has published nearly 100 technical papers. Currently he lives and teaches in Dallas. His wife studies fossil plants and his son and daughter like to accompany them in search of fossils.